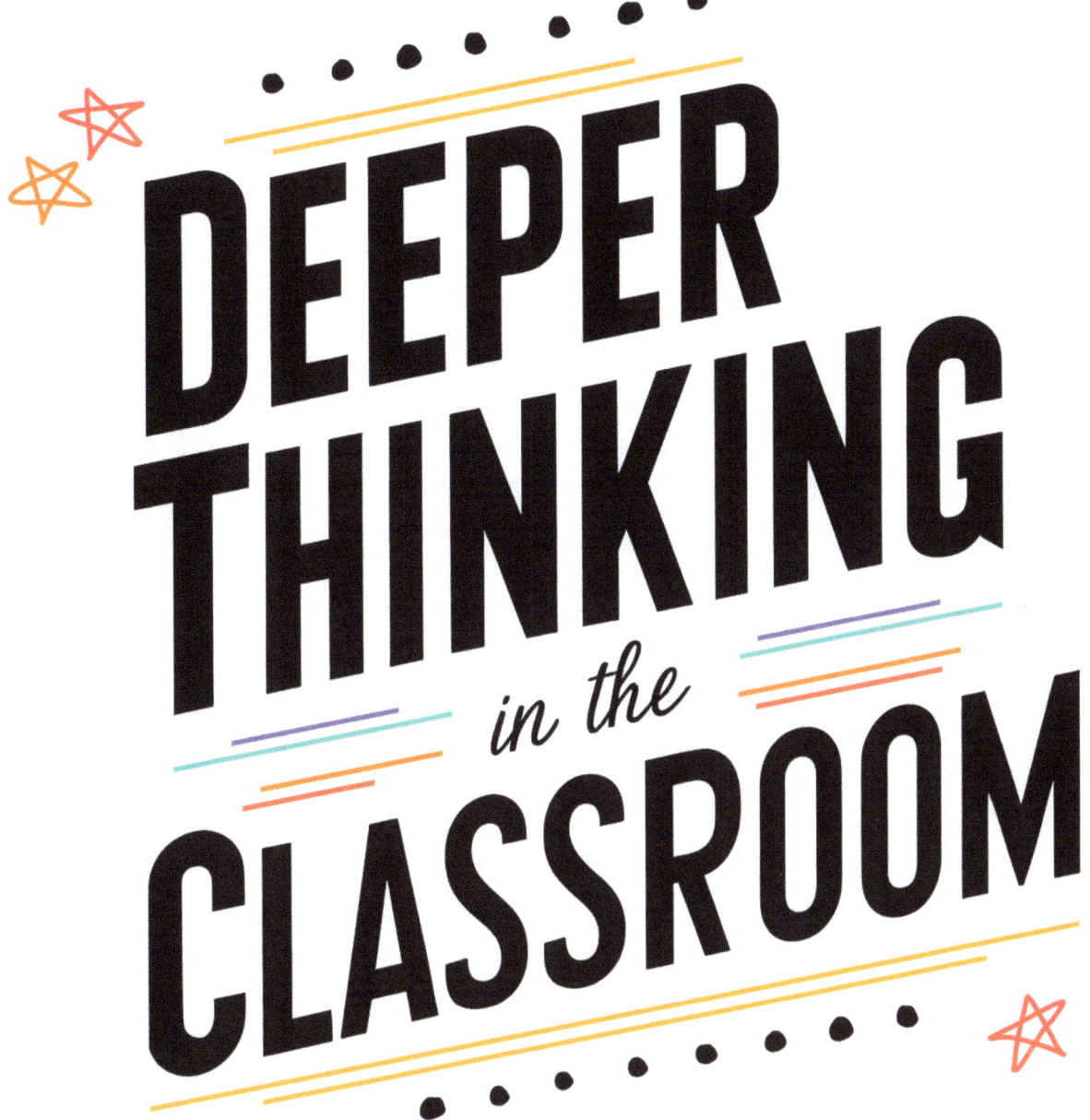

A PRACTICAL GUIDE TO THE CREATE METHOD

Written by Katie Trowbridge

With the assistance of Chelsea Stenvig and Jason Silva

Copyright © 2024 Curiosity 2 Create

All rights reserved. This book or parts thereof may not be reproduced in any form, stored in any retrieval system, or transmitted in any form by any means, electronic, mechanical, photocopy, recording, or otherwise, without prior written permission of the publisher, except as provided by United States of America copyright law and fair use. For permission requests, write to the publisher at edlinkspress@edlinks.com.

The right of Katie Trowbridge to be identified as the author of the work has been asserted by Curiosity 2 Create per the copyright, designs, and licenses.

www.curiosity2create.org

ISBN: 979-8-9897654-7-8

First printing edition 2024.

EDLINKS® Press LLC
PO Box 205
Essex Junction, VT 05453
USA
www.edlinks.com/edlinks-press

For information about purchases, special requests, and educational needs, contact EDLINKS® Press at edlinkspress@edlinks.com or visit Curiosity 2 Create at www.curiosity2create.org.

CONTRIBUTORS

Dr. Cyndi Burnett—You are my creativity and education soulmate. Who knew when we met we would become partners in crime and business? You make me laugh, keep me sane, and push me to think creatively and critically in all aspects of my life.

Dr. Kathy Kipp—Thank you for the numerous trips to Panera where we brainstormed what teachers need to be more creative in their classrooms. You always know how to support me, encourage me, and give me honest feedback. Your expertise and friendship have been invaluable.

Larissa Bennett M.Ed—I remember when you were a junior in high school serving on my First Class board. Now, you are a valued contributor to the Curiosity 2 CREATE team and our elementary school expert.

Nathan Biggs—Your continued support of and dedication to Curiosity 2 CREATE astounded me. Your ability to think creatively while always pushing me to think of new and exciting ways to bring the CREATE Method to life through content, design, and marketing has made the CREATE Method possible.

Katelyn Moon—I would be lost without your constant attention to detail and the unending support and patience you show toward my chaotic mind.

About Curiosity 2 Create

Today's educators are facing numerous challenges, obstacles, and judgments. It's no secret that the education system is grappling with a critical teacher shortage. Teachers often feel undervalued and overwhelmed, leaving the classroom for office cubicles. They yearn for the freedom to explore innovative teaching methods that ignite curiosity. Surprisingly, statistics reveal two out of three school districts struggle with teacher shortages. Our education system is in crisis.

At Curiosity 2 CREATE, our mission is to assist educators in unlocking their true passion by venturing beyond their comfort zones and into the realm of creativity. We collaborate with teachers, helping them develop engaging curricula and rediscover the joy of teaching. The CREATE Method, designed by teachers for teachers, empowers educators to refresh their existing curriculum by infusing each unit with elements of creativity, curiosity, critical thinking, collaboration, and communication.

We firmly believe that nurturing creativity in educators and students can break the downward spiral in education. Our goal is to inspire teachers, enabling them to become creative problem-solvers and critical thinkers who seamlessly integrate these skills into their classrooms. Mastering creativity enhances social-emotional wellness and fosters a supportive and engaging community where knowledge and communication thrive in a collaborative environment.

As a non-profit organization, it is essential to give back to the educational community. All profits from this book go directly to June D. Barnard's scholarship, which assists educators and school districts in implementing the CREATE Method. For more information, please visit our website at www.curioisty2create.org

Why I wrote this workbook:

When I started teaching, I envisioned that all my students loved me and my teaching style (that bubble burst early on). In the middle of my career, I just wanted students to "have fun learning" (great goal, but what I thought was fun — many of them didn't). Later, as a seasoned educator, I realized that something vital was missing in our classroom: the ability for students to think and act for themselves. Students today want the correct answer, the easy answer. They no longer see challenges and failure positively. When learning new information, the typical response from students is, "Will this be on the test?" or "Is this worth points?"

Creating the classroom I had always envisioned did not come easy. Researching innovative ways to incorporate curiosity, creativity, and critical thinking while experiencing lots of trial and error helped me build an environment where students were engaged and challenged. I want that for you and your students as well.

~Katie Trowbridge

Contents

Section One: Creative and Critical Thinking 1

    Creativity and You 6

    Divergent Thinking 33

    Convergent Thinking 37

    Cultivating a Creative Classroom 50

Section Two: The Create Method 67

    Content Curator 73

    Risk Facilitator 109

    Experience Navigator 143

    Attitude Shifter 165

    Team Transformer 195

    Evaluation Designer 227

Author Information 264

References 268

Foster creativity and critical thinking to create a joyful, connected, and innovative classroom.

SECTION ONE

We all have the capacity for creativity; it must be nurtured and encouraged.

Just a few months ago, while speaking at a conference, a teacher approached us and said, "I understand what you are saying, but I am just not creative." The entire time we spoke, this teacher had a malleable fidget device in her hands. She made several jewelry variations with this snake-like device, including a ring, bracelet, and crown. When we pointed out her creative achievements with the device, she laughed and said, "Oh, this? It is just something I do to keep my hands busy. I never thought it was a creative thing."

Creativity should be part of our everyday lives, whether it is a fidget device a painting, or cooking a new dish. Through our work and play, we can connect and express ourselves meaningfully. Teaching creativity is the key to unlocking the inner artist and innovator in all of us. It empowers us to explore our interests and develop skills that make us unique. With creativity, we can foster a more open-minded world with unlimited possibilities.

> **CREATIVITY CAN BE FOUND IN EVERYTHING WE DO—IT IS NOT JUST ABOUT BEING ARTISTIC.**

Creativity can be found in everything we do—it is not just about being artistic. Through problem-solving and exploration, we can find creative solutions to everyday challenges. Creativity can make the world more vibrant and exciting, whether by devising a clever solution to a math problem or finding new ways to save energy.

Yet, we recognize that today's youth face emotional and academic challenges. They encounter many obstacles and pressures while bombarded with limitless options for their futures. Overscheduled and overstimulated, their emotional well-being is jeopardized by their constant exposure to the world's problems. Regrettably, their ability to communicate and collaborate is eroding. Change is relentless, and our youth must prepare for the impending challenges.

According to many reputable reports, innovation, creativity, and communication are among the top skills required in today's world (IBM, 2010; LinkedIn, 2019, 2020; Psychology Today, 2015; World Economic Forum, 2016, 2022). However, here lies the predicament: since 1980, creativity has witnessed a steady decline (Kim, 2010). We must incorporate, teach, and practice these skills every year to better prepare our students to be future thinkers.

If we know what the research says and understand the need to teach thinking skills, why aren't we teaching them? When I talk to teachers across the country about their concerns with infusing their curriculum with creative thinking – I receive various responses:

- "I have too much content to teach— I don't have time for creative lessons."

- "Incorporating creativity in my classroom seems less structured – thus seems more chaotic."

- "It throws my classroom management off."

- "Assessing for creativity is impossible. I need to stick to the standards being tested."

- "I am not creative, so how can I teach creativity?"

- "My curriculum is scripted, and I don't have much freedom to change it."

That is why it was important to us to gather creative educators from all levels and content areas to assist in creating a workbook where we could embark on a journey together to rekindle the flame of creativity and reshape the future of education! Together, we aim to develop learning resources that foster collaboration and communication, nurture well-being, and build skills for a future driven by creativity. Our mission is to support our next generation of learners so that we can cultivate an inspired workforce with the courage to dream, innovate, and create!

We know teachers are the content experts, and the last thing you need is another book about pedagogical theory. Sitting in professional development and listening to a speaker lecture about the importance of a new way of thinking was sometimes rewarding. However, I remember walking out of those sessions thinking, "Now what? How do I actually use this in my classroom?" That's why it was imperative that as we wrote this workbook, we, as teachers, designed this for teachers. We can use the standards we need to teach as the framework for our creative expression.

How to Use this Workbook

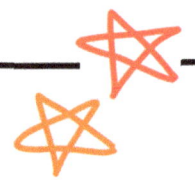

This is different from a typical step-by-step approach or another curriculum add-on. Instead, it is a remarkable method that will empower you to infuse curiosity and creativity into your existing curriculum while helping your students develop deeper thinking skills.

There are several ways you can use this workbook.

- You can work through this independently and revise a unit or lesson that needs more engagement.

- You can work independently and create a new unit or lesson using the CREATE Method guidelines.

- You can collaborate with a team teacher and revamp a unit to include problem-based learning.

- Your Professional Learning Community could choose a standard unit and work through the CREATE Method to ensure students embrace creative and critical thinking skills.

- Your department could do a book study and jigsaw each section, learning how to incorporate each letter of the CREATE Method. Then, in a department meeting, present each section in a creative and engaging way.

We want you to use this workbook in whatever way best fits your needs. That's the beauty of the CREATE Method. In fact, you don't even need to read it from front to back, which is why it is color-coded. If your most pressing need may be classroom climate, then I suggest you start with the Attitude Shifter section. It doesn't matter where you start.

As you read each section:

Stay curious and ask questions.

Engage in each activity with an open mind.

Don't fear taking risks and trying new strategies.

Embrace the possibilities and challenges presented through the workbook.

Challenge yourself to think creatively and critically while reenergizing your classroom.

Implementing the CREATE method allows you to assess your existing curriculum and identify opportunities to better your pedagogy to benefit your students. Get ready to build a solid foundation for a creative classroom culture.

• • • • • • • • • • • • • • • • •

How this workbook is organized:

The first section of this workbook establishes basic vocabulary related to creative and critical thinking. This will help you understand skills. As you go through the exercises, be open in your attitude toward creativity.

The second section of this workbook will guide you through the CREATE method. Using a unit or lesson you want to improve; this workbook will walk you through each letter and allow you the space to reflect and revise.

The third section of this workbook explains how to implement the CREATE method in urban environments and provides lesson examples that are more specific to urban experiences.

When you finish this workbook, you will have a new understanding of the importance of creative and critical thinking and know how to apply it to your existing curriculum.

• • • • • • • • • • • • • • • • •

CREATIVITY AND YOU

Reflect on why you became and remain a teacher! Before we jump into the CREATE Method, it's important for us to establish what creativity is and how it impacts creative and critical thinking and YOU! First, take some time to center yourself and remember why you chose this profession.

Stop and Reflect: Think back to when you decided to become a teacher. What were all the reasons you chose this profession? Did someone influence you? Who? How so? Think back to the first time you were in the classroom. What do you remember? What stands out most to you?

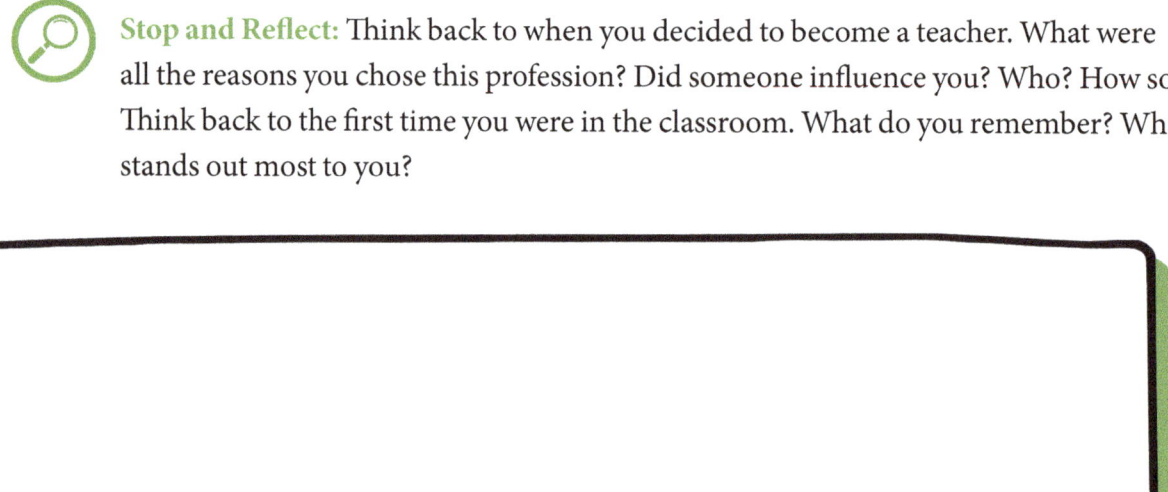

Now, switch gears a little and think back to your learning experiences as a student. Describe the learning experience that stands out to you the most. Why was this experience so memorable? When were you excited, invested, and engaged in what you were learning? What were you doing? What were you learning?

 **Practical Tip:** Keep class pictures, emails, or notes written to you by students and parents. When you need some inspiration, go back and reflect on how you made a difference. Keep lesson plans from the past—you will be amazed at how much you have grown as a teacher over the years. When you give yourself permission to be creative in the classroom by using the CREATE Method, you will be more open to taking risks and trying new strategies.

 Stop and Reflect: On a creativity scale from 1 - 10 (with one being not creative at all to 10 being a creative genius) where would you place yourself?

Why did you choose this number? Where do you find yourself being most creative?

When asked the question "Are you creative?" people often respond with a shake of the head. Yet, we would argue that everyone is creative in some way. To foster creativity, the CREATE Method encourages educators to find ways to build an environment and activities that bring out the best in each student. By tapping into creative potential while providing appropriate guidance, teachers and students will come up with innovative solutions and ideas, more effectively making the classroom a place where learning and community prevail.

What are creativity and creative thinking and how do they impact a classroom? In this section, we will cover:

- How do curiosity, creative thinking, and critical thinking work together?
- What is the importance of the teacher, student, and knowledge relationship?
- Why is it important to foster creativity and critical thinking in educative relationships?

Research from Adobe (2019), LinkedIn (2020), and the World Economic Forum (2023) indicates that critical and creative thinking leads the list of skills employees seek and feel need to be improved. Creative and critical thinking are two of the skills most sought after by universities and employers. Yet research also shows that creativity is in constant decline, and teachers need help nurturing creative thinking skills in students.

Imagine if your students:

- Looked forward to learning.
- Embraced ownership of their experience.
- Viewed insights from different perspectives with open-mindedness.
- Determined and wrote their own assessments.
- Worked with peers to solve relevant problems creatively.

Imagine if your classroom:

- Overflowed with joy, connection, purpose, and creativity.
- Focused on curiosity, creativity, and critical thinking.
- Embraced all opinions with respect, kindness, and empathy.

 Stop and Reflect: What are the first three words that come to mind when considering your ideal classroom?

The ideal classroom would be interactive, inspiring, and collaborative, a place where students can express their thoughts freely and develop their unique ideas. Through hands-on activities, students will explore their creativity by engaging with the material in a meaningful way. The environment would foster collaboration and respect, encouraging students to work together on projects, share their ideas, and develop new skills. Additionally, the classroom would be full of innovative technology, allowing students to explore different areas of knowledge in more depth. The overall goal is for all students to reach their fullest potential and become empowered to succeed in whatever they pursue.

 Stop and Reflect: Under each kettlebell below, list what keeps you from creating the type of classroom you dream of—from the easiest obstacle to the most challenging.

Remember, these challenging obstacles can be opportunities as we continue our journey through the CREATE Method. We will revisit these kettlebells later in the workbook.

LET'S DEFINE CREATIVITY

When you think of creativity, what do you think of? Draw an image that best represents your viewpoint.

There is no one clear definition of creativity. In fact, creativity scholars cannot even agree.

Here are a few examples:

- Creativity is a divine madness, a gift from the gods (Plato).
- Creativity is more than intelligence (Piers, Daniels, & Quackenbush, 1960).
- Creativity is the key to education in its fullest sense and the solution to mankind's most serious problems (Guilford, 1967).
- Creativity is those attitudes by which we fulfill ourselves (Young, 1985).
- Creativity is one of the most complex of human functions (Treffinger, 1986).
- Creativity is often mistakenly used as a synonym for originality (Balkin, 1990).
- Creativity is not a synonym for talent (Balkin, 1990).
- Creativity is thinking; it just happens to be thinking that leads to results that we think are great (Amabile, 1996, p. 1).
- Creativity is defined as the production of novel and appropriate ideas (Amabile & Conti, 1997).
- Creativity is not predominantly something that can be "forced" through creativity "techniques" (Cook, 1998, p. 1).
- Creativity is essential to human progress (Hennessey & Amabile, 2010).
- Creativity is the foundation on which innovation relies (Argabright, McGuire, & King, 2012, p. 1).

- Creativity is a basic element of innovation (Andersen & Kragh, 2012).
- Creativity is a precursor to innovation and the cornerstone of entrepreneurship (Katz-Buonincontro, 2012).

Stop and Reflect: When you look at the above list, which definition resonates with you the most? Which one do you most disagree with? Why?

Now that we have looked at various ways of defining creativity, what are the ramifications of a lack of definition? How does that impact education?

A lack of definition for creativity in terms of educational content, objectives, and expectations can lead to several negative outcomes. For example, students may be left without guidance and lack the necessary resources to understand how to apply creative problem-solving skills. This can have a detrimental effect on their academic performance and growth as learners. Additionally, teachers may need help to assess student progress and individualize instruction when the expectations for creativity are not clearly defined. With clear objectives and rubrics for creative tasks, it becomes easier for teachers to provide feedback and support to students.

Ultimately, this can lead to a lack of motivation and engagement in learning activities. It is therefore necessary to ensure that creativity has a clearly defined role within education—from its expectations and objectives all the way through to assessment. This will create an environment where creativity is nurtured and supported. **This workbook defines creativity as the ability to make something novel (new), appropriate, and useful within the context for which it is created (Stein, 1953, as cited in Runco & Jaeger, 2012).**

> *IT IS NECESSARY TO ENSURE THAT CREATIVITY HAS A CLEARLY DEFINED ROLE WITHIN EDUCATION.*

Creativity and Its Myths

 Stop and Reflect: Which of the following statements are true?

Creativity cannot be taught—you either have it or you don't.	True/False
Creativity only comes in rare "Aha!" moments.	True/False
Creative people are loners and often suffer from mental illness.	True/False
Creativity happens mostly in the right hemisphere of the brain.	True/False
Creativity cannot be measured.	True/False
Creativity and innovation are the same thing.	True/False
Gifted students are more creative than other students.	True/False

Our attitude toward creativity often impacts how our students respond to creative thinking. All of the above statements are false. Creativity is often associated with art, music, and writing, but the realm of creativity expands far beyond these. Let's debunk some common myths that hinder our understanding of creativity.

Myth 1: Creativity is an innate talent reserved for a few fortunate individuals. This suggests that creativity cannot be cultivated or developed but is bestowed upon individuals from birth. However, research has unequivocally shown that creativity can be nurtured and honed through deliberate practice and effort (Doron, 2017, pp. 150–153).

Myth 2: Creativity resides purely within the arts. While artists are renowned for their creative prowess, creativity is not confined to these expressive domains. It manifests in scientific breakthroughs, innovative business solutions, and even mundane tasks. Creativity encompasses problem-solving and complex thinking, permeating every discipline.

Myth 3: Creativity blossoms in isolation. While some prefer to work in solitary environments, collaboration and teamwork amplify creativity. Embracing diverse perspectives and ideas ignites the spark of innovation, leading to groundbreaking solutions.

Myth 4: Creativity solely revolves around generating original ideas or inventions. However, creativity thrives in refining existing ideas and processes. It's not always about reinventing the wheel but about discovering new and improved ways of doing things.

Myth 5: Creativity flourishes in unstructured chaos. While an unstructured environment may fuel creativity for some, others find structure and guidelines indispensable for inspiring their creative faculties. Striking the right balance between freedom and structure is key.

Myth 6: Creativity bears no practical value outside of certain professions or hobbies. In today's dynamic job market, creative thinking and problem-solving skills are highly sought after across all industries. The ability to think beyond convention and devise innovative solutions paves the path to success.

 Stop and Reflect: What other myths about creativity can you think of?

Now that we have looked at some of the myths surrounding creativity, it is important to assess our attitude toward creativity.

Take a look at the list below—write if you agree or disagree with each statement.

New ideas seldom become reality in education.	Agree/Disagree
There are multiple ways for a student to solve a problem.	Agree/Disagree
All students are creative.	Agree/Disagree
All teachers are creative.	Agree/Disagree
The disorganized students/teachers are usually the most creative.	Agree/Disagree
Creative students/teachers are the ones who cause the most friction.	Agree/Disagree
The classroom leaves little time for students' wild ideas.	Agree/Disagree
New ideas are just old ideas recycled.	Agree/Disagree
It's exciting when a student comes up with a different way to do an assignment.	Agree/Disagree
Creative classrooms are chaotic classrooms.	Agree/Disagree
The more intelligent the student, the more creative the student.	Agree/Disagree
Creative classrooms are full of beautiful billboards and posters.	Agree/Disagree

Adapted from Basadur, Taggar, & Pringle (1999).

They say attitude is everything, and that's absolutely true when it comes to creativity! Research has shown that the attitude a teacher expresses regarding creativity has a huge impact on how students perceive it (Doron, 2017, p. 157). So listen up, teachers! If you see creativity as disruptive, chaotic, and reserved only for a select few, guess what? Your students will feel the same way. And if you're convinced you're not creative, your students will believe the same about themselves.

Stop and Reflect: Overall, if you compared your attitude toward creativity to the weather, how would you describe the forecast right now?

Despite all the talk about the importance of creativity in the classroom, it still gets a bad rap. Teachers may think they value creative skills, but guess which skills are actually the least admired in students? You got it: the ones that are considered creative characteristics like preferring ambiguity, being impulsive, enjoying working alone. You know the drill. On the flip side, the most desired characteristics are often the ones that aren't considered the most creative like being responsible, reliable, clear and to the point, and practical.

Try it! Let's look at how creativity currently impacts your world. Under each section add at least two bullet points demonstrating how creativity is harnessed in different aspects of your day.

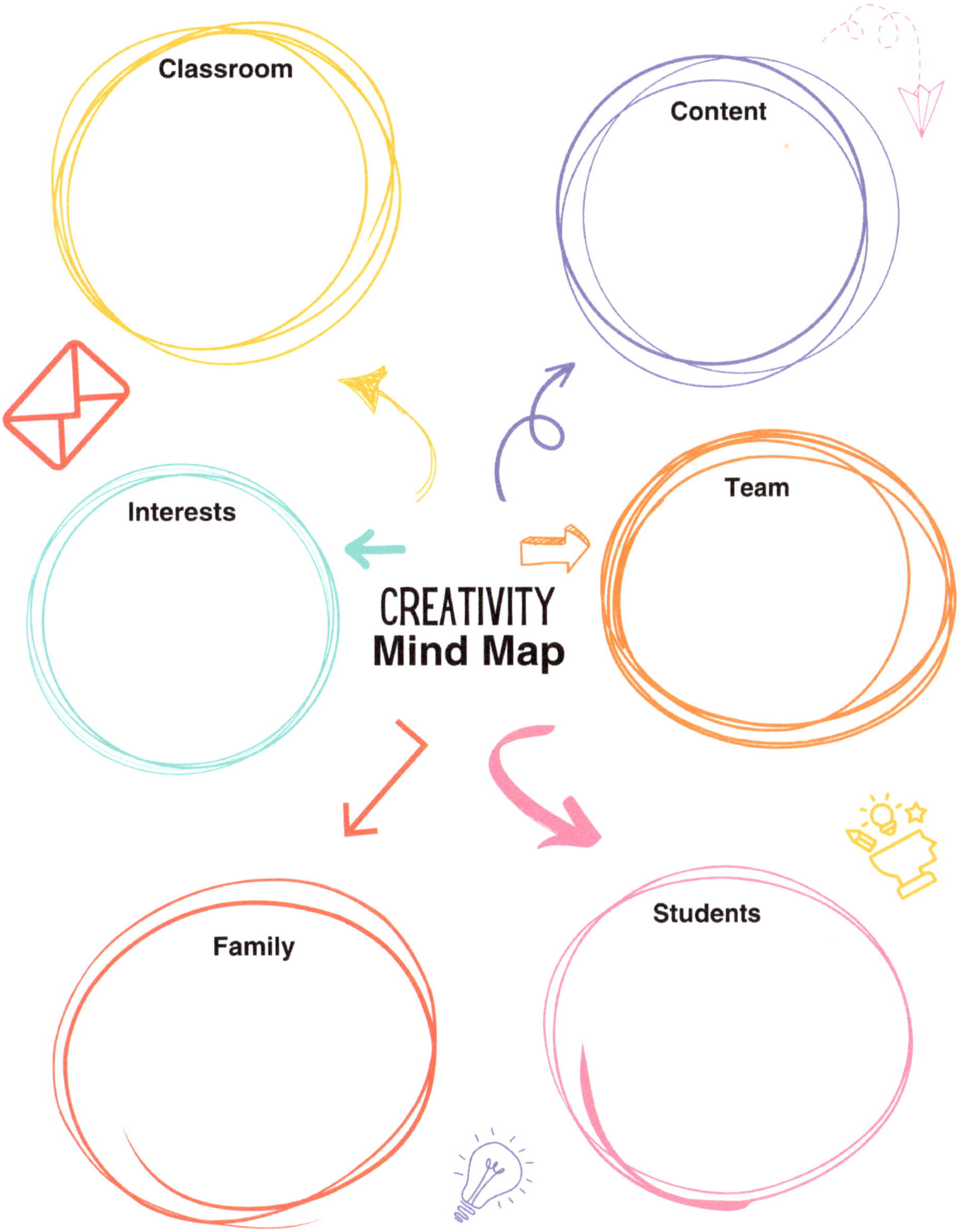

- Classroom
- Content
- Interests
- Team
- Family
- Students

CREATIVITY Mind Map

CREATIVITY AND CREATIVE THINKING

It's important, before we go any further, to distinguish between creativity and creative thinking. Though creativity and creative thinking are closely related, they have some differences in their scope and application. Think of it this way: creativity is a broader concept that encompasses the ability to produce work that is both original and valuable.

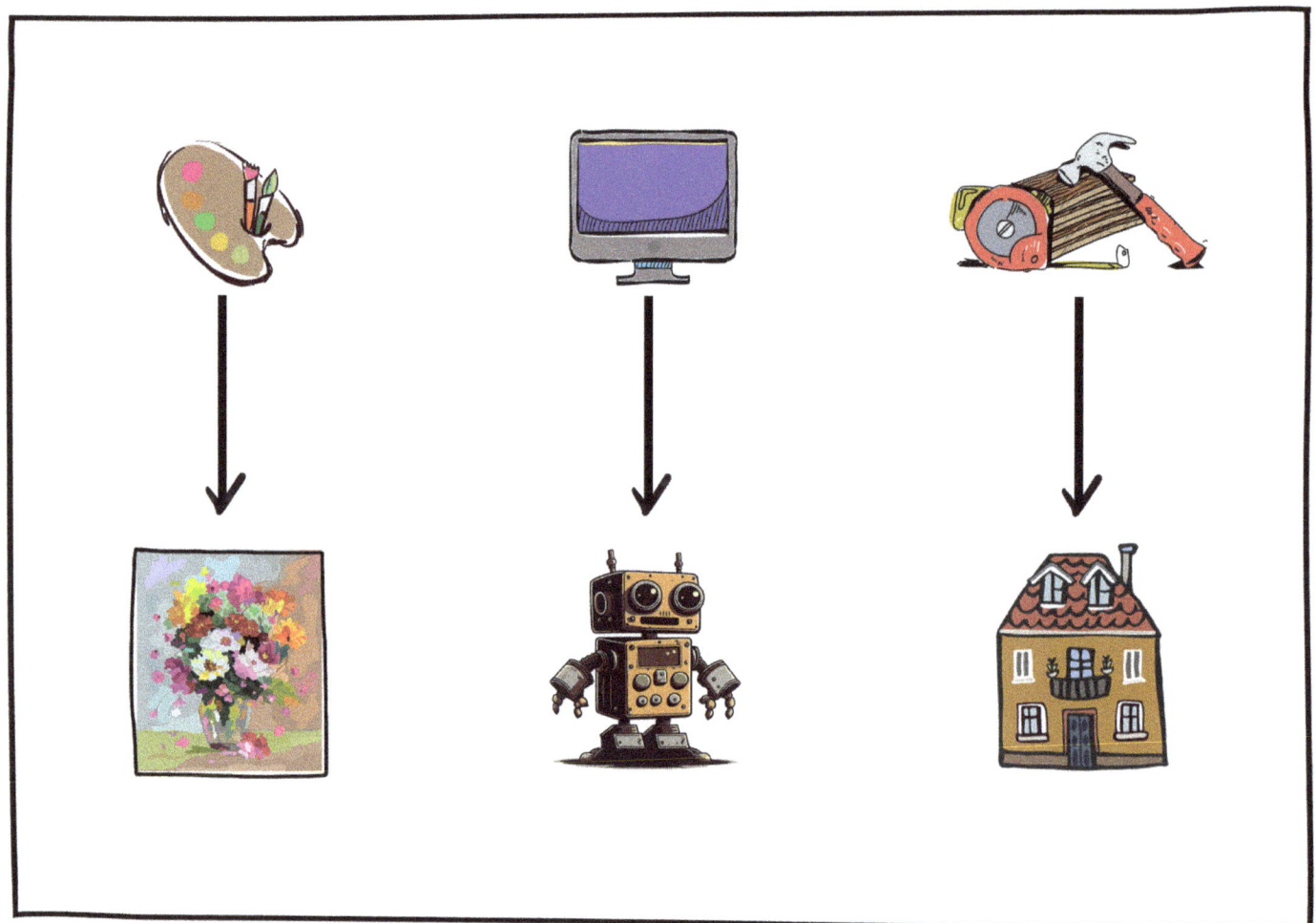

On the other hand, creative thinking is a subset of creativity. It's a cognitive process that involves generating new and innovative ideas and solutions by breaking away from established patterns and conventional thought processes.

While creativity is the overall ability and act of creating something new and valuable, creative thinking is the mental process that fuels this creation. In other words, creative thinking is one of the key tools that facilitates the act of creativity.

Creative Thinking and How It Looks in the Classroom

Ever wondered what creative thinking looks like in a classroom? We all know teaching is no ordinary gig. Educators are unstoppable problem solvers, constantly adapting lessons and brainstorming innovative ways to captivate students' attention. Trust me: we face new challenges like incentives, mandates, and standards each year, leading to continuous curriculum revision.

Now let's talk about creative thinking. As stated earlier, there are various definitions, but my favorite is by the brilliant Ron Beghetto. He describes creative thinking as a "kick-ass process" of generating original and meaningful thoughts (ideas, interpretations, or insights) in a specific task, situation, or domain (2020). That lightbulb moment in cartoons may be cool, but creative thinking is an exciting process that can be taught and practiced.

THAT LIGHTBULB MOMENT IN CARTOONS MAY BE COOL, BUT CREATIVE THINKING IS AN EXCITING PROCESS THAT CAN BE TAUGHT AND PRACTICED.

Four C's of Creativity

Creativity and content need to be balanced; they should complement each other and work together in order for real, deep learning to take place.

	Mini C	Little C	Pro C	Big C
Definition	Everything starts here - basis of learning a new skill that is personally meaningful.	Everyday creativity—production of something new and novel that requires learning a new skill.	Development of the former skill that results in a professional career.	The legends - the well-known creators who make history - Picasso, Einstein, etc.
How it helps in the classroom	Helps students develop confidence.	Helps students see learning and relearning with respect as an indicator of growth and motivation.	Helps students see what it takes to be an expert in the topic.	Helps give students a model to aspire to.
How to encourage	Give positive feedback in the classroom — "Be creative." Encourage students to share their unique ideas. Allow students to give each other feedback.	Place less focus on evaluation and more on growth. Allow students to practice the same skill in different ways. Allow students to choose ways to learn the skill. Focus on self-improvement and asking for help.	Continued practice and opportunities to get feedback from real-world experts.	Have students research legends in their field of interest. Allow students to dream and wonder: "what if I…"
Example in learning	Students learn new skills like baking cupcakes.	Student practices the skill of baking and decides to create a class project in history about food in the 1920s.	Students can submit a signature dish to a local restaurant for feedback from a professional chef.	Highest achievement a person can achieve.

Adapted from Helfand, Kaufman, and Beghetto (2016).

CREATIVE TEACHING VERSUS CREATIVE LEARNING

Teaching is a creative profession. Educators are constantly problem-solving, adapting lessons, and finding new and innovative ways to engage students. When it comes to building an experience for our students, we need to know the difference between creative teaching and creative learning. Many times, these two concepts blend. We argue that they are two separate but needed concepts in the classroom. Take a look at the following chart.

	Creative Teaching	Creative Learning
Content Creating	Teacher focused - content being delivered uniquely and engagingly by the teacher.	Student-focused - content being delivered uniquely and meaningfully by the student.
Risk Taking	Teacher creates a classroom environment where reaching outside one's comfort zone is appreciated and encouraged.	Students actively embrace and celebrate ambiguity, uncertainty, and failure while supporting each other's growth.
Questioning	Teacher generates open-ended and complex questions for students to answer.	Students generate the open-ended and complex questions and answers.
Problem Solving	Teacher creates inquiry-based projects for students to complete.	Students use choice in creating multiple solutions to various brainstormed problems.
Collaborating	Teacher-to-student Teacher-to-teacher Teacher-to-knowledge.	Student-to-knowledge Student-to-student Student-to-teacher.
Ownership of Creativity	Teacher	Student

Let's delve into the definitions of these two captivating concepts: creative teaching revolves around the methods and techniques educators employ in order to foster and enrich creative learning. It's all about educators delivering content in captivating and imaginative ways that ignite creativity in their students. This can involve implementing unconventional teaching strategies, integrating technology into lessons, or designing tasks that demand critical thinking and creativity.

On the flip side, creative learning entails a captivating process where learners actively build their own understanding and knowledge through imaginative activities and experiences. It emphasizes an approach that encourages learners to think outside the box, tackle challenges, and devise inventive solutions. This method nurtures innovation, curiosity, and open-mindedness, providing learners with the freedom to explore their interests and passions at their own pace.

> **CREATIVE LEARNING EMPHASIZES AN APPROACH THAT ENCOURAGES LEARNERS TO THINK OUTSIDE THE BOX.**

In essence, creative learning primarily focuses on the learners' process and experiences, while creative teaching centers on the educators' strategies and methodologies. Nevertheless, both are vital for fostering an environment that facilitates engaging and imaginative learning. Let's break it down even further.

Scenario One: Imagine yourself preparing a comprehensive unit employing creative teaching strategies such as integrating hexagonal thinking, gamification systems, and even decorating the classroom with an enticing theme. The lessons are meticulously planned, including thought-provoking Socratic seminars and a final assessment utilizing project-based learning. Your calendars are set, your materials are neatly organized, and you're brimming with excitement about the captivating and fun-filled learning experience that awaits. This is the epitome of creative teaching—you employ your creativity and critical thinking to craft and present captivating lessons. While some students are fully engaged, others may struggle to connect with the material. In this scenario, the teacher is perceived as the primary source of information.

Scenario Two: Now envision yourself preparing another unit, employing the same creative teaching strategies as in scenario one. However, this time, your unit calendar is flexible. You empower students to choose diverse ways to absorb the content. Students collaborate in groups, create their own Socratic seminar questions, conduct research, and design their own assessments. Brainstorming and problem-solving take center stage in the classroom. Students are engaged because they have the autonomy to select how they want to learn the assigned material. In this scenario, you act as a facilitator, guiding their learning journey.

Practical Tip: Consider a situation in which your class has recently completed the captivating novel *The Catcher in the Rye*. Rather than simply providing a standard comprehension test, you craft an educational learning objective. You design a project that requires students to analyze and delve deeper into the themes and motifs of the novel. They have the opportunity to create visual interpretations, write alternative endings, or even engage in thought-provoking class discussions. This fosters a more engaging and creative learning experience for your students and gives them ownership of the learning. Education comes alive when learners actively participate and engage in imaginative and captivating experiences.

Try it! Think of a creative teaching experience. How might you turn that creative teaching experience into a creative learning experience?

The Dance of Creative and Critical Thinking

Discover the dynamic collaboration between creative thinking and critical thinking as they gracefully dance across the stage of thought. In this enchanting partnership, each step harmoniously complements the others. But why does critical thinking often steal the spotlight?

Let's delve into the captivating world of critical thinking, as defined by the Foundation of Critical Thinking. It's a skillful and disciplined process that actively engages in conceptualizing, applying, analyzing, synthesizing, and evaluating information (Foundation for Critical Thinking, n.d.). This information can be gathered from various sources such as observation, experience, reflection, reasoning, or communication. So what's the purpose of this mesmerizing dance?

To answer that, let's explore the distinction between creative thinking and critical thinking. Creative thinking involves generating novel ideas and innovative solutions, while critical thinking focuses on evaluating these ideas. Critical thinking meticulously examines the strengths and weaknesses of ideas before deciding their implementation. Critical thinking takes a step back, dissecting and analyzing the big picture piece by piece. It ensures decisions are rooted in data, facts, and logic rather than being solely guided by emotions. This approach is essential for making well-thought-out decisions, regardless of their magnitude. Without critical thinking, we risk making impulsive choices with negative consequences.

> **WITHOUT CRITICAL THINKING, WE RISK MAKING IMPULSIVE DECISIONS WITH NEGATIVE CONSEQUENCES.**

CREATIVE AND CRITICAL THINKING ARE TWO SIDES OF THE SAME COIN: ONE IS OF LITTLE USE WITHOUT THE OTHER.

(ALGHAFRI & ISMAIL, 2014)

CREATIVE THINKING	CRITICAL THINKING
Thinking we do when we generate ideas	*Thinking we do when we judge ideas*
More Intuitive	More Ordered
Somewhat Random	Controlled
Generates Many Answers	Problem Solve
Broad in context	One Good Conclusion
Sense of Curiosity	Directed
	Independant

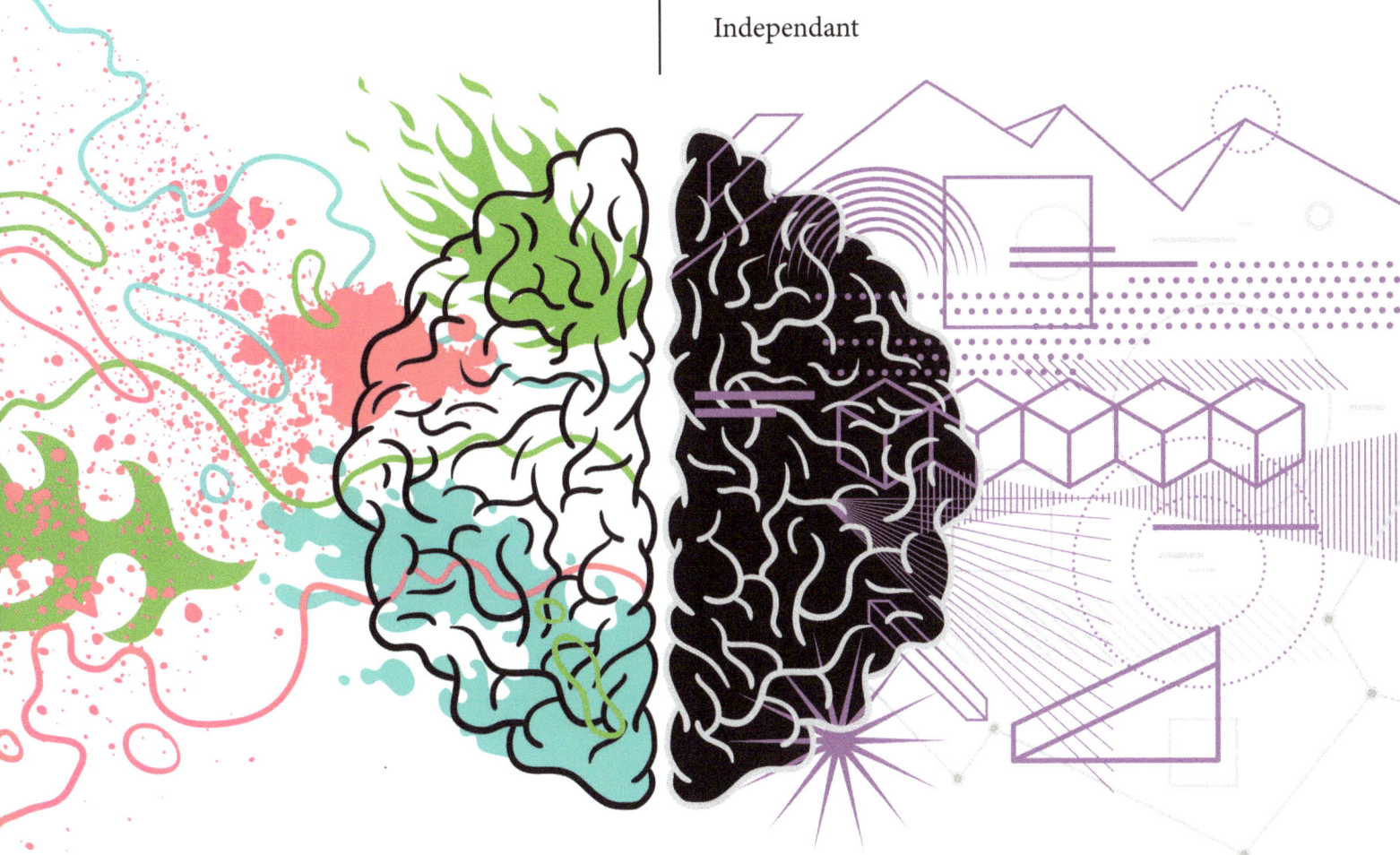

By harnessing the power of both creative and critical thinking, we can unleash truly exceptional and potentially life-changing ideas. Creative thinking encourages the exploration of diverse possibilities for problem-solving, while critical thinking helps us navigate the information presented to us. It's vital to remember that these two processes are not mutually exclusive; in fact, they work best in collaboration. By combining them, we attain a deeper understanding of the issue at hand and increase the likelihood of achieving success.

Incorporating creative and critical thinking in the learning environment has numerous benefits.

- Creative thinking promotes open-mindedness and defers judgment.
    - As educators, teaching our children to listen with an open mind can be challenging, but it is key to promoting creative thinking. As students practice deferring judgment and thinking critically, their ability to become independent thinkers will grow stronger.
- Creative and critical thinking promote problem-solving.
    - As students become stronger creative thinkers, they can address different issues and assess the components surrounding that problem to discover ways to develop a solution.
- Creativity and curiosity inspire meaning.
    - When students are connected, are curious, and genuinely care about their learning, they have a deep sense of what can be accomplished through the learning experience. Students can learn about themselves while learning the content. They can connect to the content and find purpose in their engaging lessons.
- Creative and critical thinking promote celebrating mistakes, taking risks, and accepting failure.
    - They allow us all to acknowledge and embrace our failures, knowing we are even closer to the solution because of those moments. Instead of students seeing failure as an end product, they start to see failure as just a step in the learning process.
- Creative and critical thinking promote collaboration.
- We (students and teachers) are more creative together.
  When educators and students work together to solve problems and learn from each other, ideas are more robust and abundant. When we communicate, listen to each other, and build off of each other, our creativity grows and prospers.
- Creativity and curiosity promote an engaging, open, and respectful learning environment.
    - Infusing your classroom with strong teacher-student relationships allows students to grow together, feel emotionally safe, and openly express their ideas.

> **CREATIVE AND CRITICAL THINKING TOGETHER FOSTER EXCEPTIONAL AND LIFE-CHANGING IDEAS.**

Incorporating creative and critical thinking in the learning environment has numerous benefits.

CREATIVE THINKING PROMOTES OPEN-MINDEDNESS AND DEFERS JUDGEMENT.

CREATIVE AND CRITICAL THINKING PROMOTES PROBLEM-SOLVING.

CREATIVITY AND CURIOUSITY INSPIRE MEANING.

CREATIVE AND CRITICAL THINKING PROMOTE CELEBRATING MISTAKES, TAKING RISKS, AND ACCEPTING FAILURE.

CREATIVE AND CRITICAL THINKING PROMOTE COLLABORATION.

CREATIVITY AND CURIOSITY PROMOTE AN ENGAGING, OPEN, AND RESPECTFUL LEARNING ENVIRONMENT.

In the ever-evolving landscape of education, the depth of knowledge students acquire significantly influences their capacity to think critically, solve complex problems, and adapt to new challenges. Understanding the distinctions between surface, shallow, and deep learning unravels how these different levels of understanding can profoundly impact teaching and learning in K-12 classrooms.

Surface-level learning is the most basic form of understanding. With surface-level learning, a rudimentary grasp of information is there, but students can do little with the knowledge besides recall and recognition (Bennet & Bennet, 2008). Plus, this type of learning is temporary. Think back to the math theorems you learned. Do you remember all of them? Neither do I! This level of understanding involves strategies such as repetition and memorization, which are foundational yet often seen as mundane. **When learners advance beyond this stage, they avoid falling into stagnation.** Stagnation occurs when we cannot engage dynamically with the world around us. Not diving into learning limits cognitive development and emotional growth, preventing individuals from unleashing their creativity.

> **IF YOU CAN EXPLAIN IT, YOU UNDERSTAND IT DEEPLY.**

Application in K-12 Education

- Essential for introducing new concepts and terminology.
- The foundation of critical thinking and precursor to more complex problem-solving.
- Teachers can employ flashcards, quizzes, and factual recall tests to reinforce this level of knowledge.

Shallow-level learning represents a slightly deeper understanding of knowledge. Here, students connect facts and simple concepts, applying their learning in primary, predictable ways (Bennet & Bennet, 2008). Shallow knowledge keeps students afloat with just enough practical knowledge to tackle straightforward tasks, but in-depth application can be lacking. Does this sound familiar? Just weeks after completing a unit, your students seem to have forgotten everything they had just learned! **Shallow learning often focuses on learning for the test rather than fostering a deep understanding**. To address this, educators should aim to incorporate more engaging and meaningful activities that challenge students to apply their knowledge in varied and complex contexts, thereby encouraging deeper comprehension and long-term retention.

Application in K-12 Education

- Helps students apply learned concepts to real-world scenarios with a limited scope.
- Utilizes role-playing, simple problem-solving activities, and direct application tasks in predictable settings.
- Bridges memorization and deeper, analytical understanding.

One day, I asked my class, "What is gravity?" A hand shot up almost instantly, and the student quickly related gravity to Isaac Newton and the falling apple story. "Close," I said, "but what is gravity?" Reluctantly, another student mentioned Earth's gravity of 9.8 m/s². Although I grinned (this was not what I was aiming for, as math is not my strong suit, and this was an English class), this student correctly applied the mathematical coefficient of Earth's gravity to my question. These students had recalled and related different concepts to gravity, but the question remained unanswered. "What is gravity," I said as a hand raised. The student launched into a detailed explanation of gravity involving black holes, the sun's influence, and even interstellar travel. While I was attempting to present the idea of homonyms, this student demonstrated deep-level thinking, linking multiple complex ideas in a manner they understood and could explain.

If you can explain a topic to someone else, you have a deep-level understanding of the topic.

Deep-level learning involves a comprehensive understanding beyond facts and skills. Students with deep knowledge can analyze, synthesize, and evaluate information. Applying deep-level learning often involves multiple steps across different mediums, mimicking work outside of the classroom setting (Bennet & Bennet, 2008; McGregor, 2020). Creating a lesson for a class involves taking the core knowledge and finding a way to present that knowledge in an engaging and educational way. You could explain the complex engineering process behind building boats with a handout, but wouldn't it be more engaging to build boats out of cardboard and discover as a class why they sink?

In K-12 education, fostering deep knowledge requires an environment that promotes inquiry, critical thinking, and creativity. Educators play a crucial role in designing lessons beyond the textbook, encouraging learning that compels students to engage, learn, and create. In a world that values innovation and adaptability, students equipped with the ability to think deeply will excel academically and possess the lifelong learning skills needed to navigate what life throws at them.

One of the hardest things an educator can hear is, "Why can't we learn something useful— like how to do our taxes?" My response was always, "We can, but would you pay attention?" With deep-level learning, we are not trying to give our students a comprehensive, in-depth overview of everything. With deep-level learning, we educators give students the tools they need to apply the knowledge they know to what they do not.

Application in K-12 Education

- Foster deep knowledge through activities that involve evaluation, synthesis, and creation.
- Use techniques like project-based learning, debates, and research projects to encourage the exploration of in-depth topics.
- Encourage students to question, critique, and connect ideas across various subjects.

Throughout our journey together, we will learn how to cultivate depth in thinking by adopting a multi-faceted approach using the CREATE Method. When students are encouraged to investigate their questions and lead their discoveries, they become active participants in their education. Whether through science experiments that ask students to develop their hypotheses, writing assignments that require critical analysis of literature, or social studies projects that demand an understanding of cultural contexts, inquiry-based learning challenges students to move beyond the reception of information to application.

Diving deep into learning is crucial for students' academic and personal growth. This more profound approach to learning prepares students to excel in their current academic endeavors and become thoughtful, informed citizens. As educators, we are committed to deepening our students' knowledge and their future, nurturing tomorrow's thinkers, leaders, and innovators.

Exploring Levels of Learning

Understanding the differences between surface, shallow, and deep learning helps educators tailor their approaches to maximize student engagement and understanding:

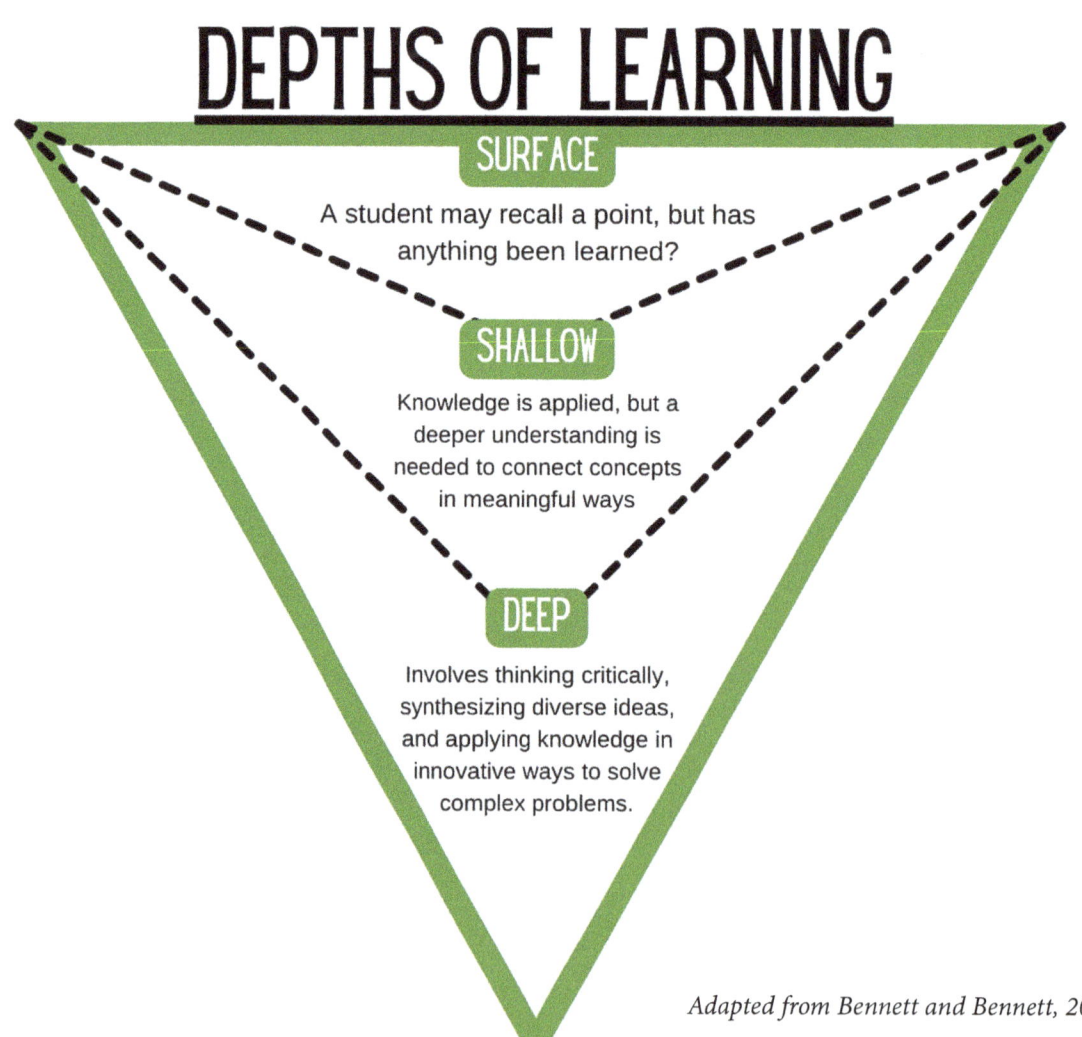

Adapted from Bennett and Bennett, 2008.

CHARACTERISTICS OF SURFACE, SHALLOW, AND DEEP LEARNING

SURFACE LEARNING	SHALLOW LEARNING	DEEP LEARNING
Aims to pass class - Short term - think about students cramming for a test.	Aims to learn foundational knowledge.	Aims to understand how the information has meaning, purpose, and connection. Long term learning.
Can recall information.	Can explain information.	Can connect the information to different concepts.
No creativity involved.	Very little creativity is involved.	Encourages creativity on all levels.
Answers questions of when, where, and who?	Answer the question of what?	Answers questions of why and how?
Easy effort.	Medium effort.	Arduous. It requires effort, time, and patience.
Answers are right or wrong.	Multiple choice assignments with limited correct answers.	Failure has a purpose - therefore, various answers are open for debate.
No action is required.	Some level of action may be able to determine the next step, but that is it - I can't see further into the future.	Intuit - makes predictions but shifts the frame of reference so the student knows how to take effective action.
The teacher gives students information.	The teacher provides students with information.	The teacher and student are reciprocal.
Routine knowledge.	Fixed knowledge.	Adaptive knowledge - Students see possibilities.
Basic level of learning.	It can be complicated.	Complex chaos - may seem messy at times, but learning is complex.
The origin of information does not matter.	Students feel someone else created the knowledge - someone in the past, so it cannot be revised.	Students are confident in their knowledge to revise old ideas and foster new ideas.
Common everyday actions— brushing teeth - getting dressed.	Students set out to do something that requires practice but is easy to master - think flashcards - learning spelling.	Students learn a multi-step, problem-based concept —how to build a cardboard boat that will float in water or create a video essay addressing a mental health issue in today's teens.

Deeper Thinking Introduction

Getting our students to start thinking for themselves can be a challenge, especially when many can find an answer to a question within seconds on their phones. But, as we previously discussed, the success of future generations will lie in their ability to creatively solve problems. They must learn to think deeply and meaningfully. People think in two common ways—divergently and convergently.

Let's take a look at how these two work together to create deep creative thinkers. Divergent thinking is the expansive process of generating multiple potential solutions for a problem (Runco & Acar, 2019). It fuels debates, inspires artistic creation, and fosters innovation, embracing the myriad possibilities that arise from a single question. Divergent thinking encourages creative thinking by allowing students to consider different, multiple, and even wild possibilities (Manning, 2016).

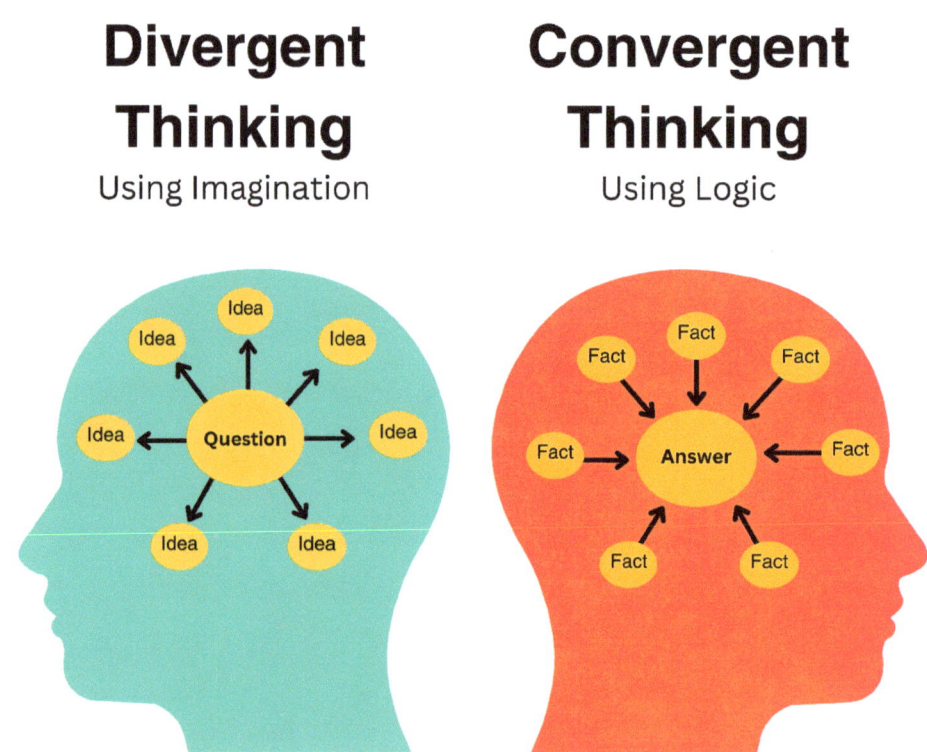

On the other hand, convergent thinking, characterized by logical reasoning and analytical skills, narrows multiple ideas into a single, optimal solution. It guides students through standardized tests, mathematical problems, and scientific experiments, fostering precision and skill development (Runco, 1993). Convergent thinking encourages critical thinking. By incorporating both divergent and convergent lanes of thought into our classroom, we can develop more meaningful, comprehensive reasoning and analytical skills—the cognitive process of distilling multiple ideas into a single, optimal solution.

Divergent Thinking

According to Sir Ken Robinson (2013), divergent thinking is the ability to see numerous possible answers to a question, recognize multiple ways to approach and interpret it, and think laterally, not just linearly. It's about embracing multiple answers, not just one.

In today's digital age, students are used to searching the internet for the "right" answer. Creative problem-solving, critical thinking, reflection, and evaluation skills are new to them. Many teachers today remember going to the library, scouring card catalogs, rummaging through stacks of books and old newspapers, all to find that perfect quote. I remember accumulating stacks of index cards while writing research papers for my high school classes.

Divergent thinking is the bedrock of creative thinking. It's essential for students to learn how to explore multiple approaches to solving a single problem. As we all know, information is everywhere. Just ask Siri or Google and you can discover the quick and simple answer to any question. Or can you? Divergent and convergent thinking are essential elements of creative and critical thinking and content curation. These thinking styles offer unique advantages and shape our approach to the content we want our students to embrace.

> **IT'S ESSENTIAL FOR STUDENTS TO LEARN HOW TO EXPLORE MULTIPLE APPROACHES TO SOLVING A SINGLE PROBLEM.**

GROUND RULES FOR
DIVERGENT THINKING

1. Defer Judgement

2. Strive for Quality

3. Seek Wild & Unusual Ideas

4. Build on Other's Ideas

Adapted from Miller, B., Vehar, J., Firestein, R., Thurber, S., & Nielsen, D. (2001) Creativity unbound. Williamsville, NY: Innovative System Group

Take a look at the ground rules for divergent thinking: to foster a classroom environment where students actively engage in divergent thinking, it is crucial to ensure they grasp and embrace the ground rules (or guidelines, if you're someone like me who tends to challenge norms). This applies not only to students but to all humans; we must learn to defer judgment. The goal is to cultivate a mindset that encourages the generation of numerous ideas, even unconventional ones. It's important to remember that some ideas might take you outside your comfort zone, but that's where growth happens. Instead of criticizing, let's remain nonjudgmental and let the ideas flow, building upon one another.

Various techniques promote divergent thinking, and with practice, students can become more comfortable. However, some students may feel hesitant or anxious about voicing wild ideas due to fear of judgment. In such cases, Post-it notes can be incredibly useful. Students can anonymously write down their ideas and place them in a common area. This allows every student to read and expand upon the ideas they find interesting.

Another effective technique is forced connections. Take any item in your classroom, such as a stapler, and ask, "How might this stapler spark some new ideas?" You can also show students images and encourage them to use those images to connect with the main problem being used for brainstorming. You can use forced connections in multiple ways—the main idea is to allow students time to think of new and creative ideas.

 Try it! How many different pictures can you draw using this shape?

What are all the different ways you might get from the earth to the moon without using a spaceship? How will you get there? Try to think of as many ideas as you can.

LET'S EMBRACE THIS ENGAGING JOURNEY OF DISCOVERY AND CREATIVITY!

Convergent Thinking

Convergent thinking, along with divergent thinking, plays a pivotal role in fostering creativity and problem-solving skills among students. With convergent thinking, students subject their ideas to critical examination. Which ideas possess the most potential? How can they be further developed and refined?

Convergent thinking allows students to cultivate critical thinking skills, and students gain the ability not only to thoughtfully analyze their own ideas but also to critically evaluate the concepts put forth by others. They learn to meticulously weigh advantages and disadvantages, consider alternative solutions, and appraise the effectiveness of their proposed solutions. This iterative process empowers students to refine their ideas in alignment with existing knowledge and insights. Let's take a look at the ground rules for convergent thinking.

> **Convergent thinking allows students to cultivate critical thinking skills.**

GROUND RULES FOR CONVERGENT THINKING

1. Be Affirmative

2. Be Deliberate

3. Check Your Objectives

4. Improve Ideas

5. Consider Novelty

Adapted from Miller, B., Vehar, J., Firestein, R., Thurber, S., & Nielsen, D. (2001) Creativity unbound. Williamsville, NY: Innovative System Group

🔍 **Stop and Reflect:** Now, using these ground rules, reflect on the ideas you previously came up with and narrow down the concepts to the ones you think should continue to the next level. Is there a shape that works best, or a way to get the moon that seems most effective?

Allowing students the time to generate creative and different ideas will lead them to generate real possibilities through critical thinking, honing in on the ones they believe should move forward.

Strategies for Divergent/Convergent Thinking

Alternative Use Activity: As students are thinking differently, show them a random image. It can be anything: a coffee cup, a toothbrush, a plant, a teddy bear—any object works for this activity. The object does not have to relate to what the students are brainstorming. Ask students to generate as many ideas as they can for how the image could be used to inspire new thoughts. Give them a set time frame such as fifteen seconds per image.

 **Practical Tip:** Students are brainstorming titles for their short stories. When they are about two minutes into the brainstorming process, hold up a stapler and ask, "What ideas come to mind when you look at this stapler?" Wait ten seconds. Show a random image and ask the same question. Repeat this process about five times. As you are doing this, students are writing the ideas they are generating.

 Stop and Reflect: How might you use the Alternative Use Activity in your classroom? What random images might you use?

Mind-mapping: Mind-mapping can be done online or on paper. This is a great activity to help students think of different components of a research paper, science experiment, or life problem. By writing the initial idea in the center and brainstorming categories and subcategories, students can visually see their train of thought.

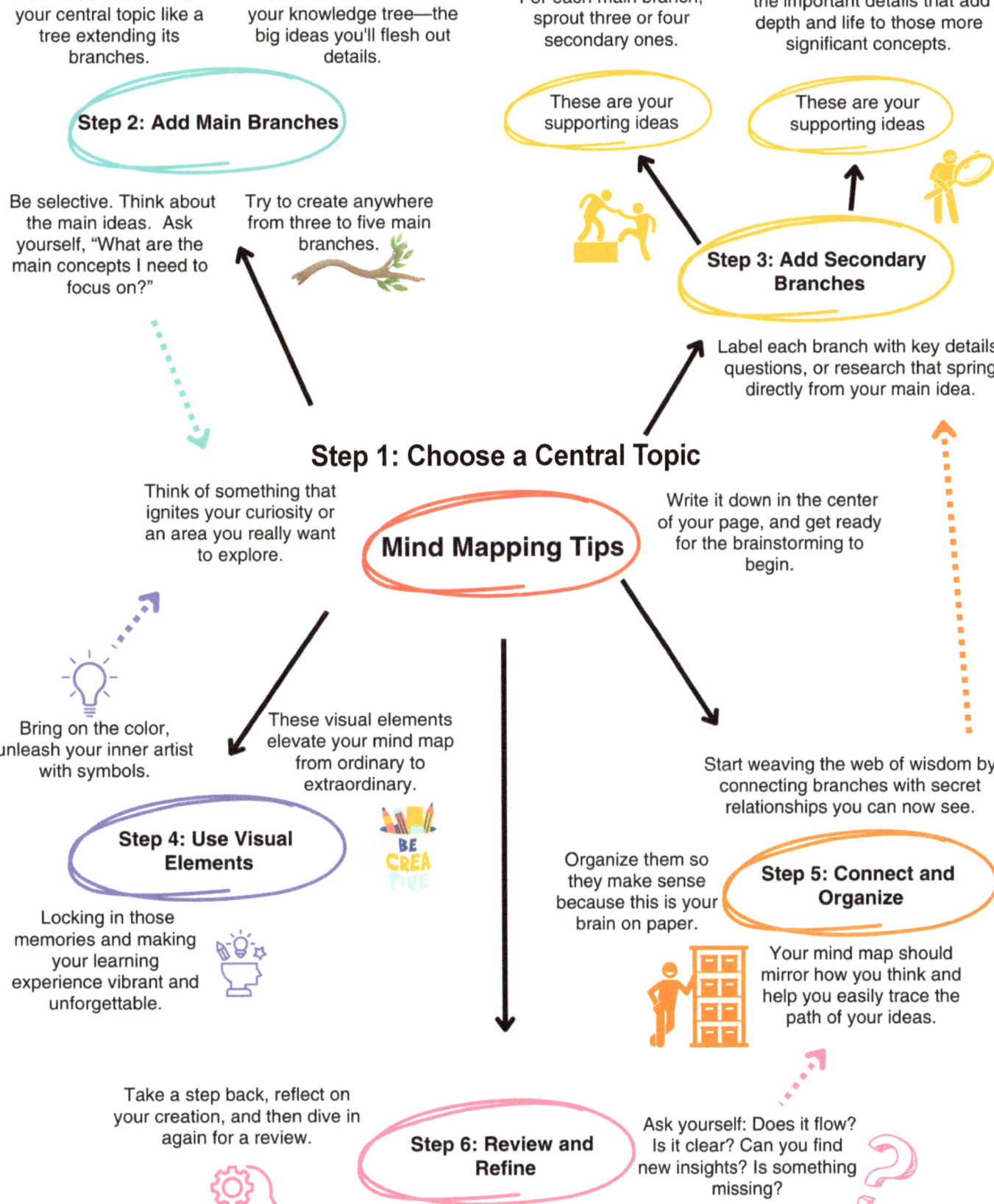

 Practical Tip: Students need to generate ideas on a research topic, a persuasive speech, or a project.

 Stop and Reflect: How might mind-mapping be useful in your classroom and content planning?

Thinking Journal: Have students keep a journal or Google Doc specifically for their thoughts. It's a safe place (never collected or graded). This can be a helpful tool to get students thinking about the subject matter and to provide them with structure when they come to class for further discussion. This strategy is designed to deepen students' understanding by tracking their growth in both creative and critical thinking. Students will read a text (poem, short story, novel, textbook chapter) and reflect on their understanding of the material. Then, through collaboration with peers, students will discuss different perspectives on the same text and discern which viewpoint best fits the meaning of the text.

If you are concerned about them completing it without a grade, use a reading conference atmosphere. Have students summarize their thoughts and highlight some of their best ideas.

Common questions to ask students to consider in their Thinking Journal include:

- Where am I most confused in the [text, assignment, problem]?
- What questions do I have about the topic?
- What might be the next steps for me to find meaningful solutions to my questions?
- What ideas do I have now that I understand the content?
- Are there any patterns when it comes to my thinking?
- What information do I wish I had to help me understand this better?

Practical Tip: Students are discussing a complex poem and need time to process. Allow students to first think about all the questions and ideas they have regarding the meaning of the poem and then write them down in their journals.

 Stop and Reflect: How might you use the Thinking Journal in your classroom?

Brainwriting: Have students break up into small groups of three or four. Each student starts with a pen and paper, and they take turns writing down an idea or thought related to the topic at hand. They then pass the paper around the group, allowing each person to continue writing on that same piece of paper. After everyone has had a chance to write, have them share their thoughts out loud and discuss what they've written.

This can be especially helpful for students who may not be comfortable sharing their ideas in a large group setting. Brainwriting is also great for brainstorming; it creates a safe space for students to express themselves and share out-of-the-box thinking, while also providing an opportunity to consider the different perspectives of the group. Brainwriting can foster problem-solving skills and build strong interpersonal skills.

 Practical Tip: Have students write together a summary of a textbook chapter highlighting what each student feels is most important to the subject or question being addressed. Give students a fun topic—flying monkeys—and have them write a short story/poem about the topic. Each person in the group would write a sentence and then pass the paper on for development. With each group member writing one sentence, a unique and creative text can be built.

Stop and Reflect: How might you use this strategy in your classroom?

Brainstorming: Using Post-it notes is a common divergent thinking activity, but allowing a structured environment can be helpful. For example, students need to brainstorm all the ways they could prevent pollution in the local river.

1. Give each student several sticky notes and instruct them to write one idea per note.
2. Gather all the notes and stick them to a board or poster.
3. Now have students read all the different ideas. Do certain patterns arise?
4. Ask students to categorize the ideas. Do some go together? From that point, you can start to converge and discover which ideas are worth pursuing.
5. Have students share their top three ideas.

 **Practical Tip:** You can use this as a jigsaw activity. Have each group brainstorm a different topic. For example, one group looks at a different character in a novel and what motivates that character. Or each group is asked to brainstorm societal issues in different time periods or countries.

Stop and Reflect: How might you use this strategy in your classroom? The next time you ponder the mysteries of creativity, remember critical thinking is the perfect partner twirling by its side, infusing depth and meaning into every inspired move.

Cultivating a Creative Classroom

Here are the characteristics of a classroom bursting with inspiration.

- Cultivate curiosity: Sparking wonder and encouraging "what if?" and "why?" questions.
- Foster open-mindedness: Embracing different perspectives and fostering a culture of acceptance.
- Develop empathy: Nurturing compassion, understanding, and connection among students.
- Promote authenticity: Encouraging individuality and celebrating diverse identities.
- Recognize diversity: Valuing differences and creating an inclusive environment.
- Celebrate mistakes: Accepting that failure allows us to grow and learn and is nothing to fear.
- Support flexibility: Adapting to different learning preferences and needs along with flexible seating arrangements.
- Encourage options: Providing choices to empower students and ignite their passions.
- Embrace creativity: Letting imagination soar and unleashing the artist within.

Building a classroom that encourages curiosity, creativity, and collaboration will inspire students to take risks and be open to new ideas.

HOW TO CULTIVATE A CREATIVE CLASSROOM

Try it! Let's use the divergent thinking skill we learned earlier to come up with an answer for the following problem. Use the boxes below to write down all the ways we might build a creative and welcoming learning environment when students seem disengaged or disrespectful?

Now, using your convergent skills, take a look at what you wrote above and see if you can categorize any of your ideas. What areas share a common theme or idea? Using different-colored markers, circle the ones that fit together best.

Stop and Reflect: Do certain ideas on your list stand out to you? Did you discover a new strategy? What will be your next steps?

Strategies for Cultivating a Creative Classroom

Your classroom environment is one that students will remember. Do you remember stepping into a classroom and feeling immediately welcomed? Did you feel like this was a place where you could relax and learn? Did you feel safe to make mistakes? Teachers often equate creative classrooms with chaos. That is one of those myths! Building a classroom that encourages curiosity, creativity, and collaboration will inspire students to take risks and be open to new ideas.

Building a creative classroom does not mean you have to spend hundreds of dollars decorating your classroom. A classroom environment that encourages creative and critical thinking depends on the flexibility of you and your students. Does your classroom:

1. **Cultivate curiosity.**
   - Encourage your students to ask: "What if?" and "Why?"
   - Teach your students how to ask questions.
   - Encourage students to discover their interests.
   - Empower students to choose their own learning path.
   - Offer choices within the curriculum?

 Practical Tip: Allow students to choose their research topics for science projects or select the next book for a read-aloud session.

2. **Foster open-mindedness.**
   - Expose students to diverse perspectives?
   - Encourage students to challenge their beliefs?
   - Foster an environment rich in respectful discussions and collaboration?
   - Model and teach embracing differing viewpoints?

 Practical Tip: Have your students create survival bags. Put students in teams of four and ask them to pretend they are on a deserted island and need to find water, start a fire to cook and stay warm, build a shelter, and call for help. Remind them they can use only the items in their backpacks or purses.

After about five minutes, have students reflect on:
- In what ways were you open-minded to the ideas others shared?
- Was it difficult to consider ideas you knew probably wouldn't work or be realistic?
- Were there any moments when you didn't share your ideas because you thought they weren't good?

3. **Develop empathy.** Empathy is being able to step into someone else's emotional world and truly understand their experiences (McDonald & Messinger, 2011).
   - Model and encourage active listening.
     - Not interrupting those who are speaking.
     - Asking follow-up questions.
   - Model and encourage examination of our innate and learned biases.

    Practical Tip: Once a week, let your students interview different classmates. Then, at the end of the quarter, have each student create a unique piece—writing, drawing, or anything that sparks creativity!—to showcase their perception of the whole class.

4. **Promote authenticity.**
   - Be authentic with students.
     - Share what you like.
     - Share your stories of success and failure.
     - Share your fears and hopes.
   - Ask students: "Who are you deep down?" "What do you believe in?" "What values define you?"

    Practical Tip: Show your students a gripping news clip or a fascinating YouTube video featuring a real-life situation. Then encourage them to reflect on how they would handle themselves if they were in that scenario. Weave a compelling tale about a young person facing a tough predicament and let your students brainstorm the best course of action. Creativity will flow, my friend!

5. **Recognize diversity.** Diversity in the classroom embraces the notion that each student brings their own unique experiences, strengths, and ideas.
   - Explore and incorporate these differences.
   - Nurture social awareness and bolster academic confidence.
   - Forge connections on various levels.
   - Foster shared experience.

Practical Tip: Have students teach something to the class. Imagine the possibilities! For instance, a Spanish-speaking student could teach the class a catchy Spanish song. And what better way to amplify the impact than by having the entire class perform it together for another class? The stage is set for a vibrant celebration of diversity.

6. **Celebrate mistakes.**

    - The fear of failure often constraints students from taking the necessary creative and intellectual risks.
    - Transform mistakes into moments of coaching.
    - Reframe the failure and mistakes into learning opportunities.

 Practical Tip: Be open and transparent about your mistakes with your students. By modeling the act of celebrating errors, you create a safe and nurturing environment where students feel comfortable embracing their own mistakes as opportunities for growth. Let's usher in a new era of fearless learning.

7. **Support flexibility.**

    - Encourage each other to be more flexible.
    - Explore different approaches.
    - Appreciate diverse perspectives.
    - Model flexibility for students.

 Practical Tip: Allow students to choose their seats or alter the routine for the day, and observe how your students react. Take this as an opportunity to spark a conversation about the significance of being flexible in life.

8. **Embrace creativity.**

    - Model finding creative solutions and collaborating with students for ideas.
    - Allow students to find innovative solutions to problems.
    - Allow collaborative opportunities.

 Practical Tip: Take your students for a walk, armed only with paper and writing utensils. As they explore, have them journal their observations, thoughts, and feelings. After returning to the classroom, facilitate a debriefing session. Encourage students to reflect on their journals and share commonalities and differences in small groups.

1. CULTIVATE CURIOSITY
2. FOSTER OPEN-MINDEDNESS
3. DEVELOP EMPATHY
4. PROMOTE AUTHENTICITY
5. RECOGNIZE DIVERSITY
6. CELEBRATE MISTAKES
7. SUPPORT FLEXIBILITY
8. EMBRACE CREATIVITY

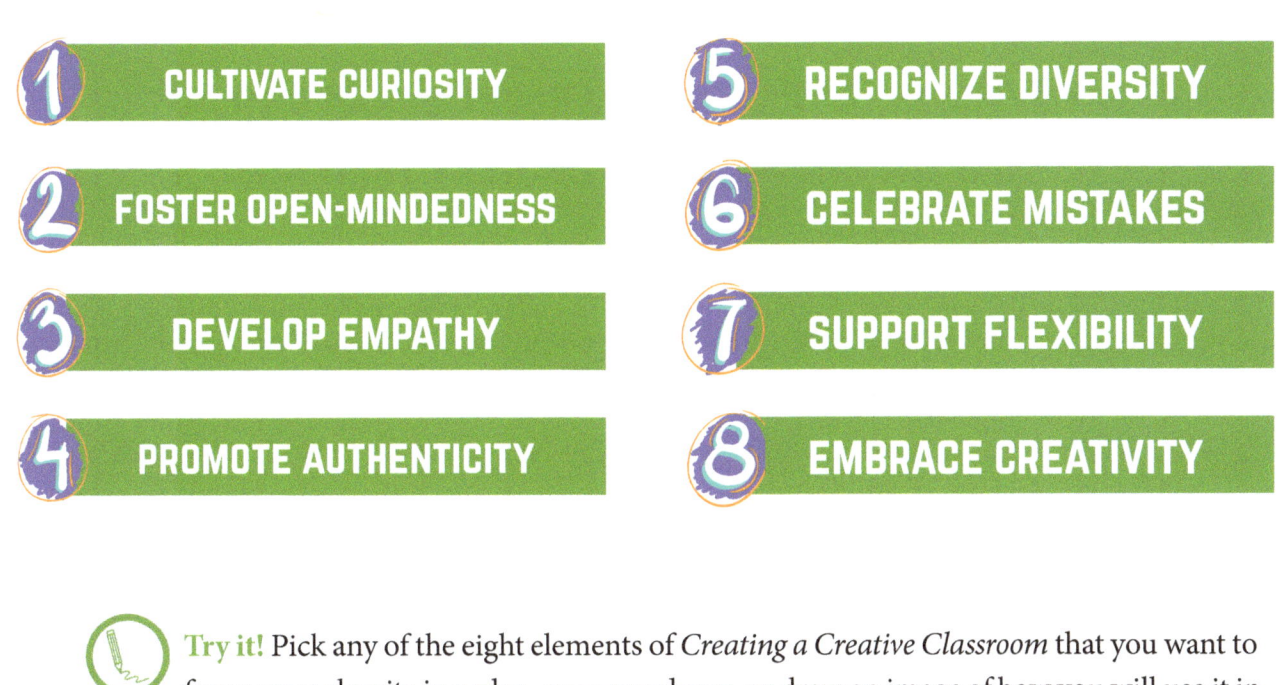

Try it! Pick any of the eight elements of *Creating a Creative Classroom* that you want to focus on and write in a plan, use a wordmap, or draw an image of how you will use it in your classroom and how you foresee it helping your classroom climate.

Reimagining Classroom Relationships to Support Creative and Critical Thinking

"[N]o significant learning occurs without a significant relationship" (Comer, 1995). This is a common quote when it comes to building rapport, and we as teachers know strong classroom relationships lead to better student outcomes; research confirms this. Solid student-teacher relationships offer security that significantly boosts students' engagement and, most important, success. Enhanced teacher-student connections profoundly impact students' psychological well-being. Studies show a direct correlation between the quality of these relationships and improvements in students' self-esteem, self-efficacy, and overall mental health (Fabris et al., 2022; Jederlund & Von Rosen, 2022; Pianta, 2001).

What if we took a more creative approach to classroom relationships? Instead of focusing solely on the student-teacher relationship, what if we expanded our approach to the classroom through the lens of the educative relationships?

Think for a moment about the three basic elements needed for *classroom* learning: the student, the teacher, and the knowledge. Now think about the power dynamic among these three learning stakeholders: who or what controls or leads the learning? Some days, what you have to teach—the knowledge!—leads the way, determining pacing, activities, expectations, and assessments. Other days, who you have to teach—the students!—is at the forefront of your decision-making, planning, and prepping. And then there are the days when who is doing the teaching—you!—tips the scale in favor of a topic you are passionate about, an idea you are interested in trying out, or in your level of energy and excitement for the lesson ahead.

Now, think about the relationships between these three classroom collaborators.

THERE ARE THREE BASIC ELEMENTS FOR CLASSROOM LEARNING: THE STUDENT, THE TEACHER, AND THE KNOWLEDGE.

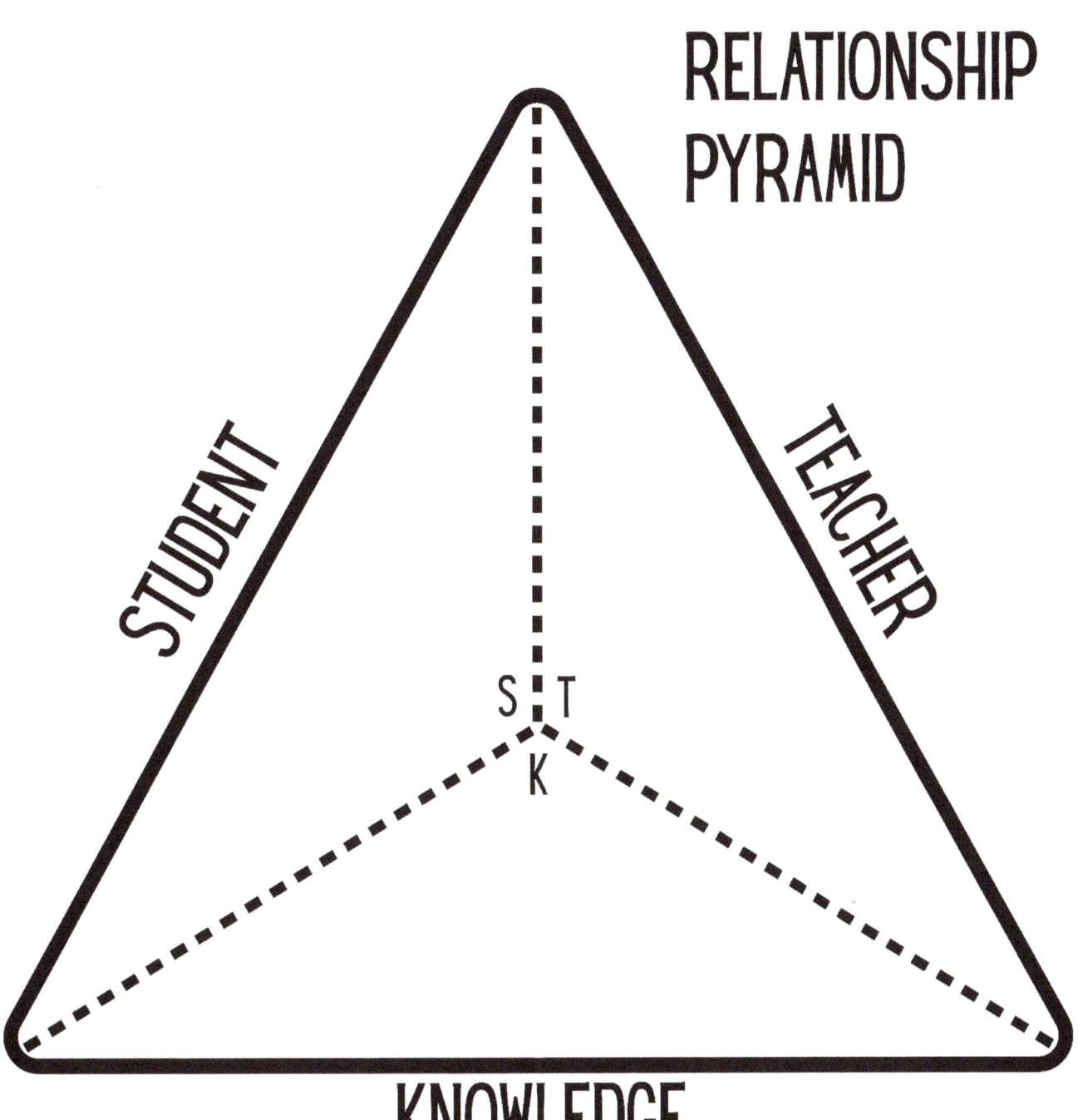

 **Stop and Reflect:**

- How would you describe the student-teacher relationship in your classroom, and how is it different from the teacher-student relationship?

- How do you feel about the content you are currently teaching (the teacher-knowledge relationship), and how do your kids feel about it (the student-knowledge relationship)?

- How are the peer relationships within your class (student-student relationship), and how well do you work with your colleagues (teacher-teacher relationship)?

- How does your personal experience support, connect, enhance, or prohibit your curriculum (knowledge-knowledge relationship), and what does this relationship look like for your students?

- How can an awareness of all of these relationships—the educative relationships—increase space for creativity?

The educative relationships are not a creative methodology or instructional strategy, but a means to an end. By turning the educative relationship prism and shifting control from one element to another—from one relationship to another—you can begin to identify different paths into your classroom and creativity. The educative relationships will help you find the space to apply all of the strategies, practices, and methods. Once you see the educative relationships at play in your classroom, you will know which relationship sets are your power players and which sets sit dormant. By constantly reimagining the power dynamic—shifting from one element to another, one relationship to another—the spaces and places for creative practice will grow exponentially!

Stop and Reflect: Instead of letting the content/curricular knowledge lead the way, what would happen if your students' individual knowledge controlled the learning path? Instead of moving through a skill set sequentially, what if your Professional Learning Community (PLC) combined experience to identify common misunderstandings and began instruction from there? Instead of being the "sage on the stage," what if you became the "guide on the side" by creating moments for student choice in content, process, product, and medium? What would happen to this activity, conversation, lesson, assessment, or unit if you shifted control?

CREATIVITY AND YOU!

How does being creative improve your mental health? Before we jump into the CREATE Method, it's important to make sure you take care of yourself. Adding creativity into your classroom will not only assist your students but it will lighten your load and allow you time to take care of yourself.

Teachers often take on the stresses of their peers and students. Burnout rates are higher than ever and we are experiencing a critical teacher shortage. That's why it is essential that as you begin to build a creative classroom environment and instruct students on how to think in a deep and meaningful way, you first embrace your creativity needs. As we move into the next section, remember:

1. Creativity is a form of self-care. Engaging in activities that support creative expression, such as drawing, cooking, painting, crafting, or writing, can have a profound effect on personal well-being. These activities can be therapeutic, relaxing, and soothing, promoting positive mood, reducing symptoms of anxiety and depression, and improving overall mental health.

2. Studies have shown that incorporating creativity into daily life can lead to improvements in cognition. Engaging in creative activities can enhance memory, problem-solving skills, and learning ability, making teachers more effective in their role.

3. Creativity encourages mindfulness, the ability to be present in the moment and focus on what is happening right now, rather than worrying about the past or future. Engaging in creative activities such as painting, writing, or gardening can be a meditative experience that encourages mindfulness. These activities allow the mind to rest and recharge, reducing stress levels and promoting a calm state of mind.

> **ENGAGING IN CREATIVE ACTIVITIES CAN BE THERAPEUTIC, PROMOTING POSITIVE MOOD, REDUCING ANXIETY AND DEPRESSION.**

4. When teachers engage in creative activities, they have the opportunity to connect with their inner selves and find purpose. Creating something new and exciting, whether it's a watercolor painting, a piece of creative writing, or a new recipe, can be an empowering experience that provides a sense of accomplishment, leading to increased self-esteem and a more positive outlook on life.

5. Creativity can promote community. Engaging in creative activities can foster connections between individuals, which is important for promoting positive mental health. When teachers participate in creative workshops or master classes, they can connect with like-minded people who share their passion. These experiences can be empowering and energizing, leading to a sense of community and support that can improve mental health.

How creativity helps your mental health

1. Creativity is a form of self care.

Engaging in activities that support creative expression, such as drawing, cooking, painting, crafting, or writing, can be therapeutic, relaxing, and soothing, promoting positive mood, reducing symptoms of anxiety and depression, and overall improving overall mental health.

2. Boosting creativity can improve cognitive function.

Studies have shown that incorporating creativity into one's daily life can enhance memory, problem-solving skills, and learning ability, making teachers more effective in their role.

3. Creativity encourages mindfulness.

Engaging in creative activities, such as painting, writing, or gardening, allows the mind to rest and recharge, reducing stress levels and promoting a calm state of mind.

4. Creativity can lead to a sense of purpose.

Creating something new and exciting, whether it's a watercolor painting, a piece of creative writing, or a new recipe, can be an empowering experience that provides a sense of accomplishment, leading to increased self-esteem and a more positive outlook on life.

5. Creativity can promote community.

When teachers participate in creative workshops or masterclasses, they can connect with like-minded people who share their passion. These experiences can be empowering and energizing, leading to a sense of community and support that can improve mental health.

There are many ways to incorporate creativity into your life as a teacher, even if finding the time and resources is a challenge. Remember creativity can have a profound impact on personal well-being and a positive effect on mental health. Whether it's painting, writing, or taking part in a creative workshop, find what works for you and make time to incorporate it into your daily life. Taking small steps toward boosting creativity can lead to significant improvements in mental health and overall well-being in the long run. Teachers today are overwhelmed—by embracing our innate sense of creativity we can rebuild some of the confidence that gets diminished in the overwhelming emotional side of teaching.

 Stop and Reflect: What is causing you to not take care of yourself? Teachers experience different stresses. Take a minute to write down your pain point.

Amidst all the stress teaching can present, there are still times of joy. Having moments to be creative helps us:

- Refresh (doing something different or something we love).
- See that there's a variety of ways to do something.
- Rebuild the confidence we lose after so many failures in the classroom and school.

Stop and Reflect: As we begin to dig deeper into the CREATE Method, let's take some time to refresh and center ourselves. Companies often have mission statements—take some time to write a strong purpose statement for the work you do.

This exercise can be hugely powerful and influence how you frame your day, your classroom, and your career. Examples could range from "I want to educate the world" to a more realistic and personal "I had a sibling who never got the proper support from educators, and I want to be that support for my students."

Now that you have reflected on the why and the what of being a teacher who strives for creative and critical thinking, it's time to write your mission statement.

Being a teacher today is challenging, but it can also be extremely rewarding. What's most important is that we teach our students how to be successful, contributing human beings. The CREATE Method can be used as a guide, assisting you on your journey to create an engaging, creative, rigorous environment for students to think, reflect and grow.

TIPS FOR INFUSING YOUR LIFE WITH MOMENTS OF CREATIVITY

1.  Be curious - ask questions and discover the answer

2.  Try something new - take a class, try a new recipe, learn a new language

3.  Take time to listen to music, a podcast, watch a funny movie, read a book

4.  Doodle

5.  Go for a walk

6.  Yoga

7.  Dance

8.  Keep tangible stress relievers on your desk - like stress balls, fidget spinners- and take time to play

9.  Keep a journal

Stop and Reflect:
What new strategies or concepts from this section resonated with you the most? How do you plan to implement them in your classroom?

Reflect on a challenge you might face when applying the ideas from this section. How can you overcome it?

Consider your current teaching practices. How can you integrate the principles discussed in this section to enhance creativity and critical thinking among your students?

Creative thinking is not a talent, it is a skill that can be learned. It empowers people by adding strength to their natural abilities which improves teamwork, productivity and, where appropriate, profits.
– Edward de Bono

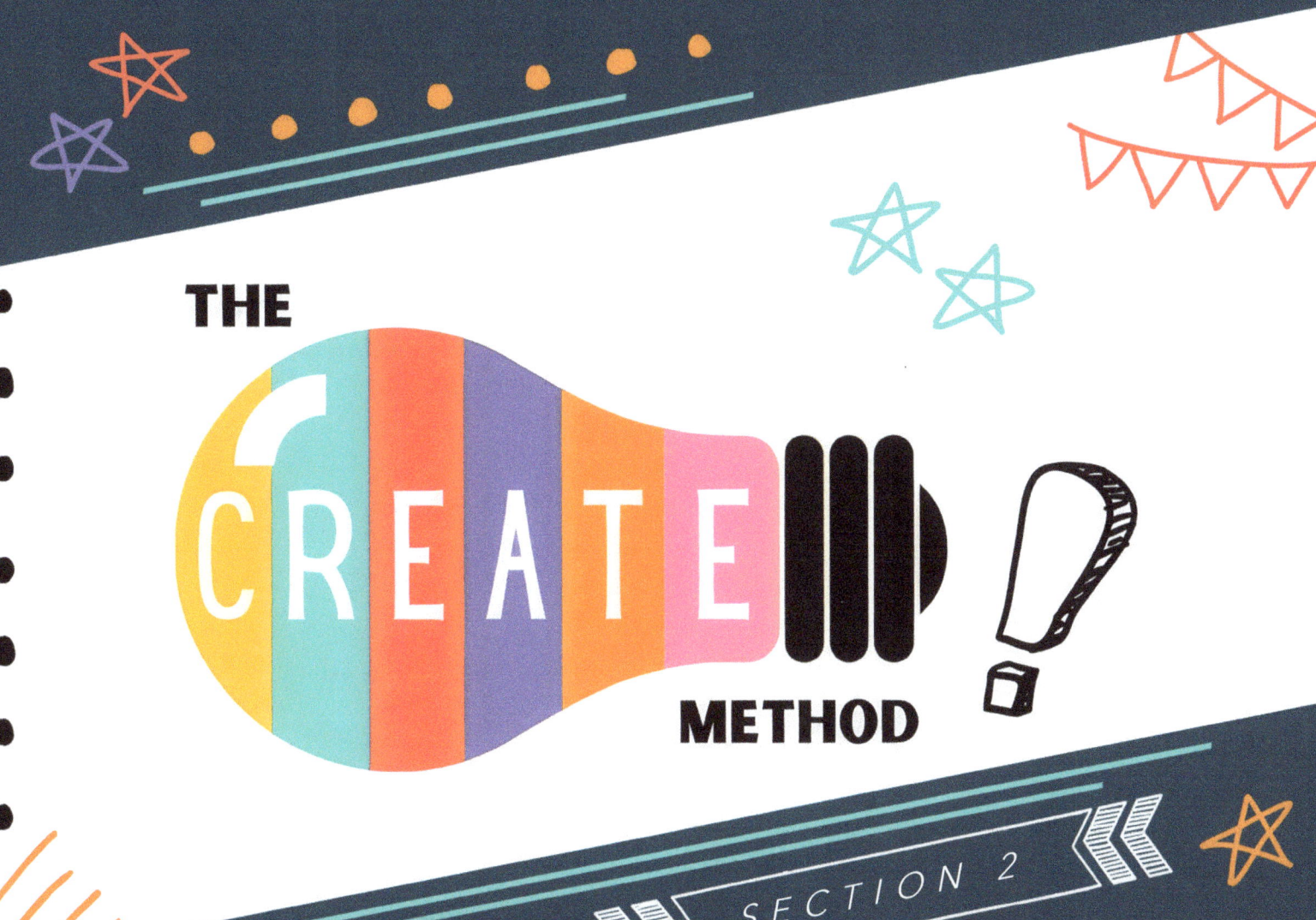

Discover the How: Incorporating Creativity and Critical Thinking in the Classroom

Understanding the reason for a situation is crucial, but we often walk away from training sessions with only theoretical knowledge, lacking a clear understanding of how to implement these ideas. It's just as important—if not more so—to know *how* to infuse creative and critical thinking into our teaching.

The key to successful creative teaching and learning is to remember it's not about the teacher but the learner. Creative teaching is about more than just employing technology or designing innovative activities. It's about meeting each student where they are and finding ways to engage them in meaningful creative learning experiences.

Many educators recognize the importance of fostering creativity in the classroom but need help to implement it. That's where this workbook comes in. We've designed this part specifically for you, to dive into a unit you already teach and rework it using the CREATE Method.

 Stop and Reflect: Choose the unit/lesson/concept/skill you want to revise or restructure, and let's fill out this guide together. Get ready to unleash your creativity in the classroom!

> **Creative teaching is about more than just employing technology or designing innovative activities. It's about meeting each student where they are and finding ways to engage them in meaningful creative learning experiences.**

LESSON / UNIT SELECTION

Unit Topic:

Why did you choose this particular unit?

Brief summary of unit:

What is the overall learning goal of the unit?

What are the priority skills being assessed in this unit?

At this point, what is the culminating summative assessment for this unit?

LESSON / UNIT SELECTION

What works in this unit?

For Students? **For Teachers?** **For Knowledge?**

What do you have control over changing?

What can you not change about this unit?

Your ultimate goal with this unit is to….

Great - now that you have a unit, let's start working through it together.

How to Renovate Your Classroom with the CREATE Method

There are many reasons why people renovate. Did an inspection reveal previously hidden problems? Do you have a solid foundation beneath a weak, flimsy frame? Classrooms are like homes—lived-in, comfortable environments built to withstand the chaos students may encounter in their learning. Like renovating a home, rebuilding a classroom requires time, dedication, preparation, and the flexibility to venture into the unknown.

You have got to make do with what you have, and sometimes, especially in construction, the worst seems just ahead. On some days, teaching can feel the same. The CREATE Method is designed so you don't have to do it all at once, offering iteration. To CREATE, you need to BUILD:

RENOVATION	CREATE METHOD
Begin and Inspect • Like an inspection before constructing a home, understanding what you are working with and what you are building toward aids the building process.	Take a step back to view and gain feedback on your classroom's activities. • What are the standards you are working with? • What skills are you building? • Why is it at the foundation of your classroom?

Understand and Plan
• When renovating, problems arise—delays, budget issues, weather, and a pandemic, for example—all of which can affect your project.
	How you see your ideal classroom requires creativity— but hey! That's the best part! Brainstorm your dream classroom and begin ideating on the changes you wish to see.
	
	What does your classroom need?
	  • What is your attention directed towards?
	  • Does your classroom need updates, upgrades?

Implement and Revise
• Is there a major issue you need to address?
• Is there an area that requires deeper focus than just patchwork?
	After assessing your classroom, list some of the end goals you may have in mind. Take a few pieces from each letter of the CREATE Method, and use what you need to patch up the areas that may require immediate attention.
	
	What are some of the immediate issues you need to address?
	  • Attitudes? Skip to the Attitude Shifter
	  • Collaboratation? Skip to Team Transformer
	  • Engagement? Skip to Experience Navigator
	  • Risk-taking? Skip to Risk Facilitator
	  • Attendance? Skip to Content Curator

Listen and Learn
• What might be hiding under the surface?
• Who do you need help from? Should you hire experts in the field to help you rework the plumbing?
• Do you need to watch an online DIY tutorial?
	By keeping an open mind and listening to feedback, we can improve our classrooms and meet the specific needs of our students.
	
	Who can you enlist to help?
	  • Students?
	  • Coaches?
	  • PLC?
	  • Online Communities?

Design and Reflect • Is your goal reached? Why? What can you do to make the next reno project even better?	This is the moment you've been waiting for! Reveal day! Take time to reflect and evaluate.

HOW CAN WE DETERMINE WHAT CONTENT IS MOST RELEVANT AND MEANINGFUL TO OUR STUDENTS WHILE MAINTAINING LEARNING OBJECTIVES?

CONTENT CURATOR

Content Curator

"My contention is that creativity now is as important in education as literacy, and we should treat it with the same status." Sir Ken Robinson (2013)

> **Essential Question**: How can we determine what content is most relevant and meaningful to our students while maintaining learning objectives? Curating content ensures the knowledge you are sharing has:
> - Depth
> - Relevance
> - Rigor
> - Engagement
> - Motivation

Strategies we will examine are:

- Storytelling.
- Choice.
- Questioning skills.
- Hexagonal thinking.

Definitions

- Content curation is selecting knowledge in an in-depth, relevant, and challenging manner.
- Curriculum frames are a set of standard frameworks in which the learning goals or outcomes are clearly defined.
- Personalized learning is a learning theory that emphasizes the need for tailored lessons accounting for students' past education, drive, culture, personality, talents, and abilities, to name a few.
- Power is where the focus of attention lies in the classroom.

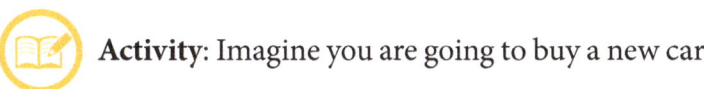 **Activity**: Imagine you are going to buy a new car.

- What information would you need before making your decision?
- Where would you go to find the information?
- What types of questions do you need to ask yourself?
- What types of questions do you need to ask other people?
- How did you know what information was reliable?

INTRODUCTION

When did you last visit a museum and truly appreciate the beauty and knowledge around you? I'm not talking about a chaotic field trip with a group of kids, but a personal experience for yourself. What did you see, feel, and learn? Why does that experience stand out to you?

Now let's take a moment to think about the immense effort that goes into creating museum exhibits. Every detail is carefully planned to provide the best viewing experience. That interactive art piece you enjoyed? Hours of curation went into making it just right. From the colors on the walls to the smallest details, everything is designed to enhance your experience.

To create genuinely captivating lessons, it is essential to understand the concept of content curation. Content curation is the practice of gathering and organizing information meaningfully with the goal of igniting curiosity in students.

What exactly is content? The word "content" can be very ambiguous. Every day we are saturated with information. Turn on the TV, listen to the radio, or search the internet, and you will be bombarded with endless streams of content. Content can refer to the information we curate, compile, and present through our teaching methods.

Content curation is essentially about finding the right sources and providing a unique insight into them. This means selecting resources that support your lesson plans while also stimulating student curiosity. When creating lessons, you need to consider the relevance of the content, its accuracy, its timeliness, and whether it will engage your students. It is important to remember any content you choose should align with academic standards as well as being age-appropriate for your classroom setting.

Once you have identified relevant content, it is essential to revise it effectively so it truly captivates your students' attention. Crafting content into an engaging narrative using visuals and multimedia can bring it to life in the classroom. At its core, good content curation is about finding high-quality resources. By doing this, you can ensure your lessons are modern, relevant, and effectively designed to meet students' needs.

Content is information—whether it's text, visual, audio, or video. Content curation is carefully selecting, organizing and sharing knowledge to make sure your students get the right information in the most efficient way possible. By properly curating content, you can create a learning experience tailored to their unique needs and interests.

Content is experience-driven. It should be engaging and well written and contain elements of surprise and delight. In order to ensure your content is effective, it's important to use keywords that attract attention and focus readers in the right direction. Additionally, by utilizing tools such as metadata tagging, you can easily sort through information for quick retrieval from the abundance of data available on the internet.

Learning Objectives for Content Curator

This section will explore:

- What it means to be a Content Curator.
- Strategies to create lessons that truly captivate our students.
- Ways you can revise your content.

A teacher as a Content Curator:

- Creates custom learning experiences for students by infusing the curriculum with curiosity.
- Keeps track of trending topics in their field, allowing them to stay up-to-date on new advancements or research and to ensure their students learn through the most up-to-date materials available.

A student as a Content Curator:

- Learns more interactively and develops critical thinking skills.
- Ignites curiosity and encourages lifelong learning.

 Stop and Reflect: Take a moment to reflect on your process for creating lesson plans.

How do you plan your lessons?

Do you have specific targets and standards?

Do you collaborate with other teachers?

Where does your content come from?

How do you sequence the learning?

Many educators cite standardized testing, large class sizes, and traditional grading systems as barriers to innovation in the curriculum. In fact, teachers are handed scripted curriculum and face frustration due to lack of personalization. These constraints can be seen as an opportunity to instill practical and meaningful thinking skills at a time when they are undervalued yet desired in the workplace. With a proven need for creative learning, we need to incorporate curiosity, creativity, and critical thinking into teaching. Content curation is a great place to start.

Stop and Reflect: Take a moment to reflect on the learning experience you chose to highlight at the beginning of the workbook. In this time when you were most engaged in learning, what made that experience different from others? What emotions were involved?

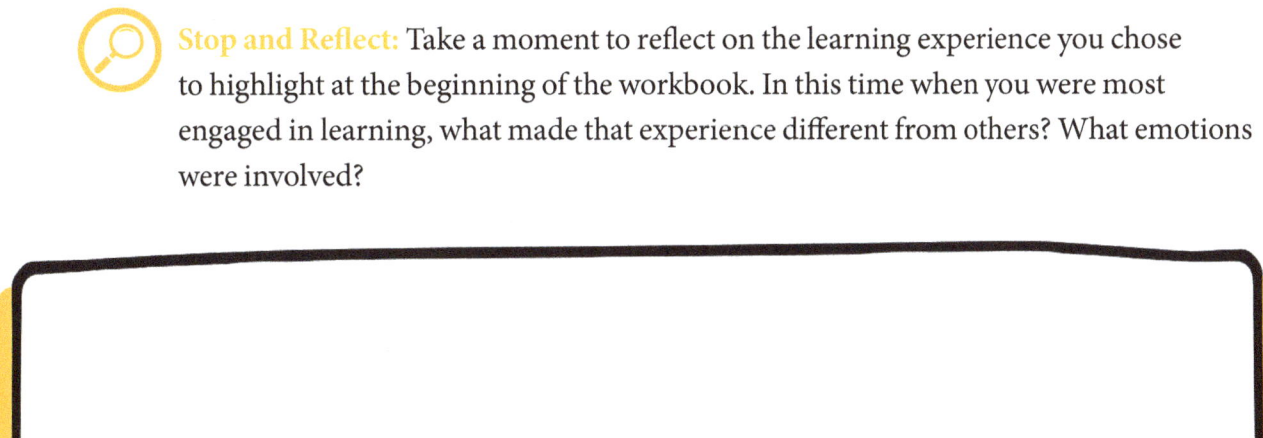

Strategies for Content Curation

Engaging students in curating content can be exciting and rigorous. Sometimes, it is easy to fall into the trap of "this is what I have always done, and it has worked before." Yet every year we encounter new students with different needs. By incorporating various strategies into our lesson plans, students and educators can find the most effective way of teaching skills.

- **Storytelling**
- **Choice**
- **Questioning Skills**
- **Hexagonal Thinking**

Curate Content through Captivating Storytelling in the Classroom

Teaching is an age-old profession; at its core, it's all about telling stories. Just like a storyteller captivates their audience, teachers weave narratives to engage and immerse students in a dynamic learning environment (Cardenas & Garza, 2007). By incorporating the art of storytelling into our content curation, educators can present information in a memorable and impactful way (Eisen, 2012).

Storytelling allows students to connect with the struggles and triumphs of characters, making learning relatable and meaningful. Using storytelling as a content-building tool also enables students and teachers to create their own stories and frame the knowledge they are learning.

 Try it!

1. Select narratives that capture students' attention, evoke emotions, and spark curiosity. Make sure they align with learning objectives and are culturally diverse. In fact, let the students choose what they want to read or create their own stories.

2. Connect stories to real-life situations, current events, or historical events to make them more relevant and meaningful. Discuss themes, characters, and conflicts, encouraging students to connect with their own lives.

3. Engage students in active listening by having them predict what might happen next, analyze motivations, and share their interpretations. Create opportunities for discussions and questions. Having a student tell how they arrived at a specific answer in science is storytelling and will allow students to connect.

4. Incorporate storytelling activities into the classroom setting as a way of sharing knowledge. Whether by having students write their own stories or by assigning characters and themes, these activities can engage students' interest in the subject. Additionally, they allow students to teach each other through sharing stories and experiences related to the topic at hand.

5. Utilize technology to facilitate interactions between students. Set up online forums, video conferences, or chat rooms for students to connect and discuss the story/content. This will give them a platform to virtually explore ideas and ask each other questions in real time. For example, instead of a traditional research essay, have the students create a podcast or video essay where they are telling a story in an informed manner. Warning here: at times technology can take center stage and students become too wrapped up with the learning of the technology rather than the content.

6. Introduce stories from diverse cultures to foster cultural appreciation and understanding. This expands students' worldviews and helps them feel included. Hearing stories from other cultures and differing perspectives encourages empathy.

What does storytelling look like in the elementary classroom? In primary classrooms, the key to effective content curation is to spark curiosity as a pathway to engagement and a love of lifelong learning. Try incorporating some of these strategies!

- Create a Curiosity Corner that can house interesting objects, books, and/or other media. The theme of the corner can change with seasons, months of the year, or curriculum unit.
- Create a Wonder Wall, a living and growing space in your classroom where students can post questions about subjects they find interesting.
- Share a read-aloud related to new concepts before diving into a lesson. This strategy works well for any content area.
- Use hands-on materials and allow students to play with/explore materials before the lesson.
- Invite students to retell the story and use math manipulatives to explore math concepts.
- Ask students of social studies to brainstorm a list of questions they would like to ask a notable person in history.
- Ask students to write a story of an animal's life cycle from the perspective of the animal at each stage of growing.

What does storytelling look like in the middle school classroom? Curating content can happen in various ways for middle school. Middle schoolers have a simultaneous desire for autonomy and a need for structure. Keep these tips in mind:

1) Give students choice whenever possible.

2) Relate everything possible to their current interests, experiences, or dreams.

3) Make it as hands-on as possible.

ELA/Social Studies

1. In a historical fiction unit, steer students in the direction of differing perspectives. For example, *Unbroken* by Lauren Hillenbrand offers a plethora of opportunities for students to explore nonfiction materials on Americans' struggles and triumphs during World War II while also considering Japanese perspectives on family life, war and freedom, or preservation of freedom and respect. Read letters, diary entries, newspaper articles, or opinion pieces from both or multiple countries or watch video clips, both cinematic and documentary, from both perspectives. Study cultural values, family life, and economic dependencies from that era in both or multiple countries. Compare and contrast viewpoints explored in the content.

2. When studying poetry, plays, or fiction, expose students to real-life examples of those trials, challenges, and conflicts so they can connect them to their experiences or perspectives. For example, while teaching *Romeo and Juliet*, have students journal/reflect on what it would be like to be told they cannot date/love someone because of their families' differing values and beliefs. Take them to see renditions of the play set in modern/differing times. Have them rewrite a summary or recount of the play in a modern-day situation they or their peers might face. Students can study spoken word poetry, finding poems, videos, and audio performances. Have them write their own spoken-word poems and have a poetry parent night when students can perform. Have students enter their poems in poetry submission contests to be published.

Math

1. Traditional mathematics classes focus on rote memorization and worksheet practice. But when we curate the content to be relevant, meaningful, and rigorous, there is a greater chance students will be engaged, remember the concepts, and be able to apply them.

2. Give students a modern-day scenario—it could be a story or scenario you have experienced—and ask how they would solve it.

3. Budgeting is another subject in which scenarios can be effective. For example: "You have $2,000. Rent is $950. Electric, water, gas, and sewage are $130. Internet is $55. The phone bill is $150. Car insurance is $130 and the car payment is $200. Gas in the car weekly is roughly $70, and you still need to eat and save some money in case you have an emergency like your car breaking down. You should leave room for a margin if you spend a little more on gas that week, depending on where you drive and how often." How can they make the money last the entire month?

4. To start the class, read aloud from a short novel or high-level picture book that relates to the math content. Have students write their own story problems using the math concepts.

Science

1. Have students reflect on the importance and process of the water cycle and create a story. They can film a video, design and write a comic strip, write a poem, or illustrate a storyboard.

9-12 **What does storytelling look like in a high school classroom?** High school students often forget the importance of telling their story. Writing a narrative and thinking through different parts of a story can seem elementary to teenagers, yet the ability to tell a good story is essential, even in adulthood.

College Essay

The college essay can prove difficult, especially when students are presented with prompts such as "When did you experience failure and how did you respond?"

- The importance of the first sentence is often underestimated. Give examples of famous first lines from novels.
    - "It is a truth universally acknowledged, that a single man in possession of a good fortune, must be in want of a wife." *Pride and Prejudice* by Jane Austen (1813).
    - "Here is a small fact: You are going to die." *The Book Thief* by Markus Zusak (2005).
    - "All this happened, more or less." *Slaughterhouse-Five* by Kurt Vonnegut (1969).
    - "Call me Ishmael." *Moby Dick* by Herman Melville (1851).
- Have students brainstorm different prompts. Give them one to two minutes per prompt. Then give them five minutes to do a brain dump and just write about anything they may be thinking about.
- Have students reflect on their writing over the past thirty minutes and choose their best sentence.
- Once they make a selection, they will write that sentence on the top of a new piece of paper (or digital document). Now instruct them to use that sentence as a starting point for the next five minutes of writing.
- If you have time, allow them to do this activity again.
- Once students have completed their free writes, have them choose their favorite, the most engaging sentence they wrote.
- They will write that sentence on a piece of paper in big bold letters and hang it on your classroom wall. No names!
- Give each student three Post-it notes. These will be used to anonymously vote on the sentence that makes them "want to know more."
- After the votes are in, discuss with students the following questions:

- What makes these sentences the most engaging?
- Why did these sentences make you want to learn more about the person and the story?
- What are the top five characteristics these sentences have that the others lack?
  - To extend the learning, have students find their favorite opening sentence and reflect on what makes it grab their attention and encourages readers to "want to know more."

Math

We often cannot see the story in numbers and equations. But sometimes stories awaken students' imaginations and allow them to remember facts and equations.

- Instead of using numbers, have students use words to tell the story of how the equation could be solved. Symbols could become characters such as a negative sign representing a grumpy person and a positive sign denoting an overly optimistic person. These two have to get along in order to solve a problem.
- Have students create a "Month in the Life" portfolio and write the story of a person and his/her budget.
  - Students can choose a person to study (celebrity, influencer, parent, nurse, teacher, etc.).
  - Ask students to determine:
- What is this person's monthly income?
- Where would they live?
- What expenses would they have? Car? Public transportation? Groceries?
- What kinds of items would they save up for?
- To extend the learning, have students tell their own future story. What might be the story of their financial situation in ten years?
- Ask students to collect a certain kind of data that interests them such as stats from their favorite sports team.

Science

- Create characters/drawings based on the different cells involved in the immune response.
- Create diary entries acting like a drop of blood as it travels around the circulatory system.
- Analyze data by writing a mystery.

Stop and Reflect: Choose one of the storytelling strategies covered above and brainstorm ways to incorporate it into a lesson.

Teaching as a form of storytelling has the power to create meaningful and impactful learning experiences. By embracing this strategy, educators can captivate their classrooms, ignite imaginations, and foster a love for learning. Through engaging narratives, teachers can spark curiosity, enhance comprehension, inspire creativity, and make abstract concepts relatable. They can also connect lessons to real-life contexts, cultivating empathy and critical thinking. By integrating storytelling techniques into content curation, educators create dynamic learning environments that inspire collaboration and empower students to be active participants in their education. Let the power of storytelling transform your classroom.

Curate Content by Offering Choice

Offering student's choice can seem overwhelming at first.

- How do I manage students reading different texts at the same time?
- How do I assess work when students are accomplishing different tasks?
- How do I have a discussion with the entire class if students are learning different content?

As we discussed, students are most likely to be engaged when they can explore content they are curious about and genuinely interested in.

 **Practical Tips:**

- Let students choose the topic they want to research or learn.
- Create a choice board that offers different ways to learn the same topic—read an article, watch a TED talk, draw a visual, etc.
- Have students pick from a list of books to read. This can be done as free reading time. Or have students read the same book in groups and discuss what they learned.
- Allow students to take part in deciding how you will teach class. Giving students options by asking "How would you like to be taught this content?" can increase buy-in.
- Allow students to choose how they will be assessed and what format they would like to use for the next assessment.
- Give students a packet of five articles around the same topic but from different perspectives, and allow them to choose which one interests them.

There are many ways to incorporate choice into your content. Start slow, try one of the above, and see how your students react. Allowing students to be a part of the learning will ignite curiosity and engagement.

 **What does choice look like in the elementary classroom?** There are lots of great ways to offer choices to empower our youngest learners.

- Learning stations are a staple of many elementary classrooms and a natural way to incorporate choice. Each center can provide a variety of activities or games that allow the students to work toward the same academic goal while choosing how they practice.
- Project-based learning can be infused into units so students can choose topics for their projects. Teachers can also provide options for project topics and allow students to vote from preselected choices.
- Allow students to choose what to read during free reading time, and stretch beyond books. Perhaps students are interested in reading magazines, newspapers, poetry, or other collections of media.
- A choice board is another fantastic tool for offering choice in the elementary classroom. A choice board can be utilized very well for "When I'm Done" options, which can include free reading time, playing a math game, writing a letter to another student, writing in a journal, etc.

6-8 **What does choice look like in the middle school classroom?** Middle schoolers are in a unique place developmentally where they want independence but still lack the ability to always make wise choices. They are often swayed by peer pressure. As a result, it is important that we provide them with choice because they desire that independence, but that we also guide them to make good choices. When they make poor choices, we give them opportunities to debrief and learn from them.

- Choice in books to read: literature circle and/or independent reading books.
- Choice to work independently, with a friend, or in a group (the only rule is to never leave a classmate out).
- Choice of topic to write about.
- Choice of a series of math problems to solve.
- Choice in how to convey knowledge in final assessment—essay, presentation, video, poem, song, podcast, play, etc. If your district requires teachers to use the same summative assessments, variety can be added via formative assessment.
- Choice of where to sit (a privilege that can be taken away if behavior deems it unsuccessful).
- Choose the order for completing the three tasks for the class period.

9-12 **What does choice look like in the high school classroom?** Many of the middle school examples also work in high school. High school students are beginning to explore, and often their curiosity can wane if not given the chance to learn about new things that interest them. When given a choice, a musically oriented student may want to learn only about certain kinds of music or musicians. Therefore, expanding knowledge by researching different topics needs to be encouraged.

- Use of choice boards can help students prepare for a test or allow them to explore different perceptions on a given topic.
- Offering students an opportunity to create their own topic is always a fantastic way to encourage creative thinking. It's amazing how students can come up with engaging and rigorous assignments on their own.

Choice Board

Directions: Choose one box and complete the activity inside

Have students complete all boxes or one box per row

Option 1	Option 4	Option 7
Option 2	Option 5	Option 8
Option 3	Option 6	Option 9

🔍 **Stop and Reflect:** Choose one of the strategies above and brainstorm ways to incorporate it into a lesson. What keeps you from adding choice?

Draw your biggest challenge and put a big X through it. Ask yourself what might be all the ways I can overcome this challenge?

Curate Content Using Questioning Skills

Teachers are not the only Content Curators in the room; so are students. Allowing students to curate their own content expands their knowledge via creative and critical thinking. When students are encouraged to discover what is important, relevant, and essential, if presented with a plethora of information, they will begin to think in a deeper way.

The first step is teaching students to ignite their curiosity by generating questions. Often, students are reluctant to ask questions in class for fear of judgment. As you continue to grow a creative classroom environment, students will feel more comfortable sharing. Asking questions does not come naturally; it is a skill that needs to be taught and practiced. At a young age, children ask multiple questions daily. Yet as they mature, curiosity and confidence can fade. By allowing students to create and answer their own questions, interest in the content can increase, and a student's ability to think creatively and critically can be practiced and observed.

For example, ask students a question such as "Why do mosquito bites itch?" Then have them brainstorm ideas:

- What do we think is important to know?
- How will we discover the knowledge we need? Where should we look? Who should we ask?
- How do we narrow down all this information? What do we think is most essential to know?

Now allow students to do their own research and share their newly discovered facts. This can be done individually, in teams, or in class competitions. Allow students to incorporate opportunities to use both divergent and convergent thinking. For instance, during a writing unit, set aside time for brainstorming and collaboration through group work, allowing students to explore different aspects of the topic, and pose questions that will help them gain a better understanding.

 Stop and Reflect: As you consider the following scenarios, reflect on:

- How do I handle this type of situation?
- What is my attitude?
- What do I say?
- How do I look (body language)?

Students continue to ask questions during a lesson I am teaching, causing me to run out of time.

Students continue to ask the same question over and over, and I am running out of ways to answer it.

Students never ask questions, yet I can see there is confusion.

I just asked a thought-provoking question to my students, and all I hear is silence.

Our attitude toward a student full of curiosity and questions is just as important as the question. Students can tell we are annoyed or frustrated through our body language and facial expressions. Eyes rolling, arms crossed, and sighing sounds all express that this student is exasperating us. When this happens, often the student will shut down and their curiosity in the content will slowly diminish.

Asking students "What do you think?" before giving your opinion allows students to look at all opinions first.

- Teaching students how to ask questions is a great place to start.
- It is imperative that we encourage questioning in a respectful and responsible manner. How do students ask questions without being rude? Interrupting? Being anxious?
- Take time to model question techniques. Have students write their own questions about stories, experiments, and equations.
- Provide students a place in which they can write questions and present them anonymously (a thinking box, or a section of the classroom that is for future ideas).
- Socratic seminars are valuable at any academic level. Allowing students to generate their own questions regarding a text is extremely important for comprehension. Socratic seminars take practice. Model the concept, then generate teacher-led questions for students to answer. As students grow in their questioning skills, allow them to generate their own questions to a text. This strategy will be discussed more in the "Experience Navigator" section.

 **What do questioning skills look like in the elementary classroom?** Elementary school students, especially those in K–2, benefit from teachers modeling and asking good questions. Engaging in thinking aloud throughout the day shows students how to engage with content, and curiosity can lead to good questions. Creating an open and safe environment for asking questions is essential; this is done by weaving questioning into all aspects of the day. If you want students to become proficient at questioning, you must provide ample opportunities for them to practice. Here are some concrete ways you can encourage questioning with your students.

- Science offers a great opportunity for students to ask a lot of questions. Especially in grades 3–5, have students work in groups to generate as many questions as they can (nothing is too strange or far-fetched!) about a new topic they are studying.
- Select a "mystery student" in the class! Students must ask yes/no questions to narrow down who or what the mystery student is.

- Create an anchor chart with prompts to help students start asking open-ended questions.
- Read aloud and encourage students to wonder/ask questions about what the characters are thinking or feeling in the story. Role-play and have students ask questions as if they were one of the characters.
- Extend thinking and processing time after content input so students can reflect on what they don't know and formulate their questions.
- Have students turn to a partner and ask a question. This provides a low-stakes opportunity for students to practice.
- Create a Wonder Wall where students can write questions on sticky notes. Each week, take a question off of the Wonder Wall and research the answer or answers!

6-8 **What do questioning skills look like in the middle school classroom?** Asking good questions is critical for social interaction, learning, and assessing what we are reading. Middle schoolers will benefit socially, academically, and intellectually when we provide intentional activities for asking good questions.

- Play "Twenty Questions" where students have to ask about a concept you have taught. After the activity, explain the three types of questions: 1) probing, 2) clarifying, 3) elaborating. Give the students examples of when to use each.
- Discuss the book *How to Win Friends and Influence People* and explain to students that one of the most effective ways to build positive relationships is by being genuinely curious and listening well so they can ask good questions. Play a version of speed-dating where students have to spend thirty seconds each asking their classmate questions about themselves and continue until all students have shared.
- Have a list of good questions to ask when reading any text and have students reference that while reading. Allow time for a debriefing on what questions they asked while reading and how that helps their perspective on the text.

What do questioning skills look like in the high school classroom? Asking open-ended and deep questions will allow high school students to begin thinking about their own opinions and how they know what they know. Allow high school students to ask their own questions instead of creating the questions for them. Starting class with "What do you think about—?" or "What questions do you have concerning—?" trains students to be independent thinkers. The essential strategy is to give students time to question the content without guidance, then after they question, discuss with peers, and process the content, step in with any missed insight.

- Share a news headline and provide thought-provoking prompts.
- Use role-play to discuss different perspectives.
- Ask, "If this is the answer, what might the question be?"
- Hold Socratic seminars/academic conversations. We will discuss this more in the "Experience Navigator" section.

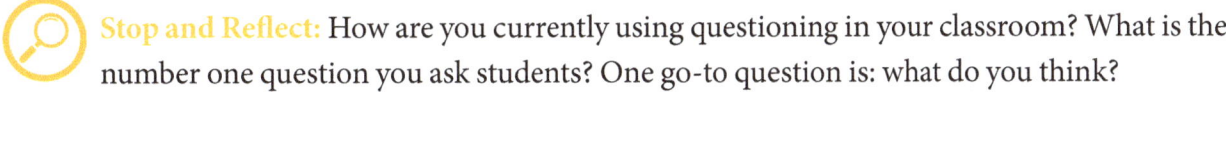

Stop and Reflect: How are you currently using questioning in your classroom? What is the number one question you ask students? One go-to question is: what do you think?

Hexagonal Thinking

Hexagonal thinking is an engaging way to inspire students to make connections and justify their thinking. This activity can be done individually, with partners, or as a small group. Small groups work well with this activity because it encourages the sharing of multiple opinions.

Hexagonal thinking allows students to think creatively and critically about how different ideas relate. It is beneficial for students to reflect on why and how different ideas connect. As students use hexagonal thinking, they will discover that although everyone has the same terms, there are numerous ways to make connections. The critical part of this activity is being able to explain your thinking.

Hexagonal thinking encourages students to:

- Think deeper.
- Communicate clearly.
- Explain their thinking process.
- Be open to different perspectives.
- Work together as a team.

Preparation: Don't let this part intimidate you. Numerous teachers have creative ideas about how to make preparation for hexagonal thinking easy and quick. Many use a hexagonal dye cutter or digital creators (several versions can be found online). The key is that each hexagon has a different term, idea, and connection related to the big idea. To add an extra challenge, give each team a few blank hexagons. This allows students to create their own ideas and connections.

HEXAGONAL THINKING ALLOWS STUDENTS TO THINK CREATIVELY AND CRITICALLY ABOUT HOW DIFFERENT IDEAS RELATE.

Hexagonal Thinking As a Warm-Up

Hand each student a copy of a hexagon. Students then write their names in the center. In each section, they should draw a picture or add a word that describes themselves. It could be an adjective (kind, curious, creative), or it could be a verb (plays sports, reads, dances), or it could be any fact about them (has three sisters, owns a dog and a cat). Once each spot is filled, have students get into groups and connect their hexagons. The goal is for the students to find connections between themselves and their peers. For example, two students might discover that they both enjoy reading or playing sports.

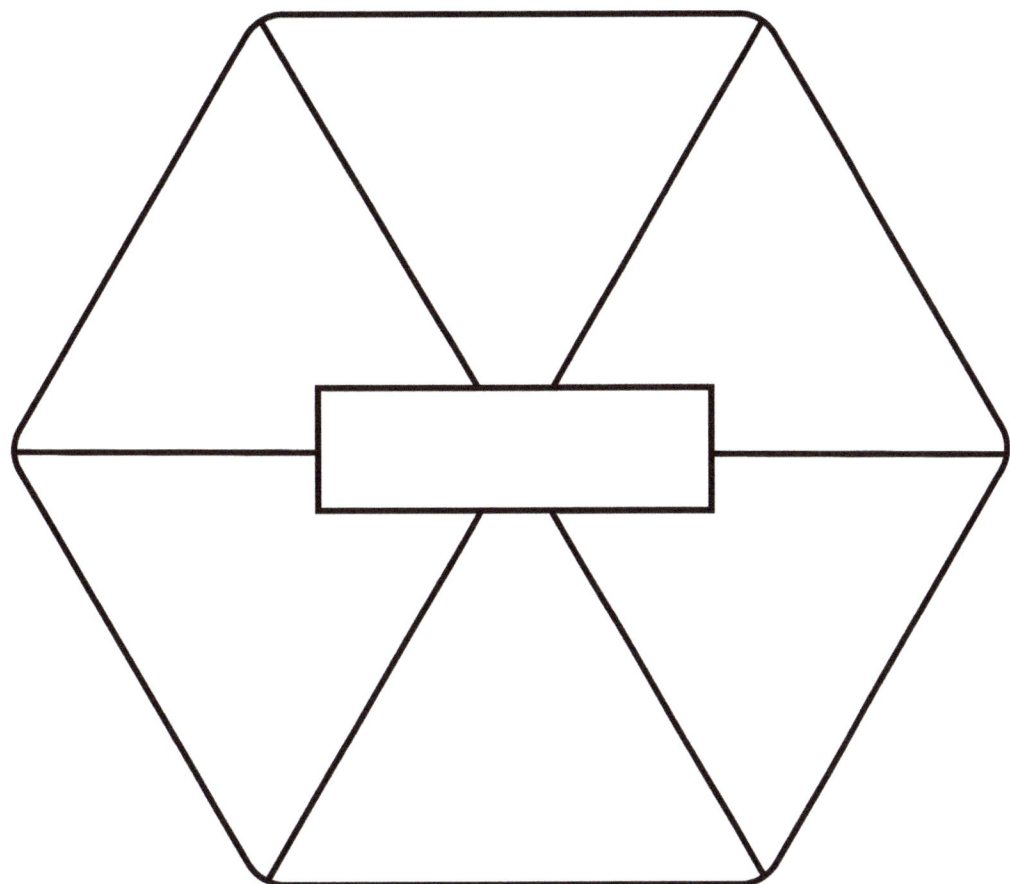

The purpose of this activity is to highlight that we are all connected in different ways and that there are commonalities among us even if we may appear different on the surface. This activity promotes self-expression, encourages students to learn more about each other, and fosters a sense of unity within the classroom. By recognizing and celebrating the similarities and differences among themselves, students will develop a greater understanding and appreciation for their peers. Once students understand the concept of hexagonal thinking and look at ideas in a different way in order to make unique and creative connections, they are ready to try hexagonal thinking in your content area.

HEXAGONAL THINKING IN CONTENT AREAS

This strategy can be used in all content areas. The same process is used—the difference comes in the hexagonal content. Choose various ideas for your hexagons:

- Current content.
- Other units.
- Other disciplines.
- Popular culture.
- Music.
- Film.
- Current social issues.

For example, if you were teaching a unit on fairy tales, you could create a hexagon with the following words:

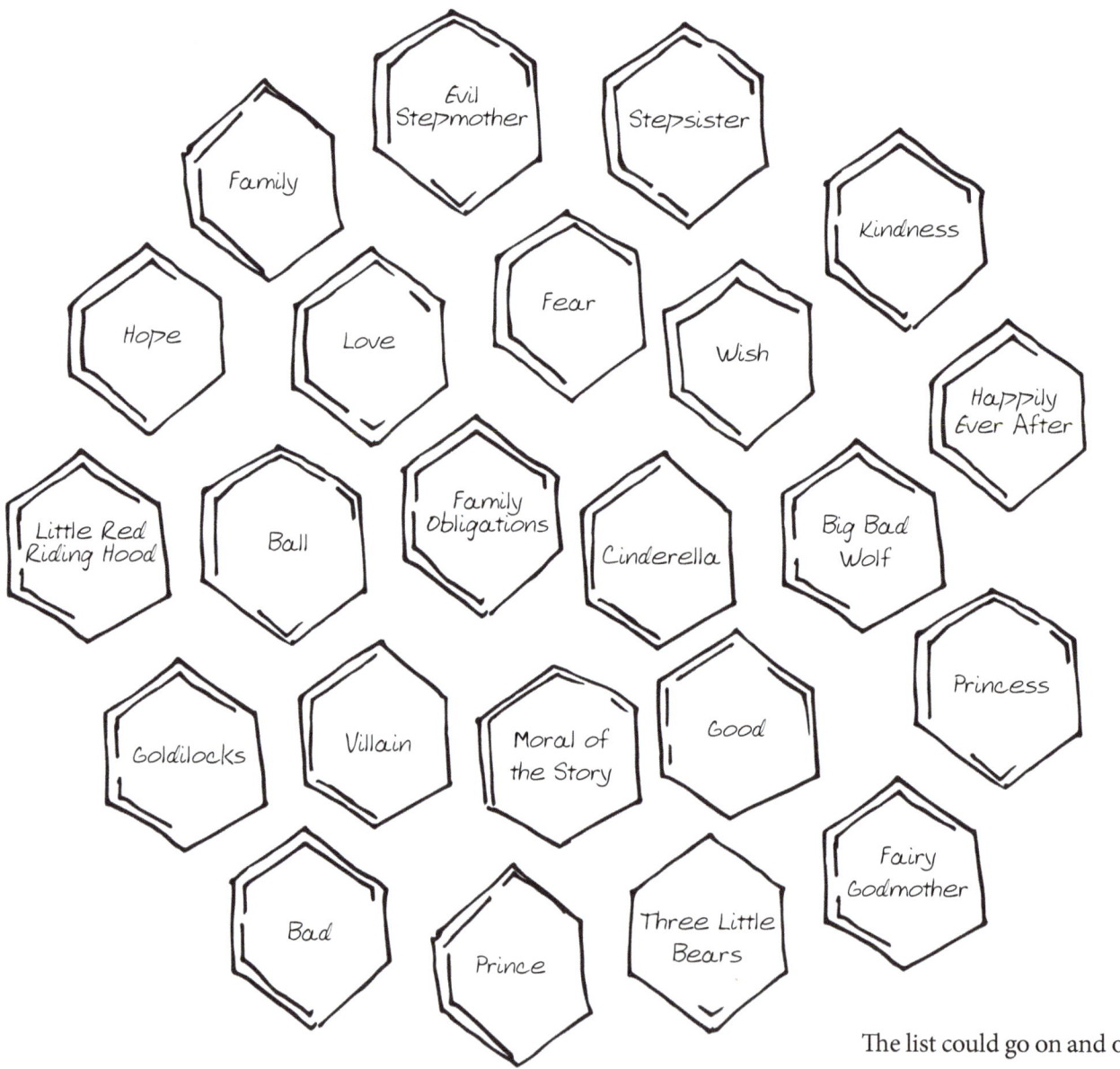

The list could go on and on.

Process

1) Group students—this can be done in pairs or small groups.

2) Give each team a set of hexagons. Each team receives the same terms.

3) Ask students to spread out their hexagons and begin discussing connections.

4) Remind students that each hexagon can connect to six other hexagons.

5) They can use arrows to show connections if needed.

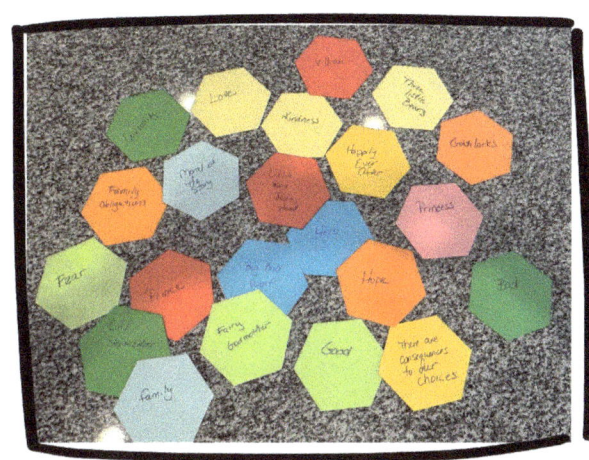

Discuss

Once all the connections are made (yes, all of them), each group needs to explain why they made each connection and prepare to share their thinking process with other groups.

Share

Much like a gallery walk, have small groups go from table to table, observing the connections made and recording any questions or observations they may have regarding specific connections. Groups may observe that each group made the same connection in one area but completely different in another.

Questions to ask while observing other connections include:

- What did you mean by—?
- A connection we both share—
- A connection we have a question about—
- A connection that made us think in a different way—

Once all groups have a chance to compile their observations, each group can share their findings and ask clarifying questions of the other groups.

Once the debriefing sections are complete, ask each group if they want to make any changes to their hexagonal organization. Once they have solidified their connection, each person should choose four or more connections and write a short paragraph describing the thought process behind the connection.

HEXAGONAL THINKING

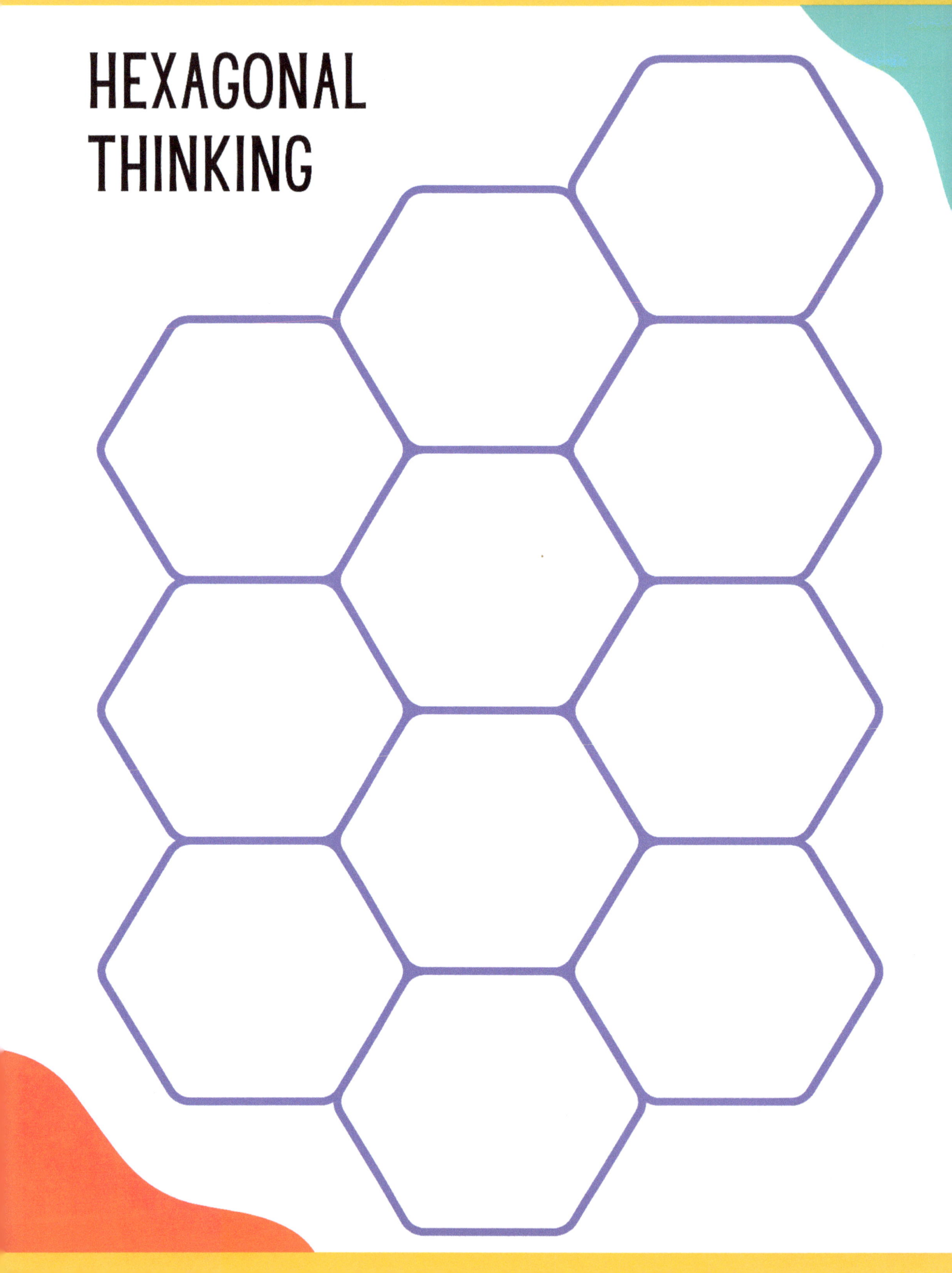

HEXAGONAL THINKING GALLERY WALK GROUP OBSERVATIONS

GROUP MEMBERS: _____

| What did you mean by... | A connection we both share . . . | A connection we have a question about . . . |

| A connection that made us think differently . . . | A connection that surprised us . . . | Overall Comments: |

Hexagonal thinking can be assessed in a formative or summative setting. In the formative setting, observe students as you walk around the room. Are any students more engaged than others? Are any students struggling to make connections? Do any students excel at this and need additional challenges?

In the summative setting, students can formally present their connections as a group. Individually, students can be assessed on their ability to write about the connections made. Using facts, textual evidence, and clear explanations, students can demonstrate their understanding of the unit or lesson.

HEXAGONAL THINKING IS AN ENGAGING WAY TO INSPIRE STUDENTS TO MAKE CONNECTIONS AND JUSTIFY THEIR THINKING.

Example of Individual Summative Reflection on Fairy Tale Hexagon Activity

Connection One

We connected love, family, and consequences to choices because all of the fairy tales we read connect family in some way. *Cinderella*, *Goldilocks*, and *Little Red Riding Hood* speak to family relationships and how they can be complex and at times turbulent. Although there is love, there can be consequences to a family relationship when decisions are made. For example, the stepmother in Cinderella made a decision to treat Cinderella as a servant, yet that decision backfired when the fairy godmother showed Cinderella that she could be anything she wanted—even a princess.

Connection Two

We connected fear to the Big Bad Wolf and to a villain because sometimes we are afraid of things we don't know. It's important to be cautious and think about what is making us afraid. Little Red Riding Hood should have feared the Big Bad Wolf more (I mean Bad is even in his name) and that way she could have saved her grandmother. Yet also overcoming what we fear can help us be brave and save the people we love.

Connection Three

I really like the connection we made between good, curiosity, and Goldilocks. This might be considered an unusual connection because Goldilocks shouldn't have gone into the three bears' house and therefore is often seen as bad. But, if you look at it another way, her curiosity allowed her to be fed and rested. Sometimes, curiosity helps us solve problems.

Connection Four

Cinderella is connected to the princess hexagon, which is obvious, but we wanted to show that she can be a hero as well. Often in fairy tales, the hero is the prince, but Cinderella had hope for her future and with the help of the fairy godmother's kindness, she was able to find love and happiness with the prince. Sometimes, it is important for us to take the lead and not depend on others to fulfill our dreams, but it is also nice to have others support us on our journey.

Reimagining Classroom Relationships to Support Content Creation

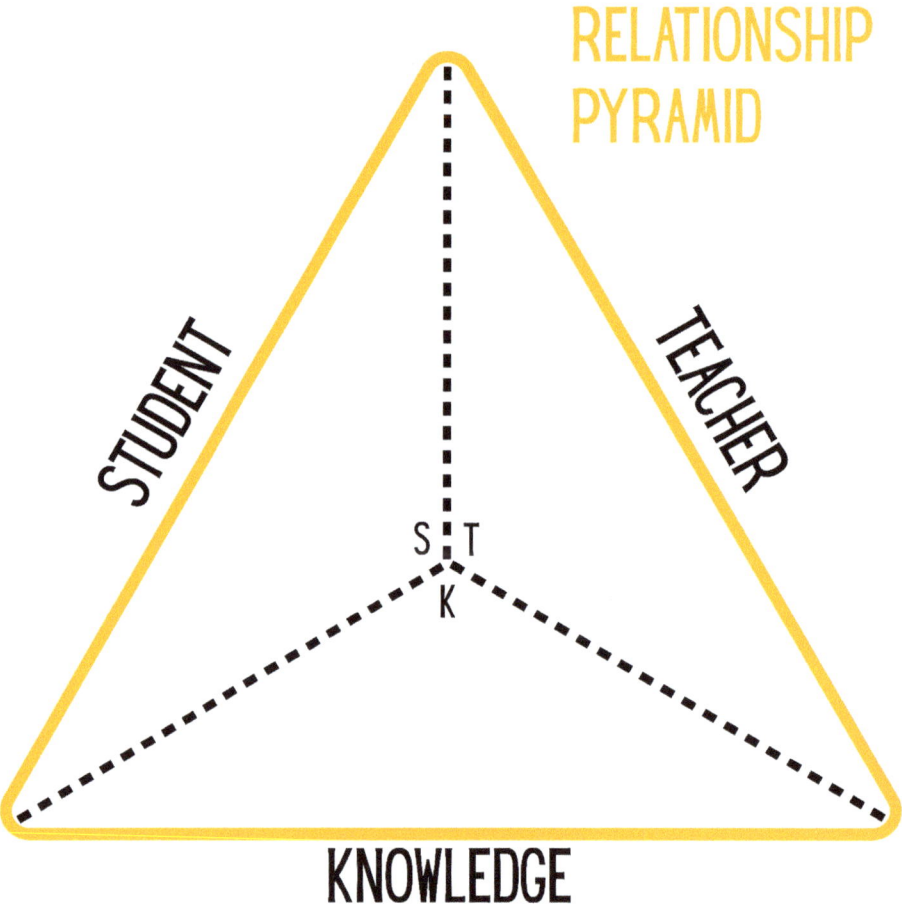

In the final section of "Content Curator," we revisit the educative relationships—all of the relationships that exist between the three basic elements needed for *classroom* learning: the student, the teacher, and the knowledge to be learned. By turning the educative relationship prism and shifting the power dynamic between the elements and relationships, you will find the spaces and places for content curation.

1. Storytelling. 2. Choice. 3. Questioning skills. 4. Hexagonal thinking.

Ways to Support Content Creation in the Relationship

TEACHER leads the relationship

T-T
1. Share the story of a lesson, start to finish, for the purpose of story development.
2. Create team bundles of resources in a common drive.
3. Observe others for the purpose of question creation/variety.
4. Compare/contrast teacher-generated content hexagons.

T-S
1. Introduce content via personal story (not academic).
2. Create subtopics for student-selected study and report
3. Provide metacognitive question stems.
4. Talk through the thinking behind the created connections.

T-K
1. Research origin stories, contributors to knowledge.
2. Identify multiple starting/ending points for topics/units.
3. Reexamine key questions and common misconceptions.
4. Define or extend boundaries for creating connections.

STUDENT leads the relationship

S-S
1. Create and share stories with key content as plot elements.
2. Mentor or peer teaching.
3. Use 5W & 1H jigsaw responsibilities.
4. Generate topics for each other to use hexagonal thinking with.

S-T
1. Tell a story to connect skill and interest to content.
2. Create a rubric that emphasizes students' priority skills.
3. Generate the guiding questions for a lesson, topic, and unit,
4. Identify topics/connections to use for hexagonal tasks.

S-K
1. Create a worksheet/activity for next year's class.
2. Select area of interest for research and evaluate for credibility.
3. Use prior knowledge to fuel question creation.
4. Search for content based on connections of interest.

KNOWLEDGE leads the relationship

K-K
1. Compare personal experience to real-world/textbook content.
2. Look at various content sources to compare knowledge.
3. Compare questions generated in class to content standard questions.
4. Create topics to connect from personal experience to content.

K-T
1. Use content-based stories to start instruction.
2. Ask curricular committees or PLC to provide options.
3. Start with real-world applications as a basis for instruction.
4. Use explicit/implicit content connections to drive instruction.

K-S
1. Use current event stories for anticipatory instruction.
2. Provide choice boards for formative assessment.
3. Identify practical use for knowledge to generate buy-in.
4. Acknowledge personal knowledge drives connections.

 **Stop and Reflect:** Reflect on the relationship pyramid and the relationship dynamics between student, teacher, and knowledge. Where can you shift the power for your content and your classroom to support content creation?

Try it! Let's take a look at the unit/lesson plan you decided to revise. As you go through your materials, ask yourself a few questions:

- Where do students have the independence to learn about something they are interested in?
- Where do students have the opportunity to use divergent thinking?
- Are you allowing time for brainstorming, collaboration, and creative exploration?
- Where might you be able to add choice?
- Where are you purposefully unlocking the power of relationships?

Use the chart below as your application piece so that when you are ready to write a lesson plan from your ideas, it is already formatted and easy to find.

Lesson Idea/Creativity Skill
Heighten Anticipation (ignite curiosity and a sense of wonder): *How will you get students excited or curious about the lesson or content?*
Deepening Expectations (deep diving into the lesson; students are consistently actively engaged): *How will you make it hands-on? How will they explore different perspectives? How will it be relevant and meaningful to them?*
Hands-on Interactive Ideas: *What can you bring in, have them create, construct or interact with?*
Connect It to Real-Life Experiences: *List all of the ways this applies to their life, experiences, or dreams. How will you make this connection for them?*
Extend the Learning (how students will apply new-found knowledge and curiosity into the world outside the classroom) *What activities can students do outside the classroom to continue the learning?*

 **Activity:**
Without using words, draw a picture of the importance of curiosity in the classroom.

Stop and Reflect:

What new strategies or concepts from this section resonated with you the most? How do you plan to implement them in your classroom?

Reflect on a challenge you might face when applying the ideas from this section. How can you overcome it?

Consider your current teaching practices. How can you integrate the principles discussed in this section to enhance creativity and critical thinking among your students?

How can we encourage students to push outside their comfort zone and enter their creative zone?

RISK FACILITATOR

Risk Facilitator

"Only those who will risk going too far can possibly find out how far one can go." ~ T. S. Eliot (1931)

> **Essential Question:**
>
> How can we encourage students to push outside their comfort zone and enter their creative zone?

This "Risk Facilitator" section emphasizes that sharing knowledge can:

- Be uncomfortable at times.
- Be transformational.
- Be prone to failure.

Strategies we will examine are:

- Self-efficacy.
- Productive struggle.
- Celebration of failure.
- Creative problem-solving.

Definitions

- Academic resilience is students' ability to effectively navigate and bounce back from adversities or challenges that could disrupt their academic progress.
- Comfort zone is the environment within which students feel most at ease due to their familiarity and strength with tasks or topics.
- Risk-taking refers to students' willingness to engage in tasks or activities that extend beyond their existing knowledge, relationships, and beliefs.
- Productive struggle is effortful and purposeful learning that is of an appropriate challenge.
- Self-efficacy, introduced by psychologist Albert Bandura (1977), is an individual's belief in their capacity to execute behaviors necessary to produce specific performance attainments and refers to a student's belief in their ability to perform a task or understand a concept.

 **Activity**

Imagine you are at a camp's high-adventure facility and you have to choose between three activities: the solo challenge (you are harnessed to a rope and have to climb up a telephone pole, stand on top of it, and jump for a trapeze wire), the rock climbing wall (you have to climb all the way to the top and belay your way down; you may not come down until you reach the top), or the high ropes course (you need to complete a series of obstacles harnessed to a rope at thirty feet in the air and may not come down until you complete it).

- Which one would you choose and why?

- Which ones sound exciting?

- Which ones sound terrifying?

INTRODUCTION

As educators, we have the incredible opportunity to shape the way our students perceive the world and their place in it. One of the most critical ways we can do this is by creating a classroom environment that champions academic risk-taking. Encouraging our students to step outside of their comfort zones, embrace the uncertainty of failure, and push themselves to new heights fosters personal growth and cultivates essential traits like creativity and curiosity. When students feel safe to take academic risks, they're more likely to take chances and explore new ideas, which can lead to groundbreaking discoveries and accomplishments. As teachers, we have the privilege of being the facilitators of this growth, and it's up to us to do everything in our power to encourage and support our students in their academic journeys.

In order to create a classroom that promotes academic risk-taking, it's essential to establish a culture of trust and open communication. This means fostering an environment where students feel comfortable sharing their thoughts and ideas without fear of judgment or criticism. By actively listening to our students and valuing their input, we can encourage them to speak up and take ownership of their learning.

Another crucial component of promoting academic risk-taking is providing a variety of opportunities for students to take risks. This can include assigning challenging tasks, encouraging debates and discussions, or allowing creative expression through projects and presentations. By offering diverse learning experiences, we can cater to different types of learners and empower them to explore their strengths while also developing new skills.

It's also essential to acknowledge and celebrate when our students take academic risks, regardless of the outcome. Success should not be the only measure of risk-taking; instead, we should emphasize the process and the effort put into taking on a challenge. By acknowledging their efforts and highlighting their growth, we can encourage our students to continue pushing themselves in their academic pursuits.

In addition to fostering a culture of trust and providing diverse opportunities for risk-taking, it's crucial to model academic risk-taking ourselves as educators. When we openly share our own mistakes and failures and show resilience in the face of challenges, we demonstrate to our students that taking risks is a natural part of the learning process. Being vulnerable and transparent about our experiences with academic risk-taking can inspire our students to do the same.

Promoting academic risk-taking in the classroom is crucial for the personal and intellectual growth of our students. By creating a safe and inclusive learning environment, providing diverse opportunities for risk-taking, acknowledging and celebrating efforts, and modeling risk-taking ourselves as educators, we can empower our students to take on challenges with confidence and curiosity. Let's not forget that promoting academic risk-taking also means creating a growth mindset among our students. By teaching them that intelligence and abilities can be developed through effort and perseverance, we can encourage them to take on challenges without the fear of failure. This mindset shift can help our students see mistakes as opportunities for growth rather than a reflection of their abilities.

Furthermore, promoting academic risk-taking builds a sense of community among students. When students feel supported by their peers and have a strong sense of belonging in the classroom, they are more likely to take academic risks and explore new ideas without fear of judgment. As educators, we can facilitate this by encouraging collaboration and teamwork, promoting a positive classroom culture, and celebrating individual and collective successes.

It's important to remember that academic risk-taking looks different for every student. What may be challenging for one student may come easily to another. As educators, we must recognize and celebrate the unique strengths and abilities of each student while also encouraging them to push themselves outside of their comfort zones. By doing so, we can foster a classroom environment where all students feel empowered to take risks and reach their full potential.

Remember academic risk-taking is not just about achieving success or reaching academic goals; it's about fostering personal growth, developing essential skills and traits, and inspiring a love for learning. By continuing to champion academic risk-taking in our classrooms and empower our students to make their mark on the world their confidence levels will skyrocket.

Academic risk-taking includes:
- Tackling complex tasks.
- Participating in classroom discussions and activities.
- Venturing into new areas of curiosity.
- Actively seeking feedback from peers.
- Embracing failure.
- Actively using creative and critical thinking.

> **WHEN STUDENTS FEEL SAFE TO TAKE RISKS, THEY EXPLORE NEW IDEAS AND ACHIEVE GROUNDBREAKING DISCOVERIES.**

Learning Objectives for the Risk Facilitator

This section will explore:
- What it means to be a Risk Facilitator.
- Strategies on how to create lessons that encourage students to embrace mistakes.
- How you can incorporate risk-taking into your classroom.

A teacher as a Risk Facilitator:

- Creates a curriculum that is new and innovative despite the chance that the lesson could flop.
- Becomes vulnerable with their students regarding their own celebration of failures.
- Believes in themselves and their ability to be creative.

A student as a Risk Facilitator:

- Embraces and celebrates failure.
- Challenges themselves to overcome learning obstacles on their own before asking for help.
- Believes in themselves and their ability to be creative.

Stop and Reflect: Take a moment to think about a lesson that flopped. Why did it flop? What was your reaction to the failure? What was your students' reaction?

Strategies for Risk-Taking

Encourage Self-Efficacy

Students with a high sense of self-efficacy (belief in their ability to succeed in the classroom as it relates to real life) are more likely to engage in academic risk-taking behavior as they believe in their abilities to navigate unfamiliar territory, face potential difficulties, and ultimately master new skills or knowledge. By contrast, students with low self-efficacy may be less likely to engage in academic risk-taking due to their fear of failure or the belief that they lack the necessary skills to succeed. For these students, stepping out of their comfort zone feels threatening rather than challenging.

Encouraging self-efficacy can empower students to venture out of their comfort zones, embrace challenges, and turn potential failures into learning opportunities. Recognizing this can significantly enhance teaching strategies, promoting an educational environment that encourages exploration, resilience, and the continual pursuit of knowledge.

Practical Tips for Supporting Self-Efficacy

1. Help students set realistic goals. When setting creative goals, it's important for students to be realistic and specific. This will not only give them a clear direction to work toward but also make the goal seem attainable.

2. Celebrate small achievements. This can boost students' self-efficacy by showing them that they are making progress and capable of achieving their larger goals. Using a simple checklist can help students see all the small steps they made along the way.

3. Embrace failure as a learning opportunity. As mentioned earlier, failure is an inevitable part of any creative process. Instead of seeing it as a setback, encourage students to view it as a learning opportunity. This can help them develop resilience and improve their self-efficacy.

4. Surround yourself with positive influences. Positive influences, whether supportive friends, mentors, or inspirational figures, can have a significant impact on self-efficacy. Encourage students to surround themselves with people who believe in their abilities and encourage them to pursue their creative passions.

5. Practice self-reflection. Self-reflection can help students identify their strengths and weaknesses and develop a better understanding of their capabilities. This, in turn, can improve their self-efficacy by allowing them to focus on areas where they excel and work on areas where they need improvement.

6. Take risks. Encourage students to take risks in their creative pursuits. This can inspire confidence in their abilities and expand their skills and knowledge.

7. Seek out constructive feedback. Constructive feedback can be a valuable tool for students to improve their skills and boost their self-efficacy. Encourage students to actively seek out feedback from peers, teachers, and mentors and use it as a guide for growth. This will be developed more in the "Evaluation Designer" section.

8. Set aside time for creative exploration. Sometimes, the best way to build self-efficacy is to try new things and explore different creative avenues simply. Encourage students to set aside time for unstructured play and experimentation, allowing them to discover their strengths and passions. I keep a box of fidget spinners, Play-Doh, puzzles, card decks, and LEGOs on each desk.

9. Keep a positive mindset. A positive mindset can go a long way in developing and nurturing self-efficacy. Encourage students to practice gratitude, optimism, and self-compassion in their creative endeavors.

10. Take breaks and practice self-care. Burnout can negatively impact self-efficacy, so it's important for students to take breaks and prioritize self-care. Encourage them to find a balance between their creative pursuits and other aspects of their life.

What does self-efficacy look like in the elementary school classroom? Elementary students can learn to monitor their own growth and learning through similar processes that older students and adults use! Elementary-age students can set goals for their learning, and monitor their progress over time with a little bit of modeling and accountability from their teacher.

- K–2 students can set goals around learning sight words and check their progress weekly or monthly against their goal. After setting their goal, students can create their plan for working toward this goal (How many words will they practice? How often?). Setting goals and monitoring progress create natural opportunities for discussion about overcoming obstacles as well (What will you do or change if you aren't making progress toward your goal?).

- Students can keep a journal (can be used as a warm-up, center activity, or free-time activity). Teachers can provide prompts and respond to students writing to provide reflections, encouragement and feedback.

What does self-efficacy look like in the middle school classroom? Middle schoolers are at a critical age when self-efficacy starts to fade due to assignments becoming more challenging. In fact, by the time most students have started middle school, they rarely see the assignments or work as meaningful. Many may already experience the feeling of defeat in the classroom. Our role is to help rebuild self-efficacy so they can continue learning with confidence in their ability to push through even when they do not know or have experienced failure.

- Present famous failures to them and discuss how failure is not a stopping point but rather a new beginning.
- Have them set realistic small goals at first and then celebrate loudly when those are achieved. The goals and celebrations could be public, like a bulletin board in the classroom, or private, like a goal journal. Maybe start privately with a journal and then move to a bulletin board once their confidence is built.
- Have a reference anchor chart titled "What to Do If I Am Stuck": 1) Reread the instructions. 2) Ask a peer for help. 3) Research possible solutions/answers. 4) Ask my teacher (this allows them to search for answers before needing to rely on the teacher, which helps build their confidence).

What does self-efficacy look like in the high school classroom? A learning portfolio can increase a student's ability to reflect on their growth throughout their class and their high school years. Students can keep a digital or paper portfolio filled with important milestones. Perhaps they can reflect on certain assignments, feedback opportunities, and projects and use them a resource in the future. To demonstrate a culmination of what was learned in your class, a student could write (or record) a detailed reflection of the growth they experienced throughout the semester.

Ask students to review the work in their portfolio and, using specific examples from their work, reflect on:

- What was your biggest challenge?
- Where do you see the largest growth in this class?
- What surprised you the most this semester?
- Where did you find yourself taking risks?
- When did you fail and how did you overcome it?
- What are you most proud of this semester?

As seniors prepare to graduate, this is a fantastic opportunity for reflection and self-efficacy.

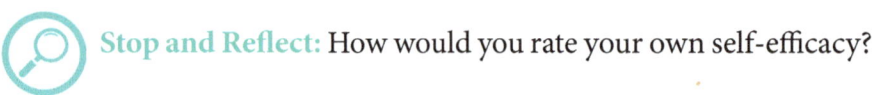 **Stop and Reflect:** How would you rate your own self-efficacy?

Look back at the tips for self-efficacy. Choose two you would personally like to improve. Why did you choose those two?

Productive Struggle

"*Effortful practice that goes beyond passive reading, listening or watching—that builds useful, lasting understanding and skill*" (Bullmaster-Day, 2014).

Motivation is a crucial factor in the learning process, and it significantly influences the extent of active, personal engagement in learning (Oxford, 1992). Teachers can leverage this understanding to guide their students toward productive struggle.

Productive struggle:

- Puts creative learning ownership on the student.
- Allows educators to be guides in the learning process.
- Gives students the power to be the conductors of their own knowledge.
- Is a critical component of effective learning.
- Refers to effortful learning that encourages students to persist in solving complex problems.
- Fosters resilience.
- Produces a natural extension of understanding where each student's unique learning strategy and motivation is embraced.

When teachers understand their students' motivations, they can design learning tasks that are appropriately challenging, pushing students to step out of their comfort zones and engage in deeper cognitive processing. Especially when personalized, this engagement in challenging tasks, or productive struggle, is where significant learning occurs (Wulf & Lewthwaite, 2016). It's not about making learning so difficult that students give up, but rather about finding the right balance of challenge and support so students are motivated to persist in the face of difficulty (Suárez et al., 2019).

For a productive struggle to be impactful, there must be a balance between how much you support the learning and how much the student is challenged. Remember, sometimes, as educators, our scales are high in complexity and challenges but low when it comes to support. Yet our students' scale shows support high and challenge low. Students ache for the right answer, and as an exhausted educator, it may be easy to give them what they want. But we are doing a disservice to our students and us if we do so. By allowing productive struggle, we become the guide to supporting students to discover the right answer.

Stop and Reflect: Using the scales below, how would you describe your balance with productivity with the unit you are revising? Is support or struggle too high in any area? How can you balance the scales?

Productive struggle can unleash the power of student motivation! When students are learning tasks that connect with their own interests and dreams, they become intrinsically driven to tackle challenges head-on. They see how the tasks align with their personal goals and that keeps them going, even when things get tough. This sense of purpose and ownership fuels their motivation to embrace the struggle and uncover new depths of learning and understanding.

Try it! On your bulletin board, have students brainstorm strategies to use when facing a challenge. For the younger kiddos, give them prepared ideas and ask them to find where each one belongs. For the older ones, give them blank sticky notes and have them brainstorm ideas on what to do—and what not to do—when they feel stuck. This can be done electronically using Jamboard or Padlet.

What does productive struggle look like in the elementary school classroom? One of the keys to productive struggle in the classroom is ensuring that the classroom culture is strong. Students need to know the classroom is a safe space to try new things, to be vulnerable, and to not know the answer right away. By encouraging productive struggle, we avoid students shutting down and disengaging completely when they don't know the answer to a problem. A great way to support students is by cocreating an anchor chart that lives in the classroom titled "What to Do When I'm Stuck." On this chart, you can provide strategies for students to try, such as:

- Represent the problem in a different way. Can I use manipulatives? Can I draw the problem? Will writing about it help me?
- Chat with a partner. What questions can I ask my friend? Can they be the teacher for a moment and help me clarify my misunderstanding?
- Do I need to do research? What don't I know, and where am I getting stuck?

> **WHEN TEACHERS UNDERSTAND THEIR STUDENTS' MOTIVATIONS, THEY CAN DESIGN LEARNING TASKS THAT ARE APPROPRIATELY CHALLENGING, PUSHING STUDENTS TO STEP OUT OF THEIR COMFORT ZONES AND ENGAGE IN DEEPER COGNITIVE PROCESSING**

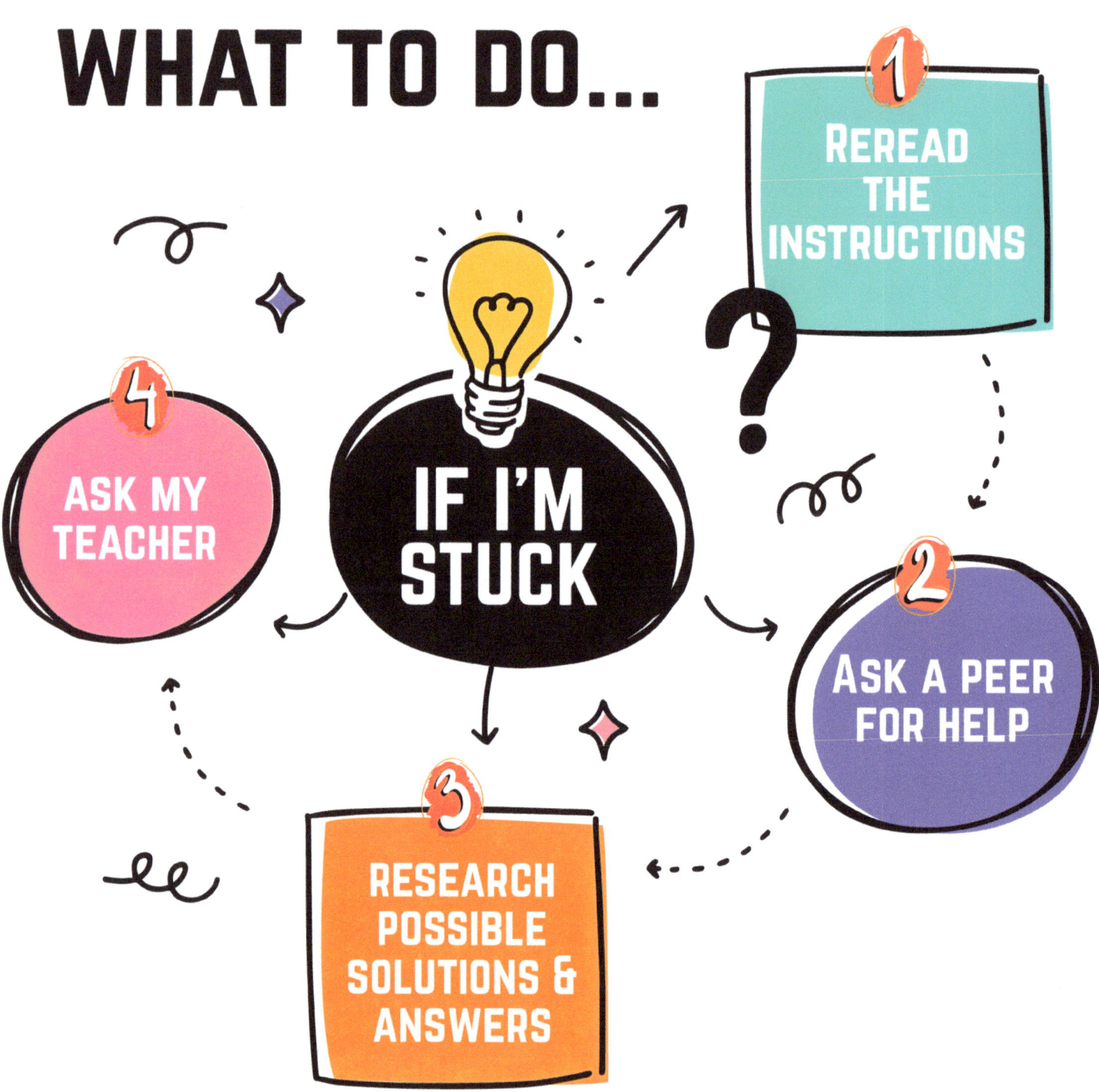

What does productive struggle look like in the middle school classroom? Middle schoolers often want the right answer and they want you to give it to them. When a student asks questions, you can respond with "What do you think?" and then "How do you know? How could you check that?" These questions do a few things:

- Encourage students to develop independence.
- Make the students responsible for checking their own learning.
- Allow students to struggle with the reality that there is rarely one right answer, but a plethora of options in which they may need to choose the best, most effective, or quickest depending on the scenario.

FOR A PRODUCTIVE STRUGGLE TO BE IMPACTFUL, THERE MUST BE A BALANCE BETWEEN HOW MUCH YOU SUPPORT THE LEARNING AND HOW MUCH THE STUDENT IS CHALLENGED.

When You Are Stuck

What To Do	What NOT To Do

- Think of a different idea to try
- Think of a question you want to ask
- Break it apart in smaller chunks
- Distract others from their work
- Think about what's worked before
- Ask someone for help
- Only try one idea and then quit
- Take a short break
- Give up
- Let someone else do all of the work

 **What does productive struggle look like in the high school classroom?** You know the student—the one who wants you to stand over their shoulder and make sure every step they take is the right next step. (Am I doing this math problem correctly? Is this the best next sentence?) Allowing students to productively struggle at this age is vital to their future success. Being able to state, "I don't know, but I will figure it out on my own" is essential as students prepare for college and careers.

- Allow students the opportunity to challenge themselves by providing difficult math problems, science experiments, and texts.
- Create a challenging "problem of the week" and offer a reward to those who answer it correctly.
- Get your students thinking by writing a riddle on the board; let them take time to see if they can solve it.

The important factor is to allow students the opportunity to productively struggle without any consequences. High school students, especially when grades and test scores can impact their future decisions, tend to resist productive struggle. But, given the chance to challenge themselves knowing it will not impact their grade—and might even be fun—well, that's a whole different story.

 Stop and Reflect: In what area of your curriculum do you see students using productive struggle?

RECOGNIZE AND EMBRACE THE FEAR OF FAILURE

As educators, we are often burdened with the fear of failure. Will we be the educators our students need? Don't let failure and doubt hold you back from reaching your full teaching potential! Sometimes, we want our classrooms or our lesson plans to be perfect. We put unnecessary burdens on ourselves and our students.

 Stop and Reflect: What is a goal you fear to accomplish because you might fail?

Fear of failure can hinder learning, preventing the exploration of new ideas and pushing limits. But honestly, failure doesn't have to be a negative thing. In classrooms where educators encourage risk-taking and embrace failure, a whole new world of learning opens up. By shifting the focus from perfection to innovation, the learning experience becomes dynamic and exciting. Failure is no longer something to be punished; it becomes an essential step in the journey of learning.

Imagine a classroom where asking questions and taking on challenges is not only accepted but rewarded, and where failure is seen as one step closer to success. This environment will foster a mindset that embraces failure as an impersonal and integral part of the learning process. A growing body of research suggests that embracing failure in the classroom can be a powerful tool for learning and innovation (Dawson, 2023). In this context, failure can serve as a powerful catalyst prompting learners to question, explore, and ultimately deepen their understanding (Heljakka, 2023).

Not only do our students struggle with taking risks, so do we. What would happen if we tried a new learning strategy or took a risk? What if it flopped? How would we, as teachers, feel being open and vulnerable about our own failures? This is a powerful learning tool for our students. Sharing our failures with our students allows us to not only build rapport but also to show we all encounter failure. Simply sharing a story such as "I tried to make a new recipe last night—and it was horrible! I totally forgot to add a key ingredient!" then laughing about it with your students allows them to feel safe and comfortable sharing their own mistakes.

So let go of your fear and be ready to fail forward. By redefining failure as a crucial component of learning, we can open doors to creativity, growth, and ultimately success. Don't be held back by the fear of failure; instead, let it propel you toward greatness!

F	A	I	L	S
FREEDOM	**ATTITUDE**	**INDIVIDUALITY**	**LEARNING**	**STRENGTHS**
Failure in the classroom can liberate students from the fear of making mistakes. It teaches them it's okay to fail and failure is a part of the learning process.	Encountering failure can change a student's attitude toward learning by making them understand that it's not just about getting the right answers but also about learning.	Failure can encourage students to find their unique ways of understanding and solving problems, fostering individuality.	Failure serves as a powerful tool for invoking deep learning as it forces students to analyze their mistakes and understand where they went wrong.	Failure can help students identify their strengths as they navigate challenges and find ways to overcome them.

Curiosity Thrives Where Failure Begins

What does celebrating failure look like in the classroom? Failure seems to have become a taboo word, and not just to students but also to parents, administrators, and teachers. Fear of failure is real, and many times it causes self-doubt and anxiety. Often students will choose to not participate out of fear of being wrong and therefore judged by their peers and teachers. Offering opportunities to celebrate failure and to embrace it as a learning experience is vital as we build trusting relationships with our students and inspire them to take academic risks. Feedback, as we will discuss more in "Evaluation Designer," is a key component to embracing failure. If students know they can fail and it will not negatively impact their grades, they will be more likely to try something new.

CONTRACT TO FAIL

By this hereby contract, in _____ classroom, all failure, preceding learning, is not only permitted, but encouraged.

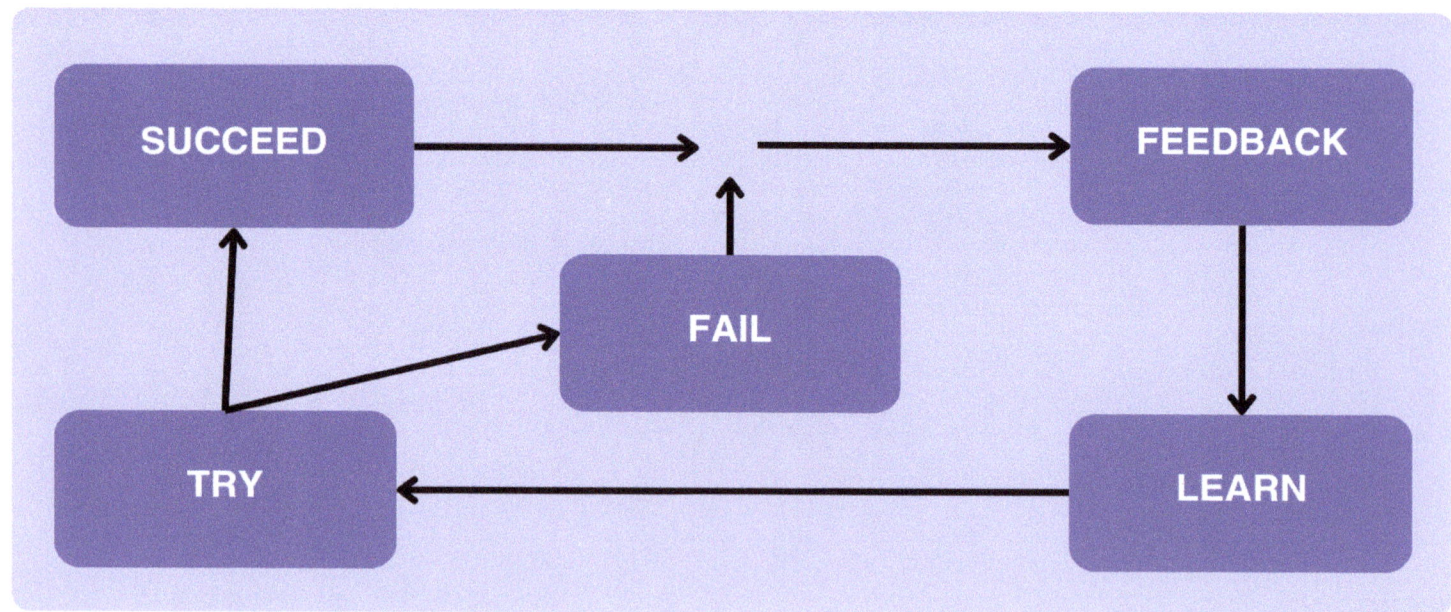

Successful Stories of Failure

Oprah Winfrey – Faced failure early on in her career before starting her self-titled talkshow.

Soichiro Honda – Was turned down by Toyota Motor Corporation for a job before founding Honda.

Ludwig van Beethoven – Was told he had no talent for music, yet became one of the greatest composers.

Michael Jordan – Was cut from his high school basketball team, went on to play professional baseball.

By redefining failure as a crucial component of learning, we can open doors to creativity, growth, and ultimately success.

Practical Tip: When someone shares a mistake or failure with the class, have the whole class clap, cheer, hoot, and holler like that student just scored the winning touchdown. Celebrating failure in our classroom fosters deeper thinking skills including reliance, perseverance, and empathy (Bolander Laksov & McGrath, 2020).

Stop and Reflect: In what area of your curriculum do students frequently fail? How might you add strategies to allow students time to celebrate those failures instead of feeling defeated?

FAILURE IS THE CATALYST FOR CRITICAL UNDERSTANDING, DEEPER LEARNING, AND PERSEVERANCE.

(BOLANDER LAKSOV & MCGRATH, 2020)

CELEBRATE FAILURE IN THE CLASSROOM!

	Meaning	Description
F	Freedom	Failure in the classroom can liberate students from the fear of making mistakes. It teaches them it's okay to fail and failure is a part of the learning process.
A	Attitude	Encountering failure can change a student's attitude toward learning by making them understand that it's not just about getting the right answers but also about learning.
I	Individuality	Failure can encourage students to find their unique ways of understanding and solving problems, fostering individuality.
L	Learning	Failure serves as a powerful tool for invoking deep learning as it forces students to analyze their mistakes and understand where they went wrong.
S	Strengths	Failure can help students identify their strengths as they navigate challenges and find ways to overcome them.

Provide Opportunities for Creative Problem-Solving

Teaching creative problem-solving has numerous benefits that can serve students well in their ability to think creatively and critically. This skill fosters independent thinking and innovation, critical skills in our rapidly changing world. It equips learners to approach challenges from different angles, often leading to unique solutions. It develops resilience and adaptability as they learn to navigate obstacles and setbacks and adjust their strategies accordingly. This resilience can enhance their overall mental well-being by reducing stress and anxiety. Additionally, creative problem-solving aids in building self-confidence as students recognize their ability to tackle issues and produce effective solutions. This increased self-assurance can positively affect their social interactions and academic performance.

> **Creative problem-solving fosters independent thinking and innovation.**

Teachers and students face problems on a daily basis, so learning how to take a risk and creatively solve problems is a valuable skill, not only in the classroom but also in life. There are several different ways to teach creative problem-solving.

Steps for Creative Problem-Solving

1) Identify the problem. What needs to be solved?

2) Using divergent and convergent thinking, brainstorm different ways to solve the problem openly and honestly.

3) Try to solve the problem. How might we go about solving this problem in the most reliable but novel way?

4) Narrow down the most relevant and realistic solutions.

5) Create a plan or a prototype that uses the ideas generated.

6) If failure is experienced, try, try again!

7) Evaluate the plan. What worked? What new ideas did you discover?

8) Reflect. What might you do differently next time? What went well?

STEPS FOR CREATIVE PROBLEM SOLVING

Follow these steps!

1
Identify the problem. What needs to be solved?

2
Using divergent and convergent thinking, brainstorm different ways to solve the problem openly and honestly. How might we solve the problem?

3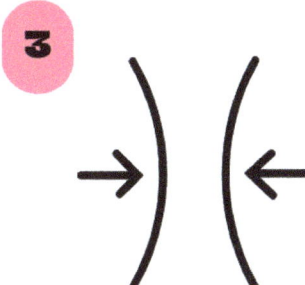
Narrow down the most relevant and realistic solutions to the problem.

4
Try to solve the problem. How might we go about solving this problem in the most reliable but novel way?

5
Create a plan or a prototype that uses the ideas generated.

6
If failure is experienced, try, try again!

7
Evaluate the plan. What worked? What new ideas did you discover?

8
Reflect. What might you do differently next time? What went well?

9
REPEAT

 **What does creative problem-solving look like in the elementary school classroom?** With a little bit of practice, elementary students can excel at creative problem-solving! The trick is changing their mindset so they know it's okay (and exciting!) to think and brainstorm outside of the box. Here are some ways students can practice creative problem-solving.

- In a third-grade science unit, you might ask students to brainstorm a list of reasons organisms' characteristics change over time. Be ready to prompt students after they give you what they perceive as the right answer!

- In social studies, you might ask students to consider how history might've been different if an important event had a different outcome.

- Ask students to work together in pairs or small groups to reimagine a common item: a bicycle, a wheelbarrow, a water bottle. How can students use creative thinking to reimagine these items? You'll be amazed at what they come up with!

 **What does creative problem-solving look like in the middle school classroom?** We live in a time when students just want the correct answers and the steps to get them there quickly with the least amount of work. Teach students that finding solutions can be fun, that there are benefits to trying something new, and that there is rarely a correct answer in real life, but there are many possible solutions to a problem.

- Normalize challenging the way things are done in your classroom culture. If students question why a mathematical problem is done a certain way, ask them how they would do it or how many other ways there are to do it. If in ELA or social studies, students challenge something that is read or a theory for a historical event's motivation, allow them to talk through their reasoning and engage in the conversation.

- Have quick team-building activities that require collaboration and trial and error. For example, spread a sheet or blanket on the floor of your classroom (you may need two sheets of blankets and have two teams depending on the size of your class). Give the students six minutes to turn the sheet over, but tell them no one can touch the floor. Have a purposeful debrief getting students to reflect on how they came up with the solution, what ideas were shared, why they chose the solution they did, and if there are other ideas that they could try or that might work better.

- Set up imagination games. For example, have all the desks turned upside down when students enter. Tell them in order to earn their desk back upright, they have to come up with a different use for a desk. It can be as wild and unusual as they want. Debrief with the idea that many creative solutions took one person to see things differently and to be brave enough to try it.

What does creative problem-solving look like in the high school classroom? In any classroom, simple community-building activities like playing a game of Clue or creating an escape room can introduce the concept of problem-solving. Oftentimes, as students walk into the classroom they are complaining about something—the music at the dance was horrible, the tickets were too expensive, or their parents are being too strict. Take five minutes and work through one of those problems with the class. How might we find a better DJ for the dance? How might we convince parents that curfew could be a half-hour later? This will build community and rapport and allow students to get centered and ready for class.

Science

Have students go to the local river and discover a problem. Maybe the local river is polluted or a certain fish is dying. Whatever the problem is, have students brainstorm some questions.

- What might be all the causes of pollution in our local river?
- How might we, as a classroom, improve the river's health?
- How might we get the community involved?
- How might we educate our community about the impact of pollution?
- How might we stop the pollution from getting worse?

Once students use divergent and convergent thinking to discuss this problem, they can create a new way to clean up the river such as a community awareness plan.

ELA

Have students study a certain issue in today's youth? It could relate to fitness, mental health, social justice, etc. It could relate to a theme you are discussing during a novel study. Have students brainstorm questions.

- What might be all the ways students feel stressed today?
- What might be all the ways we can help students feel a sense of belonging?
- What might be a way teenagers can utilize communication skills with their parents?

Once students use divergent and convergent thinking to discuss this problem, they can do research and create a video or podcast educating peers on the problem and solution.

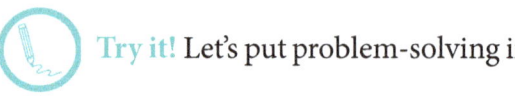 **Try it!** Let's put problem-solving into practice.

What is a problem you are currently facing? It could be personal or professional. Identify the problem.

What needs to be solved? Using divergent thinking, brainstorm different ways to solve the problem openly and honestly. Remember to stay open!

Take a look at the ideas you just brainstormed. Using convergent thinking, narrow down the most viable ideas.

Try to solve the problem. How might you go about solving this problem in the most reliable but novel way?

What steps do you need to take first? It might be researching, taking a class to acquire new skills, asking peers or mentors for help, etc.

Implement your plan! Give it a try!

Reflect on how the plan was implemented. What worked? What needs improvement? What new ideas did executing this plan inspire? If failure is experienced, try, try again!

Reimagining Classroom Relationships to Support Risk Facilitation

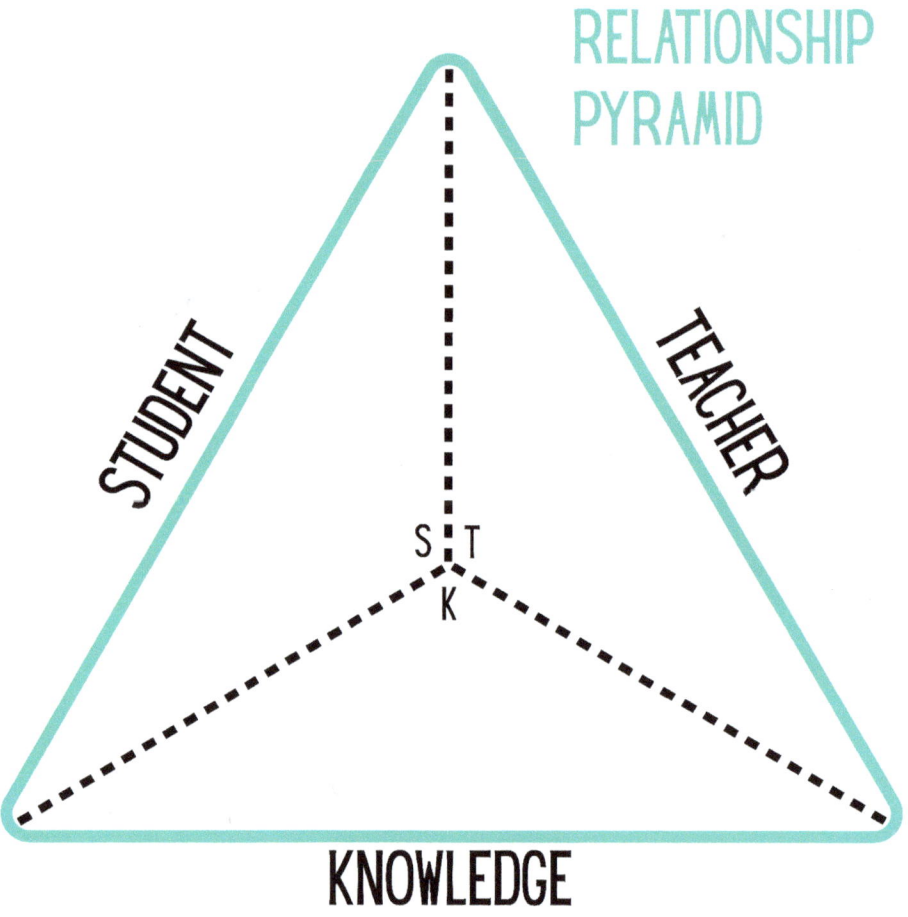

In the final section of "Risk Facilitator," we revisit the educative relationships—all the relationships that exist between the three basic elements needed for classroom learning: the student, the teacher, and the knowledge to be learned. By turning the educative relationship prism and shifting the power dynamic between the elements and relationships, you will find the spaces and places for risk facilitation.

> What would happen to an activity, conversation, lesson, assessment, or unit if you shifted control? Instead of starting with the element or relationship you typically do, shift the prism.

1. Self-efficacy. 2. Productive struggle. 3. Celebration of failure. 4. Creative problem-solving.

Ways to Support Risk Facilitating in the Relationship Pyramid

TEACHER leads the relationship	T-T	1. Implement daily success talks to celebrate strengths. 2. Work together to divide and conquer units based on interest. 3. Discuss strategies that are good in theory but not in practice. 4. Exchange classes for a day across grade/subject/class level.
	T-S	1. Model positive self-talk. 2. Share the evolution of the correct answer for your content. 3. Introduce failure or "not yet" thinking as a class rule. 4. Use a daily challenge as problem solving bell ringer.
	T-K	1. Identify areas of expertise, confidence, and comfort. 2. Set the challenge of at least one new activity or lesson per week. 3. Keep a failure journal as inspiration. 4. Research classroom pain points to crowdsource solutions.
STUDENT leads the relationship	S-S	1. Use positive peer feedback to promote strengths. 2. Utilize cooperative learning to encourage a group mindset. 3. Share formative feedback in groups so all benefit. 4. Look at peer mediation strategies.
	S-T	1. Use interests and strengths as a starting point for learning. 2. Develop a language around asking for help. 3. Narrate product creation in order to identify learning. 4. Identify class or school issues and present alternatives.
	S-K	1. Develop learner statements around areas to take risk. 2. Choose options that aren't strengths or favorites. 3. Keep progress logs to show mastery of content takes time. 4. Create a plan for growth within the self, the skill, and the content.
KNOWLEDGE leads the relationship	K-K	1. Articulate prior knowledge but acknowledge areas for growth. 2. Consult student data to support curriculum revision. 3. Identify gaps in personal and content knowledge. 4. Look at outliers in the knowledge area to inspire or caution.
	K-T	1. Revisit knowledge wins and comfort zones. 2. Use classroom patterns/ preferences to identify comfort zones. 3. Use historical data to guide instructional choices. 4. Look for interdisciplinary connections and crossovers.
	K-S	1. Use a pre-assessment/post-assessment tool to reinforce progress. 2. Provide "unknown" options to allow for discovery. 3. Study historical "greatest failures" in content area. 4. Present known solutions to see the problem solving process.

 Stop and Reflect: When you think about risk-taking and building rapport, what comes to mind? In which relationship do you traditionally take risks? In which area do you see an opportunity to grow?

With its roots deep in various theories, academic risk-taking breaks the barriers of traditional education, pushing students out of their comfort zones and creating an exciting and dynamic learning environment. By encouraging students to take risks, ask questions, and dive into the unknown, we not only develop their cognitive abilities but also nurture essential personal attributes like resilience, creativity, and self-confidence.

When we incorporate concepts like zones of proximal development, self-efficacy, inquiry-based learning, and sparking curiosity and creativity, we transform classrooms into epicenters of discovery, resilience, and innovation. In this fast-paced and uncertain world, it's crucial for educators to integrate academic risk-taking into their teaching practices, making learning an active journey of exploration and growth.

Try It! Use this chart as your application piece so that when you are ready to write a lesson plan from your ideas, it is already formatted and easy to find.

Lesson Idea/Creativity Skill

Heighten Anticipation (ignite curiosity and a sense of wonder): *How will you get students excited or curious about the lesson or content?*

Deepening Expectations (deep diving into the lesson; students are consistently actively engaged): *How will you make it hands-on? How will they explore different perspectives? How will it be relevant and meaningful to them?*

Hands-on Interactive Ideas: *What can you bring in, have them create, construct or interact with?*

Connect It to Real-Life Experiences: *List all of the ways this applies to their life, experiences, or dreams. How will you make this connection for them?*

Extend the Learning (how students will apply new-found knowledge and curiosity into the world outside the classroom) *What activities can students do outside the classroom to continue the learning?*

 **Activity:**
What goal do you dream of accomplishing? Using what you learned throughout this section, how might you push outside your comfort zone and enter your creative zone?

Stop and Reflect:

What new strategies or concepts from this section resonated with you the most? How do you plan to implement them in your classroom?

Reflect on a challenge you might face when applying the ideas from this section. How can you overcome it?

Consider your current teaching practices. How can you integrate the principles discussed in this section to enhance creativity and critical thinking among your students?

How can we make the learning experience meaningful, relevant, and beneficial for all students?

EXPERIENCE NAVIGATOR

Experience Navigator

"Teachers provide the true north, and help students find a worthy course … one that will challenge their skills on the open learning seas." ~David Truss (2019)

Essential Question: How can we make the learning experience meaningful, relevant, and beneficial for all students?

Experience Navigator ensures knowledge is shared in a way that is:

- Relevant.
- Meaningful.
- Engaging.
- Challenging.

Strategies we will examine are:

- Torrance Incubation Model.
- Project-based learning.
- KWL.
- Socratic seminars/academic conversations.

Definitions

- Experiences are the process of actively engaging in meaningful activities, interactions, and observations to acquire knowledge, skills, and understanding within an educational setting, while also paying respect to prior experience and learning.
- An Experience Navigator is an educator whose focus is to foster an environment of exploration and course correction rather than rigid adherence to a predefined path.
- KWL (Know, Want to Know, Learned) is a strategy teachers commonly use in classrooms in order to activate prior knowledge, set learning goals, and reflect on what has been learned throughout a lesson or unit.
- Project-based learning (PBL) is a teaching approach focusing on students engaging in real-world projects so as to develop knowledge and skills through active, hands-on learning.

 **Activity**

What is one of the best experiences of your life? Why was it such a great experience? How did it make you feel? Would you do it again? Tell the story of the experience using as many descriptive words as you can. For example, maybe you went skydiving once and it was an amazing experience, but you may never want to do it again!

INTRODUCTION

Embark on a thrilling educational journey as an Experience Navigator. Instead of a strict commander, envision a friendly guide who sails alongside students on the vast seas of knowledge. This innovative educator is not just a source of information; they act as a facilitator and mentor, empowering students to chart their unique learning paths.

Like a ship's captain navigating uncharted territories, an Experience Navigator encourages exploration instead of rigid conformity. They inspire students to look beyond the horizon, sparking a culture of inquiry and discovery. With their guidance, learning becomes an exciting adventure, igniting curiosity and creativity.

An Experience Navigator stands out by creating a classroom environment where ideas flourish. They provide a safe space for students to think in a unique and novel way while expressing their creativity. Every student's distinct qualities are recognized and supported.

The conventional teacher-student relationship is transformed into an interactive and captivating exchange. Students become active participants in their learning journey. They don't simply absorb information; they actively engage with it, experiment with it, and question it. This active involvement allows students to take ownership of their learning and fuels their motivation to explore beyond the classroom walls.

An Experience Navigator:

- Embraces ambiguity.
- Participates in classroom discussions and activities.
- Ventures into new areas of curiosity.
- Actively seeks feedback from peers.
- Embraces failure.
- Actively uses creative and critical thinking.

Learning Objectives for an Experience Navigator

This section will explore:

- What it means to be an Experience Navigator.
- Strategies to create lessons that encourage students to experience learning.
- How you can incorporate more meaningful and relevant experience into your classroom.

> **BECOME AN EXPERIENCE NAVIGATOR: IGNITE CURIOSITY, INSPIRE ENGAGEMENT, AND TRANSFORM LEARNING INTO AN EXCITING ADVENTURE.**

A teacher as an Experience Navigator:

- Creates a curriculum that allows students to experience the study material in different ways.
- Becomes a tour guide, allowing students to create personalized learning experiences.
- Embraces challenging and ambiguous classroom moments.

A student as an Experience Navigator:

- Embraces and celebrates ambiguity.
- Challenges themselves to look at learning as a creative and personalized experience.
- Believes in themselves enough to take control of their own learning experience and know when to ask for guidance.

Stop and Reflect: Looking back at your current curriculum and students, where are opportunities for experiencing learning versus sitting and absorbing?

Strategies for Incorporating Experience Navigator

Torrance Incubation Model (TIM)

Unleash your students' creativity in the classroom with the Torrance incubation model (TIM) for creative teaching and learning. Developed by renowned education pioneer E. Paul Torrance, the father of creativity in education, and further refined by researchers Keller-Mathers, Murdock, and Burnett, this model seamlessly integrates creative thinking skills into your lessons without adding extra time or pressure (Murdock & Keller-Mathers, 2008).

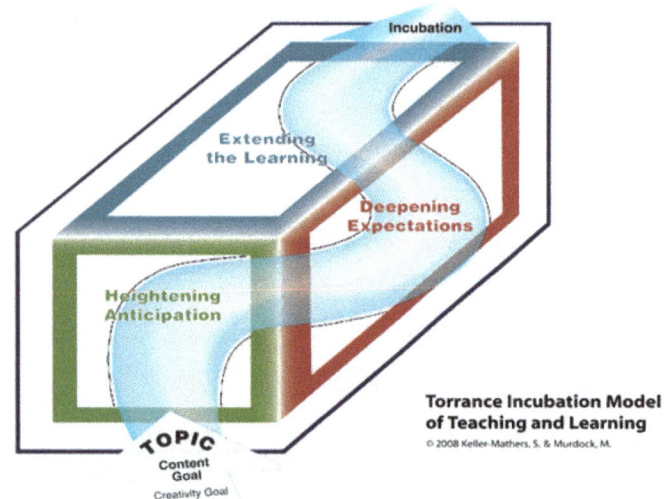

Imagine teaching your students how to use a microscope while also inspiring their creativity. With TIM, you can do just that. Begin by defining your lesson and learning outcomes, then select a creativity skill you want to develop. Drawing from a set of twenty identified creativity skills, as compiled by Burnett, choose the most relevant one to infuse throughout your lesson (Murdock & Keller-Mathers, 2008).

The Torrance Incubation Model consists of three stages that will captivate your students and transform their learning experience.

Stage One: Heightening the Anticipation

From the moment your students walk into your classroom, ignite their curiosity and create a sense of wonderment. If you hang images of various magnified objects around the room, students will be intrigued and eager to find out more. Encourage them to guess what the images are, sparking engaging conversations about how different perspectives can shape our understanding.

Stage Two: Deepening Expectations

Dive deeper into the lesson, keeping students actively engaged in exploring and understanding the content. Continuously integrate the chosen creativity skill of looking at things from different angles. Have students draw what an object might look like under a microscope at different magnifications, revealing how their perspective changes as they zoom in and out.

Stage Three: Extending the Learning

Take learning beyond the classroom walls and empower students to apply their newfound knowledge and creativity in real-world situations. Task them with finding three objects at home that they want to examine from different perspectives. By bringing these objects to class, students reinforce the concept of looking at things from various angles while applying their creativity skills in a meaningful way. With TIM, teachers can effortlessly infuse creativity into their lessons and empower students to develop their creative thinking abilities while meeting lesson objectives (Murdock & Keller-Mathers, 2008).

WHAT'S MY VISION?

COMMON CORE STANDARDS
Speaking and Listening

CREATIVITY THINKING SKILLS
Getting Glimpes of the Future

ESSENTIAL QUESTION:
How can creating a plan help us focus on the possibilities?

TARGETS:
Students will be able to c reate concrete goals for the semester/year,

Students will be able to reflect on differing possibilities.

ASSESSMENTS:
FORMATIVE
Students will present their vision boards to the class.

TIME NEEDED:
2 class periods
(120 minutes)

MATERIALS:
- Brainstorming Sheet
- Slide Deck
- A blank slide deck with enough slides for each student.

6-12

Overview of Lesson

Executive functioning is important at any age. Setting goals and reflecting on them helps us grow as individuals and envision the possibilities that may lie ahead.

This lesson can be used at the beginning of a school year to help build community. It is also vital that students start to see the diversity that exists in their school.

There are several options for this lesson. Students can set goals for the semester, year, five, and ten years. Depending on the age of the students and the focus of the lesson.

Heightening Anticipation

1) Ask students:

How many of you have been asked what you will do next year? What school you will go to? What you will major in or what do you envision for a career?

How many of you have an answer for that?

How does that make you feel? Why?

2) It would be helpful for you to share your experiences with these questions. Being vulnerable and open with your students gains trust and builds rapport.

Overview of Lesson

1) Give each student a brainstorming sheet

2) Walk students through the slide deck explaining that a vision board is a way to imagine what you want in your future; it's a time to set goals and think big by imagining all the possibilities.

3) After the lesson, give students time to complete the free personality tests and begin to brainstorm.

4) The vision board can be completed in class or at home depending on the schedule.

5) Inform students that they will present their vision boards to the class.

NOTE: It is extremely helpful if the teacher creates a vision chart. It allows students to see an example, hear an example of the presentation, and get to know the teacher more personally.

Heightening Anticipation

After the presentations are over, encourage students to make their vision board a .png and use it as wallpaper for their computers or print it out and hang it in their room.

At the end of each quarter, have students revisit their vision boards and reflect on what has been accomplished and what is yet to do. This is also a great time to talk about how goals change and the importance of being flexible.

Stop and Reflect: How might using TIM impact the way you design your lesson?

Project-Based Learning

Project-based learning (PBL) empowers students to shape their education, explore their passions, and take their learning to new heights. With PBL, students become the architects of their own education as they choose their project themes and dive into comprehensive investigations. They're not just absorbing information—they're constructing knowledge, solving problems, and making a difference.

PBL isn't just about creativity—it's also about nurturing curiosity. By tackling real-world problems that resonate with students' lives and interests, teachers spark curiosity and fuel a lifelong love for learning. Failure becomes a stepping stone, not a setback, as students learn from their mistakes and grow.

Experience navigation, like PBL, thrives on curiosity. By designing real-world challenges and posing intriguing questions, users are motivated to explore, interact, and discover. They can take intellectual risks, challenge the status quo, and think outside traditional boundaries. The process is both engaging and empowering. Ultimately, by embracing PBL and experience navigation, teachers and users alike can make learning a meaningful journey of exploration and discovery. Through creativity, collaboration, and curiosity, they can shape their own destiny in the world of education technology (Cremin et al., 2015).

By taking this approach, they not only enhance their own learning experience but also have a positive impact on the lives of others. Whether it's designing an innovative solution to a real-world problem or inspiring another student to reach for their dreams, the possibilities are seemingly endless. As such, PBL and experience navigation will continue to be powerful tools in transforming the way we learn and equip us with the skills needed to succeed in an ever-changing world.

At their core, PBL and experience navigation are about creating a safe space for exploration and inquiry. They encourage students to ask questions, take risks, investigate solutions, and collaborate with others to develop their own understanding of a concept.

Key Concepts of Project-Based Learning (PBL)

- Knowledge isn't simply absorbed, but rather constructed, shaped, and then applied to real-world problems.
- Comprehensive investigations are carried out over a span of several weeks or months, centering on a particular question, problem, or challenge.
- Student autonomy and decision-making are emphasized.
- Students have the flexibility to learn at their own pace as they freely select their project themes guided by their personal interests and passions. They are accountable for planning, executing, and reflecting on their work.
- Teachers evolve into Experience Navigators: they no longer control but guide the learning process, equipping students with the necessary tools, resources, and support to foster a learner-centric environment.

- Creativity and curiosity are fostered due to this approach's emphasis on exploration and problem-solving.
- Creativity is stimulated by prompting students to look at problems from various perspectives and to explore multiple solutions while posing open-ended questions and incorporating different disciplines.
- The process is valued over the product (Cremin et al., 2015).
- Challenging questions or intriguing scenarios are utilized so as to stimulate curiosity.
- Failure is seen not as a setback, but as a valuable learning opportunity.
- The approach relies on the curiosity of its users to be truly effective.

 Try it! What is a project you want to work on around the house? What learning will take place while you complete it? For example, are you getting ready to plant a garden? Then you may need to ask:

- When is the best time to plant?
- What type of soil should I use?
- What type of plant food do I need?
- Which vegetables will grow best in my location?
- How often should I water my plants?

🔍 **Stop and Reflect:** Use that same thinking for your content. What project could your students work on in the classroom and what learning would take place? For example, students need to learn about mapmaking. Have students make a map of the school that is easy enough for kindergartners to understand.

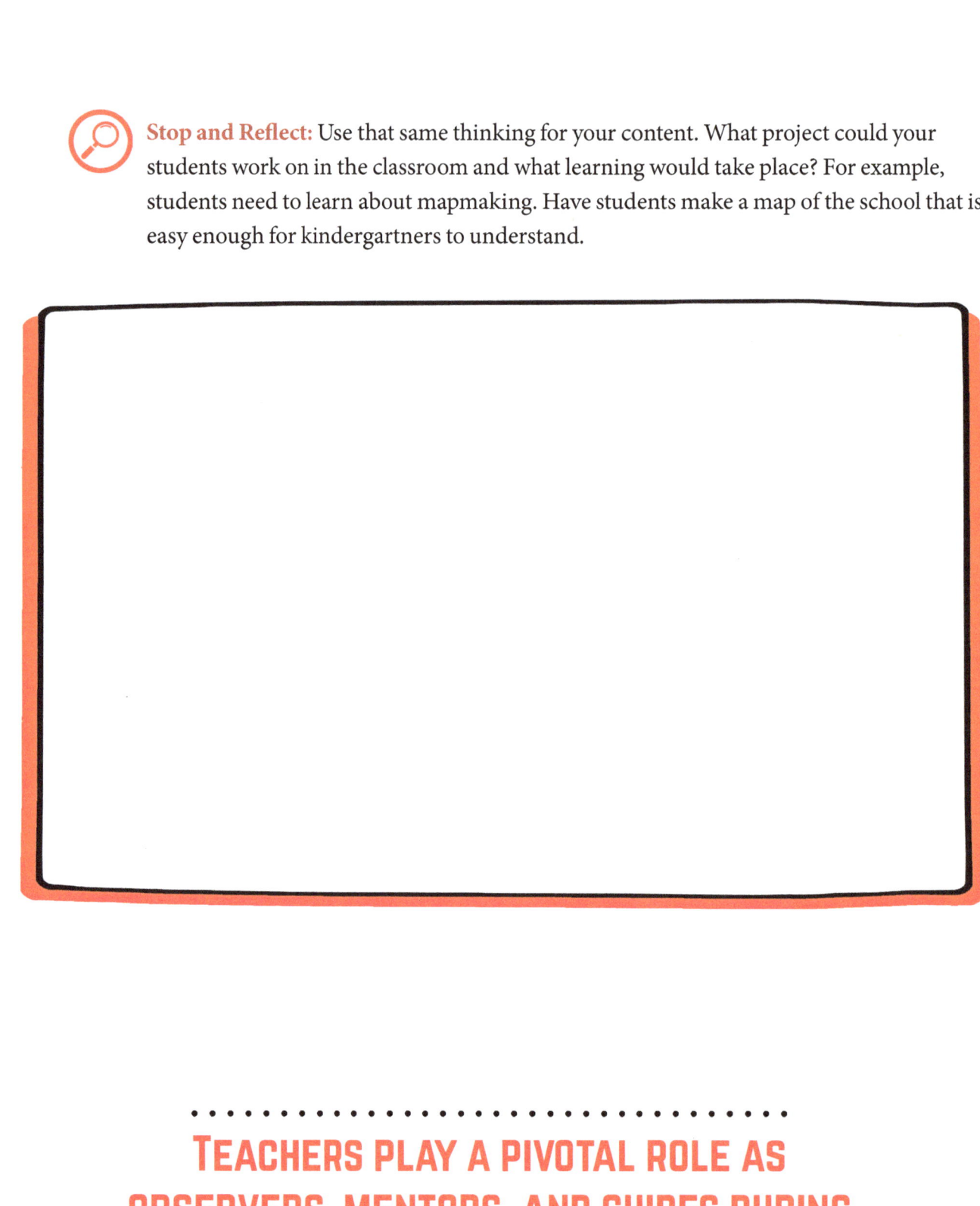

Teachers play a pivotal role as observers, mentors, and guides during this transformative journey.

KWL

A teaching strategy that has stood the test of time is KWL, or Know, Want to Know, Learn. This incredible tool gives students the power to shape their own learning experience, fueling their curiosity and helping them reflect on their newfound knowledge. With KWL, students actively engage in the learning process. They start by tapping into their existing knowledge about a topic, exploring what they want to learn, and finally reflecting on what they've learned. This approach not only deepens their connection with the subject matter but also enhances retention and individualized learning.

Teachers play a pivotal role as observers, mentors, and guides during this transformative journey. They provide structure and support, encouraging inquiry and reflection while ensuring learning objectives are met.

To help educators incorporate the KWL strategy effectively, we've created a detailed chart that covers each stage of the process. This blueprint will inspire a sense of ownership and open doors to a new level of learning.

Experience navigation relates and expands on KWL through:

- Identifying prior knowledge: Both methods start by determining what the learner already knows. In KWL, this is the "Know" part. In experience navigation, this is understanding the learner's prior experiences with the topic.
- Setting learning goals: The next step in KWL is to identify what the learner wants to know, which can be paralleled in experience navigation by setting learning goals based on the learner's interest and curiosity from their prior experiences.
- Guiding the learning journey: Experience navigation involves creating experiences that guide the learner toward achieving their learning goals, similar to how KWL guides the learner to acquire new knowledge that fulfills their "Want to know" queries.

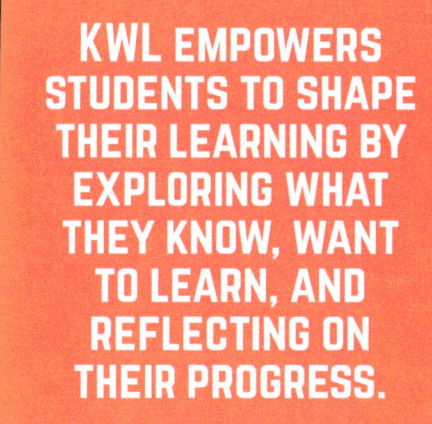

KWL EMPOWERS STUDENTS TO SHAPE THEIR LEARNING BY EXPLORING WHAT THEY KNOW, WANT TO LEARN, AND REFLECTING ON THEIR PROGRESS.

Reflection: The final step in KWL is identifying what has been learned, and this is mirrored in experience navigation by reflecting on the experiences and understanding what knowledge or skills have been gained from them. Ensure the experiences at hand are a learning experience and tell students reflecting on them can empower them throughout their learning journey.

What I...	Description	Building	Implementing	Execution
Know	The phase when students list what they already know about a topic	The teacher prompts students to share their existing knowledge on the topic and helps organize this information coherently. This promotes confidence and allows students to identify their existing knowledge.	This step is incorporated at the beginning of a new topic or lesson, creating a foundation for further learning and giving the teacher insights about the class's prior knowledge. This allows students to build from previous lessons learned to encourage creativity.	The teacher facilitates brainstorming or mind-mapping activities, encourages class discussion, and notes students' inputs on a visible board or digital document.
Want to Know	The phase when students specify what they wish to learn.	The teacher encourages students to ask questions and share what they would like to learn about the topic. This boosts motivation by focusing learning on students' interests and inquiries.	The teacher incorporates this step by prompting students to think about what they want to know after they have established what they already know. This primes them for the learning process.	The teacher guides students to form questions or statements about their learning objectives and records these for reference throughout the learning process. Divergent thinking activities such as brainstorming or mind-mapping works well during this phase.
Learned	The phase when students review, reflect on, and describe what they've learned.	After the lesson, students are prompted to share, both orally and in writing, what they've learned. This reinforces learning and builds a sense of accomplishment by reviewing new knowledge.	This final step is incorporated at the end of the lesson or topic to consolidate the new knowledge. It offers students a chance to reflect on their learning.	The teacher asks students to summarize what they've learned, either individually or as a group and guides them in connecting new knowledge to the questions they had at the beginning. The teacher might also use quizzes or projects to assess understanding. The critical emphasis here is reflection. Allow students time to reflect on what they have learned and how it has impacted them.

Stop and Reflect: Create your own KWL chart. What is something you have always wanted to learn? Woodworking? Knitting? Cake decorating? Get started on that journey now by completing the chart below.

What I...	Description	Building	Implementing	Execution
Know				
Want to Know				
Learned				

Socratic Seminars/Academic Conversations

Using questions along with discussion can increase a student's ability to think creatively and critically. Socratic seminars allow students to think and respond to a text and their peers. Teachers can implement this engaging and rigorous discussion strategy in multiple ways.

Components of an Academic Conversation

1) The conversation should revolve around a central text. It could be an article, short story, novel, textbook chapter, poem, piece of artwork, song, or movie. You could use one central text or have students synthesize different texts.

2) The teacher acts as a facilitator. As students grow in their questioning skills, the teacher's role changes from facilitator to observer.

3) The role of the student is to discuss the text using specific facts and life experiences. There is virtually no right or wrong answer. You want students to have an intellectual conversation with each other.

4) This is not a debate. There should not be two sides but multiple perspectives backed up by text-to-text, text-to-world, and text-to-self.

5) These conversations can be graded (see the rubric in the appendix).

How to Organize an Academic Conversation

1) When starting, it is best if the teacher prepares the questions. These questions should be open-ended and offer a chance for students to discuss multiple perspectives. As students progress, the responsibility for generating questions shifts to the student.

2) Depending on the number of students, you can create one large circle or two circles, with the inner circle doing the discussion and the outer circle taking notes. Halfway through your time, you can switch the inner and outer circles.

3) Students need to come prepared. You can give students questions ahead of time so they can do their research and prepare for the conversation or you can require students to come to the conversation with three to five generated questions.

4) Start with an opening question for the class to answer and then sit back and listen to the responses. Introducing a larger theme or issue within the text will give students clear direction on how to start the conversation. It could even be "What does the title tell us about the meaning of the text?" There may be times when you, as the teacher, have to step in to either push the conversation forward or challenge the students with a question.

5) During the conversation, encourage variety in voices. During the first few conversations, you may require hands to be raised so you can ensure balance within the conversation. As your students progress, they will run the entire discussion and you can observe, take notes, and give feedback.

6) After the conversation, encourage students to use the rubric as a self-assessment. What did they excel at, and what goals do they want to achieve during the next seminar?

7) Remember this isn't about quantity but quality. Students can earn a top score just speaking once, but that one comment was insightful, full of textual evidence, and propelled the entire conversation in a different, more complex manner.

8) Encourage students to not piggyback on other students' ideas. Original thought is key.

9) Oftentimes, your most vocal students will try to dominate the conversation. If this happens, limit the number of times a student can speak.

10) Remember to stay neutral; it's natural for teachers to respond with "great idea," but oftentimes that will discourage other students from sharing their ideas.

Using academic conversations can greatly enrich your classroom experience. Students who rarely speak will often shine during academic discussions. These can occur multiple times during a unit. Besides allowing students to be their own Experience Navigator, academic conversation encourages creative and critical thinking, communication, risk-taking, and problem-solving.

Note about using Socratic seminars in K–5 classrooms: High-level academic discourse and Socratic seminars can absolutely happen in the elementary classroom! The process as described above does not change greatly, but the timeline does. Younger students will need more practice with the procedures and protocols to engage meaningfully in these discussions. Additionally, students may need more support in preparing questions or understanding the expectations for discussion and roles within the group.

Stop and Reflect: Socratic seminars/academic conversations can be used at any point with any curriculum. What are all the ways you could use this strategy in your next unit?

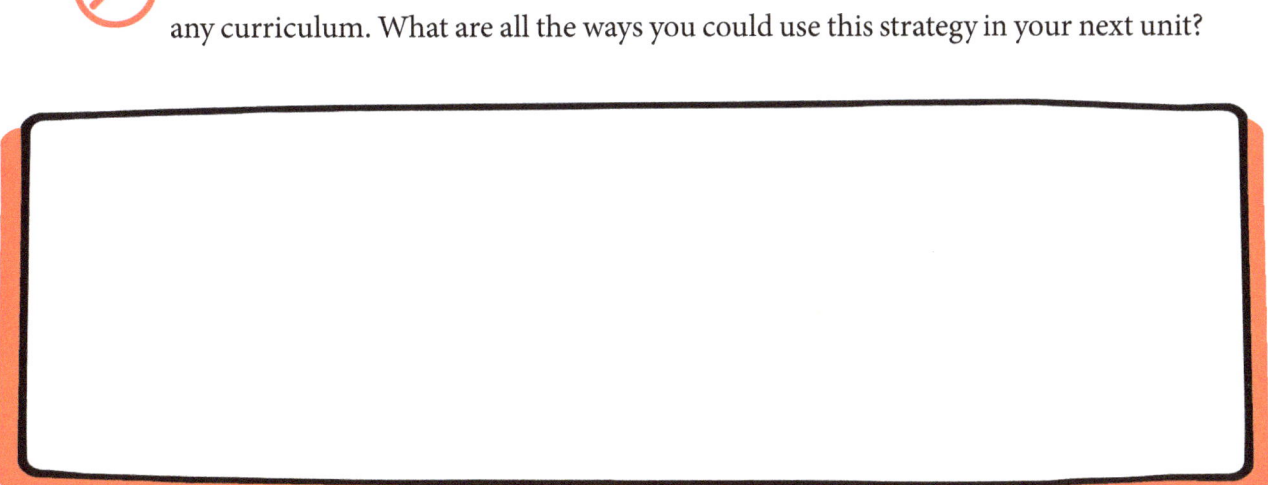

As educators become Experience Navigators, this type of learning mustn't be a one-and-done. Navigating knowledge, strategies, and student needs must continue throughout the year.

Reimagining Classroom Relationships to Support Experience Navigator

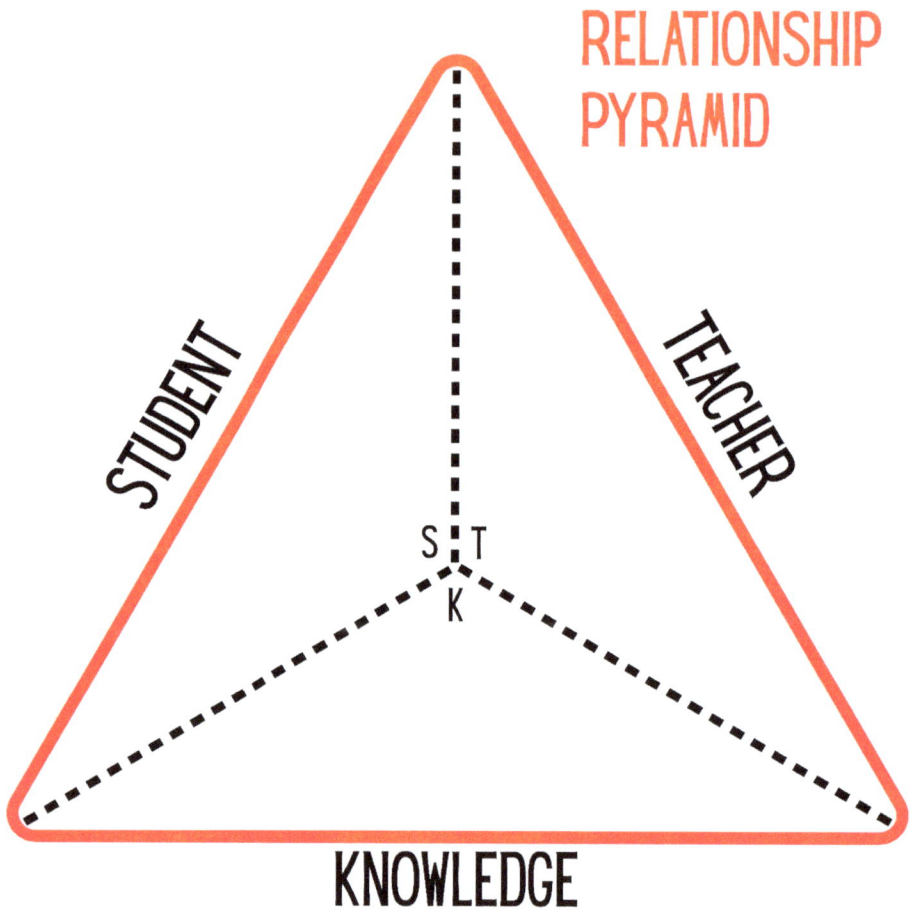

In the final section of "Experience Navigator," we revisit the educative relationships—all the relationships that exist between the three basic elements needed for classroom learning: the student, the teacher, and the knowledge to be learned. By turning the educative relationship prism and shifting the power dynamic between the elements and relationships, you will find the spaces and places for experience navigation.

> What would happen to an activity, conversation, lesson, assessment, or unit if you shifted control? Instead of starting with the element or relationship you typically do, shift the prism.

TEACHER leads the relationship	T-T	1. Highlight the uniqueness of classroom happenings. 2. Identify school-wide issues and connect via content areas. 3. Encourage book groups, lesson studies, and peer observation. 4. Offer in-house PD on topics like Edtech and AI.
	T-S	1. Meet the students where they are in terms of interest. 2. Identify real world content connections. 3. Use socratic seminars. 4. Keep class logs on student interest, successes, connections.
	T-K	1. Identify areas of personal high interest within the content. 2. Match school and community issues to skill and content. 3. Audit content classes to broaden subject experience. 4. Seek professional development and enrich content expertise.
STUDENT leads the relationship	S-S	1. Pick challenge teams that compete to extend the learning. 2. Take a compare/contrast approach to problem solving. 3. Lead and participate in academic conversations. 4. Partner up to take subtopics through KWL steps.
	S-T	1. Identify spaces for excitement around learning priorities. 2. Reimagine a unit using PBL and personal perspective. 3. Propose moments for academic conversation. 4. Identify subtopics to explore independently.
	S-K	1. Research a self-selected topic of interest. 2. Approach self-as-learner with the PBL format. 3. Annotate content. 4. Create a self-generated learning path through the content.
KNOWLEDGE leads the relationship	K-K	1. Use Google searching to establish knowledge entry points. 2. Discuss how prior knowledge impacts learning. 3. Compare personal questions to content questions. 4. Flip "K" to start with the content to be learned, etc.
	K-T	1. Use outside resources to identify "newsworthy" moments. 2. Draw on historical problems within content to model solutions. 3. Listen to experts discuss topic to guide questioning. 4. Research how learning has progressed in the topic.
	K-S	1. Set up content station starting points for students to select. 2. Create a future timeline of the topic using past advancements. 3. Compare various viewpoints on topic to identify key questions. 4. Balance personal, class, and societal learning need.

Try it! Use this chart as your application piece so that when you are ready to write a lesson plan from your ideas, it is already formatted and easy to find.

Lesson Idea/Creativity Skill
Heighten Anticipation (ignite curiosity and a sense of wonder): *How will you get students excited or curious about the lesson or content?*
Deepening Expectations (deep diving into the lesson; students are consistently actively engaged): *How will you make it hands-on? How will they explore different perspectives? How will it be relevant and meaningful to them?*
Hands-on Interactive Ideas: *What can you bring in, have them create, construct or interact with?*
Connect it to real-life experiences: *List all of the ways this applies to their life, experiences, or dreams. How will you make this connection for them?*
Extend the Learning (how students will apply new-found knowledge and curiosity into the world outside the classroom) *What activities can students do outside the classroom to continue the learning?*

Stop and Reflect:

What new strategies or concepts from this section resonated with you the most? How do you plan to implement them in your classroom?

````
````

Reflect on a challenge you might face when applying the ideas from this section. How can you overcome it?

````
````

Consider your current teaching practices. How can you integrate the principles discussed in this section to enhance creativity and critical thinking among your students?

````
````

How can we teach open-mindedness and acceptance while embracing differing perspectives?

ATTITUDE SHIFTER

Attitude Shifter

"You can't use up creativity. The more you use, the more you have."
~ Maya Angelou (Caged Bird Legacy, LLC., 2023)

Essential Question: How can we teach open-mindedness and acceptance while embracing differing perspectives?

Attitude shifting ensures knowledge is shared in a way that promotes:

- Belonging.
- Purpose.
- Compassion.
- Open-mindedness.

Strategies we will examine are:

- Dealing with ambiguity.
- Purpose-driven learning.
- Reflection versus mindset.

Definitions

- Attitude is the psychological foundation of our actions and reactions, greatly influencing our behavior and interactions with others (Emmanuel & Delaney, 2014).
- Mastery learning involves building toward attaining a high level of understanding or proficiency in a particular area.
- A mindset is the established set of attitudes or beliefs an individual holds.
- Purpose-driven learning is an educational strategy that focuses on meaningful and relevant learning experiences. It emphasizes connecting learning to personal interests, values, goals, or societal issues in order to make it more engaging and impactful.
- Understanding by Design (UbD) is a backward design process developed by educators Grant Wiggins and Jay McTighe that provides a framework for curriculum design, performance assessments, and instruction that leads to a deep understanding of the subject matter and transfer of learning (Wiggins & McTighe, 2005).

 **Activity**

If your students made a slogan for your classroom, what do you think it would say? Draw/write what it would look like.

Teaching Style

If your classroom style was compared to a fashion style, how would you describe your outfit? Draw it. What attitude does your classroom fashion style illustrate and why?

Personal Style

If you could pick an actress/actor to play you in a movie, who would you choose? Would your students choose the same person? Why or why not? What type of characteristics would you want your actress/actor to exude? What attitude would he/she/they convey?

One component of being an Attitude Shifter is changing the way we view ourselves as educators, considering the activities listed above. How do those questions spark ideas to liven up your classroom or teaching style based on who you are?

Introduction

Attitude Shifter is embracing a curious and creative mindset that requires shifting how we perceive the learning process, ourselves, and others. There's a fallacy that education is about learning content in order to achieve a grade that furthers our intelligence so that we can earn the degree that will earn us respect and maybe a high-paying job. At least that's how many students view it. One of the biggest shifts in the perspective of education is to view learning as a lifelong process to achieve personal satisfaction and that the classroom is a safe place to engage in exciting new adventures that teach us about our world, ourselves, and our impact. Sure, skills need to be taught, but how we view those skills and the rationale behind learning them matters. We can narrow down the idea that education is really about nourishing curiosity and creativity in order to make learning exciting, relevant, and engaging.

Attitude Shifter includes:

- Being open to new ideas and perspectives.
- Deferring judgment.
- Listening with an open mind.
- Being vulnerable with others.
- Reflecting on how and why you feel the way you do.
- Taking responsibility for one's attitude toward different situations.

Learning Objectives for an Attitude Shifter

This section will explore:

- What it means to be an Attitude Shifter.
- Strategies for creating lessons that encourage an open-minded, purpose-filled environment.
- How you can incorporate a sense of belonging and reflection into your curriculum.

A teacher as an Attitude Shifter:

- Creates a curriculum that allows students to reflect on different perspectives while keeping an open mind.
- Becomes a facilitator, allowing students to debate, listen, and research with compassion, empathy, and purpose.
- Challenges students to reflect on what they have learned and their attitude toward the learning process.

A student as an Attitude Shifter:

- Embraces and celebrates different perspectives.
- Challenges themselves to be open-minded and empathetic toward ideas that may differ from theirs.
- Demonstrates confidence even when the material being presented may be complex and make them feel uncomfortable at times.

Stop and Reflect: How are we viewing the learning process? Fill in how each person views the learning process and their attitude toward students as learners.

	Attitude Towards Learning Process…	Attitude towards students as learners…
Students	*Students view the learning process as a grade-based dynamic in which they need to learn to adapt to each teacher's unique expectations in order to pass the class.*	*Students view themselves as in this classroom to get a grade to move on to the next class.*
Teachers (us)		
Parents		
Administrators		

Studies show that students exhibit teachers' attitudes. Your perception and view of creativity and critical thinking will carry over into your classroom climate. If teachers illustrate an open-minded attitude, defer judgment, and encourage belonging, students will feel comfortable and safe to think in creative and critical ways. This can be challenging and time-consuming, but if educators incorporate the following tips and cultivate a creative classroom, the entire environment will shift.

Causes of Disengagement and Disrespect

Before we start exploring strategies for Attitude Shifter, let's make sure we understand how the environment impacts the way students learn. As we travel the country talking to teachers, we often hear, "Students today just don't care. They aren't interested in class and they can be so disrespectful to me and their peers." So let's start there.

According to the *Harvard Business Review*'s interview with students, students are disengaged for several reasons: trauma, exhaustion, feelings of hopelessness, and the way they're being taught (2023). The first three are part of Maslow's hierarchy of unmet needs.

Trauma:

- Cause: A critical component of working with anyone, but especially students who have been affected by trauma, is having high empathy with high expectations and high support. We all have the shared trauma of experiencing COVID-19. None of us are free from trauma; we just live through different types.
- Impact on learning: A student is verbally volatile, mistrustful, and often disruptive. We can be empathetic and even provide resources for the student to be heard and help that student with claiming techniques when triggered, but we do not allow that student to be violent. We provide high support for what that student has experienced, but we also have high expectations for behavior that is and is not allowed in the classroom.

Strategies:

- Allow students to keep journals in your classroom or with them and give them time to write.
- Allow students to take a break listening to calming music in a corner or while working on an assignment. Sometimes, music regulates emotions.
- Depending on your environment and what your administrator allows, you could have the student go run an errand in the school for you, go for a quick couple of laps in the gym, or have a buddy-teacher the struggling student can go to for a few minutes to "help."
- Have a peace corner where students can go away from others to calm down when feeling the need to orient themselves.

Stop and Reflect: How are you allowing students to express their trauma?

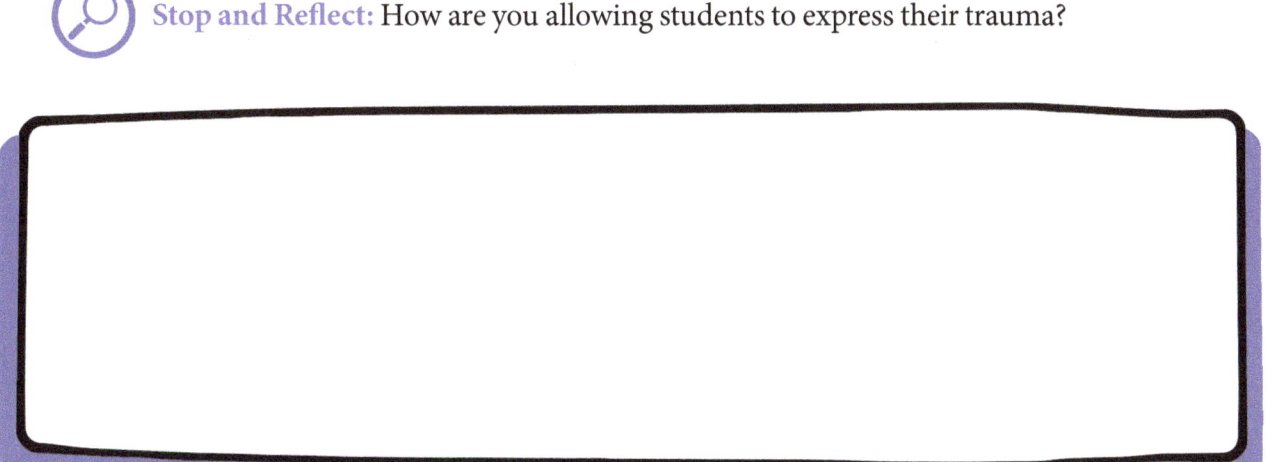

Exhaustion:

- Cause: Students who are exhausted do not have one of their basic needs met and therefore may not be able to complete a task until their body is in a state of rest. There are many scenarios in which a student could be exhausted: the student has to work a job after school to help the family pay bills, or the student is up at night listening to parents fighting and/or trying to calm down younger siblings, or maybe that student was up all night studying for the five Advanced Placement tests they are taking.

- Impact on learning: Exhaustion can cause lack of focus and inability to fully comprehend what is being taught. Oftentimes, students are exhausted and therefore do not see the purpose of learning something that is not relevant to their current hectic lives.

- Suggestions: Work out with your administration a safe place for students to sleep in the school. Maybe the nurse has an empty bed, a teacher on their prep period has a beanbag in their classroom, or the dean has a place in their office. If there is not a safe place anywhere in the school, can there be a place for your students to rest in your classroom? Essentially, the only way to help exhaustion is to allow students to rest. Some teachers are worried that it will start a culture of "it's okay to sleep in my class" for all students. The truth is quite the opposite; the practice opens the door for a classroom conversation, specifically about individual needs.

Stop and Reflect: How are you allowing students to express their exhaustion?

Feelings of Hopelessness:

- Causes: A sense of hopelessness comes from not feeling adequate, a sense of belonging, or even feeling significant insecurity, which indicates that students' need for adequate love and belonging are not being met.
- Impact on learning: When there is a sense of hopelessness, students are not just unmotivated to learn; they also cannot even see the purpose, have no drive, and in some cases are simply in an emotional survival mode. The first step is to help them find something to hope for.
- Suggestions:
  - Help them see their strengths and impact on their family, classroom community, and the world.
  - Help them rediscover their interests, strengths, and accomplishments so far.
  - Help them set some small, attainable goals and make a big deal of reaching those goals.
  - Often what they need is someone to believe in them when they do not believe in themselves.

Stop and Reflect: How are you allowing students to express their feelings of hopelessness?

Case Study: Two Teachers, Two Outcomes—Shifting Our Attitudes

Case Study 1: Teacher A walked into the classroom and felt overwhelmed by the chaos—shouting, name-calling, disrespect, threats, students on phones, and fights. Teacher A made a list of rules, followed by a list of consequences:

Teacher A introduced the rules and consequences, and some students began to laugh; some instigated disrespect, and others got up anyway. The behavior in Teacher A's room continued to spiral, leaving the teacher feeling burnt out. After about three weeks, Teacher A acknowledged the behaviors had continued and, in some cases, became worse.

RULES

1. Do not speak when others are speaking.

2. Do not make a threat.

3. Do not get up unless given permission

4. do not use your phone unless you've been given permission

5. Do not use words that are degrading or disrespectful

CONSEQUENCES

If you speak out, speak disrespectfully, get up, or use your phone without permission, you will be required to write sentences, make a phone call home, and receive a check. Three checks and you will be given an in-class detention.

If you threaten, the administrator will be called and you will be removed from the classroom.

Case Study 2: Teacher B walked into the classroom and felt overwhelmed by the chaos—shouting, name-calling, disrespect, threats, students on phones, and fights. Teacher B decided to show the students they had more in common with each other and the teacher than they realized. Here is what Teacher B did.

Step One:

1) Asked the class to write down what they hate and love about school. Teacher B was not surprised the hate list was longer than the love list.

2) Asked the class to write about their dream or ideal school, considering what they hate about it and what they would change so other kids wouldn't experience what they have.

3) When they stopped writing, Teacher B asked a few more questions:

   a) What would your school feel like when you first walked in?

   b) What would the teachers do when you arrive? How would they greet you?

   c) What would the beginning of the class look, sound, and feel like to make you want to learn something?

   d) What kinds of things would you want to learn?

   e) In what ways would the teachers teach you so that you would enjoy it?

4) Students began expressing their thoughts and feelings through writing and discussion.

Step Two:

1) Teacher B had the whole class stand up and asked one student if they would like to share.

2) Teacher B explained that if anyone agreed with or wrote down what the student had shared, they would remain standing.

3) Any idea that had the whole class still standing would be written on the board.

4) After the whole class had a chance to be heard and about twenty items were written on the board, Teacher B explained to the class that they all agreed on the kind of environment in which they would want to learn.

Step Three:

1) Teacher B then had the class write down how they, as students, could help build that classroom environment through their own behaviors, actions, and ideas, and he allowed students to share.

2) Teacher B had an anchor chart paper, as you can see below.

3) Students copied the chart on their paper and filled in their personal commitments; they paired up and merged commitments.

4) Then their pair paired up with another group and merged their commitments and so on, until the entire class had a unified list of student commitments.

Together as a class, they shared it, and Teacher B added it to the chart. Based on what students articulated they needed in the school and classroom to learn and how they could contribute to their learning environment, they followed up with a discussion on appropriate consequences, which they labeled it accountability.

This is what they decided on:

Teacher Commitments

- I will greet each student by name with a smile every class period.
- I will speak with the utmost respect to each one of my students, understanding that they each have feelings and are walking roads I know nothing about.
- I will listen to personal and educational grievances by all students either face to face or in a note so all students are heard.
- I will ensure my lessons are practical, lively, and purposeful so all students can take away something from my class.
- I will ensure my classroom is a safe place where physical, emotional, and educational needs are met.
- I will humbly hear and reflect on any mistake I have made that a student has pointed out and will apologize if necessary.

Student Commitments

- I will come into class with a positive attitude to the best of my ability.
- I will listen to others as I want to be listened to.
- I will speak respectfully to my teachers and classmates.
- If I am wronged, I will take a minute to cool down and try to articulate it as calmly and respectfully as possible.
- I will let my teacher teach, understanding we can't have fun if we interrupt, argue, or fight.
- I will tell my teacher beforehand if I am having an off day and commit to trying my best to leave it at the door.
- I will apologize to my teacher or classmate I have wronged and attempt to make it right.

Accountability

If any of the above commitments are broken, we, with mutual respect, have the right to call each other out. We will take time in a chair in the corner to calm down, write or reflect on how we went wrong, and apologize if we messed up. We accept any consequences, natural or imposed, with a mature attitude.

After about three weeks with the classroom commitments established, while not all the behaviors were gone, Teacher B saw a significant improvement. Teacher B was establishing positive relationships with students and guiding positive relationships among classmates. Here's the point: the more teachers include students in setting up classroom standards, the more buy-in there will be.

This is also a great activity for helping students refine their questioning skills. Using divergent and convergent thinking by asking students, "What characteristics might a creative and curious person contain?" can open up a discussion regarding how the classroom functions as a team and how teams work together to ensure a successful and safe learning environment.

Stop and Reflect: In an honest assessment of self, are you now or have you ever before been more like the teacher in case study 1 or 2? Why do you think that is?

Compare and contrast the teachers from Case Study 1 and 2

CASE STUDY 1   **CASE STUDY 2**

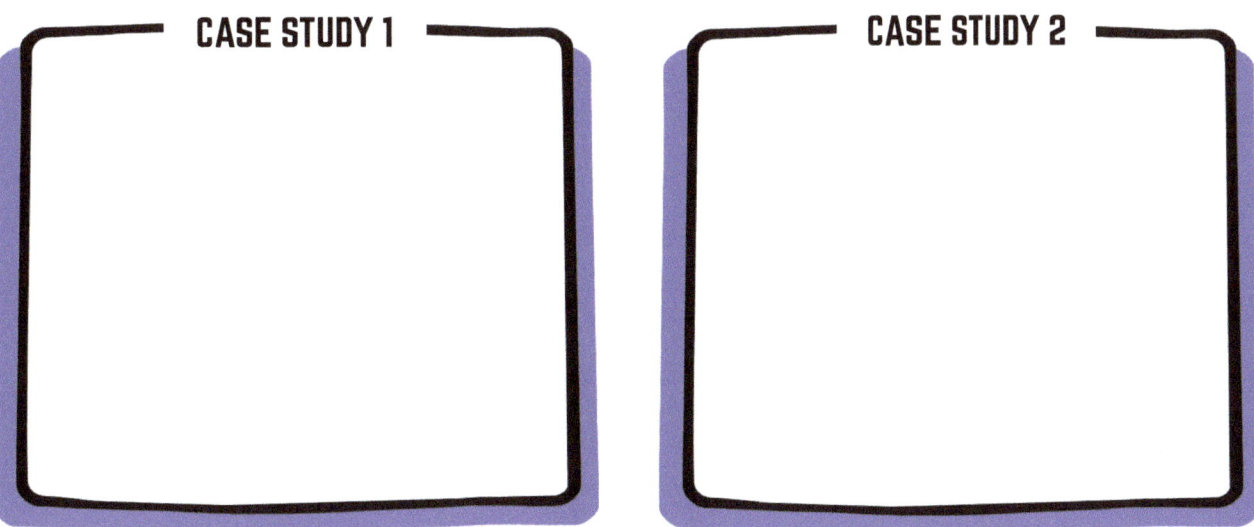

Who's attitude needed to by shifted? Why?

Strategies for Attitude Shifters

Dealing with Ambiguity

We are living in a time of uncertainty. The careers our students are planning for haven't even been invented yet. With the emergence of artificial intelligence, political unrest, and economic distrust, life is becoming chaotic and, at times, overwhelming. Managing ambiguity is an essential life lesson that makes us uncomfortable at times but ultimately increases our ability to be curious and think deeper.

In today's society, students crave the "right answer" and, as we discussed earlier, fear failure. Yet there is a vast sea of knowledge, and our responsibility as educators is to teach students how to navigate uncharted waters. How do we navigate through the turbulent waters, especially when we don't know what direction we want to head? When students feel anxious due to uncertainty, they often shut down or overreact. We must guide students through these challenges and help them feel comfortable questioning the unknown.

A classroom environment that welcomes ambiguity:

- Acknowledges the emotions that can arise from the unknown, reflects on them, and determines ways to adjust those feelings if needed.
- Assigns challenging projects (productive struggle) and allows students to reflect on how it feels to not know what to do.
- Embraces a sense of mystery. Students explore different ways to solve problems that maybe even the teacher hasn't thought about. Sometimes, students can surprise you!
- Celebrates chaos. As students learn how to manage the unknown and navigate through their ever-changing feelings, knowing they belong, are safe, and will not be judged by their teacher or peers is essential. The classroom may seem chaotic at times, but learning is nonlinear.
- Allows for times of discomfort and frustration, recognizing that these feelings are acceptable and lead to curiosity and deeper understanding.

What does ambiguity look like in an elementary school classroom? Ambiguity is a natural part of an elementary classroom because younger students are curious and tend to look at subjects and problems with a more creative lens than most adults! Here are some ways to encourage ambiguity in your classroom:

- **ELA:** Students (especially in K–2) may be worried about their progress in learning how to read and write. Teachers can support students by meeting with them in small groups and focusing on what those individual students know. Teachers can also mix up their groups so students don't feel static or stuck and will see that learning is flexible and nonlinear.

- **Science:** Wonder about topics out loud and ask students questions you don't know the answer to.
    - What will happen if I feed my flowers orange juice instead of water?
    - Why is it cold in winter, even when it's sunny?
- **Math:** Include "challenge problems" as a part of a weekly or daily warm-up activity. Challenge problems can include concepts students haven't learned yet or are from the next grade level. Allow students to productively struggle!
- Create a class PBL project that students will work on together throughout a couple of months.

What does ambiguity look like in a middle school classroom? Rather than being concerned about not knowing a topic or skill, most middle schoolers do not want to appear uneducated or ignorant. As a result, ambiguity is an important topic for middle schoolers. One of the most essential first steps in approaching ambiguity is teaching them how normal and okay it is to not know the answer. A lack of knowledge does not indicate that one is not smart but that there is room to discover and learn. Once a professor assigned a project at the beginning of the semester and as students began working on the project, he changed the specifications and expectations as they went. When they were frustrated and asked why, he stated that in real professional life, the projects or expectations we work on will often change, and we will have to adapt and still complete the project on time.

- **ELA/Social Studies:** Ask an open-ended question where you genuinely do not know the answer.
- Why are the ice caps melting, and why does it matter?
- What would life look like if Germany or Japan had won World War II?
- **Math/Science:** Give the answer to a problem and ask students to find a way to get to it.
- Have students solve real-world problems, including research, discussion, and trial and error. For example, many countries that have a democracy, have complained of both political parties being corrupt during elections. Is that accurate? What makes a political party corrupt? What can be done about that?

 **What does ambiguity look like in a high school classroom?** What do you want to be when you grow up? Although this question is asked of even young children, the answer is given more weight when high school starts. Basically, we are asking fourteen-to-eighteen-year-olds to decide what they want to do with the rest of their lives. High school is full of anxiety and uncertainty about the future. What happens after they graduate? There can be conflict between what the parent wants for the teen and what the teen wants. All of this ambiguity causes stress and anxiety. Our classrooms need to be a place where students can explore and acknowledge the unknown without facing consequences.

- Allowing students to research careers and hear from experts in various fields will give them the opportunity to ask questions of others and themselves.
- Ask students to look at social issues and generate questions regarding what we know and don't know. Then discuss the emotions surrounding the unknown.
- Assign open-ended assessment questions, allowing for different interpretations of an assignment. This will open the class up for discussion, questions, curiosity, and ultimately deeper thinking.

 Stop and Reflect: How can I create an environment that embraces, balances, and celebrates the known and the unknown?

Purpose-Driven Learning Strategy

As teachers, we all desire our students to engage in purpose-driven learning. However, it can be disheartening when we hear the familiar grumble of "Why are we doing this?" or "When will I ever use this in real life?" echo down our classroom hallways. Our mission as educators is to instill joy in learning in our students, but it can be challenging when the purpose isn't always apparent. We must find ways to show students the relevance of their learning and how it can impact their future. By helping our students find their purpose for learning, we can unlock their full potential and empower them to achieve their goals. So let us ask ourselves, teachers, what is the purpose behind what we teach, and how can we make it meaningful for our students?

One way to make learning purposeful for our students is by connecting it to their personal interests and future aspirations. By incorporating real-life examples, case studies, or projects that align with their passions or career goals, students are more likely to see the relevance of their learning. This can be achieved through activities such as hosting guest speakers, taking field trips, or even conducting virtual simulations. If learning is relatable and applicable to their lives, students will be more motivated to engage and take ownership of their learning. Their attitude toward learning will change from "Why?" to "Why not?" as they see the value and potential impact this attitude shift can have.

 **Practical Tips:**

- Create a safe and inclusive learning environment where students feel respected, supported, and valued in the classroom. They are more likely to take risks, participate actively, and engage with the material.

- Create purposeful learning through providing activities that promote collaboration, critical thinking, and empathy among students. Then they will begin to feel a sense of belonging in the classroom, and their intrinsic motivation to learn increases, leading to better academic performance, personal growth, and solidified attitudes.

- Create an inclusive environment by explaining how each lesson or concept fits into the bigger picture of their education or future careers. Then students will understand the relevance and importance of their learning, making it more meaningful and engaging for them.

- Create opportunities for students to actively engage in problem-solving and critical thinking. Then students can greatly enhance the effectiveness of their learning. Instead of memorizing facts and information, students can apply their knowledge to solve real-world problems or scenarios.

- Create opportunities for collaboration among teachers from different departments or students from different classes. This will illustrate to students that all of their subjects work together to create a greater purpose.

It is crucial for us to continuously strive to make learning more purposeful for our students. By connecting it to their interests, helping them see the bigger picture, and providing opportunities for active engagement, we can empower students to take ownership of their learning and unlock their full potential. Let us never underestimate the power of purpose in education and its ability to shape bright, curious, and motivated individuals.

What does purpose-driven learning look like in an elementary school classroom? Part of purpose-driven learning in elementary school is to be explicit and clear about what you're teaching and why. Many teachers regularly post the learning objectives and standards that are linked to the lesson, but often we miss telling our youngest learners WHY they are learning something. Try getting into the habit of telling students why you're teaching them something, and ask them if they can make any connections to other lessons, topics, or interests. Younger elementary students might answer they are learning phonics "so that they can read" or "so that I'll be ready for first grade," but older elementary students can start seeing the connections of their learning beyond the classroom. Here are a few other ways you can incorporate purpose-driven learning into your classroom.

- Create a research project for fourth and fifth grade students asking them to identify future careers they think are interesting. Have them work backward to identify what types of skills and knowledge they would need to do that job well, and map from there the connections to their lessons.

- Create opportunities for reflection during lessons and post assignments. Ask students "Why do you think we learned this today?" and have them write or draw on a Post-it note that can be shared on a bulletin board. Making that connection and purpose visible in the classroom will solidify and extend the learning.

- A common misconception in kindergarten classrooms is that students are "just" playing. As educators, we know students are engaged in far more in during choice time or center time. Highlight for students some of the important learning they are engaged with: "You are learning how to work with a group!" or "You are learning how to share and take turns!" Using language like this serves as a reminder to our students, and anyone else who visits our classrooms, that nonacademic work is often just as important as the curriculum and content we cover!

6-8 **What does purpose-driven learning look like in a middle school classroom?** Why are you having the students complete the assignment? Why are they learning the skill or topic? Why are they reading that book or article? Everything we spend time on in the classroom must serve a purpose because we have limited time to revive and cultivate curious and creative minds. One of the challenges with middle school is that so much of students' mental and emotional focus is on developing socially. As a result, we must weave social-emotional lessons into everything we teach.

- Choose materials, activities, and assessments that effectively serve an academic, creative, and social skill simultaneously.
  - **ELA/Social Studies:** When reading the novel *The Hunger Games*, you can teach the academic skill of making inferences about characters by citing evidence while also teaching the creative skill of looking at it another way, while also teaching the social-emotional skill of the cost of conformity and noncompliance.
  - **Math/Science:** When teaching a procedural/theory/concept, also teach the creativity skill to produce and consider many alternatives and the social/emotional skill of how to consider we might be wrong and how to handle it with others when we are. Create a bulletin board with the title "When am I ever going to use this?" and fill it with articles and visual of every-day science.
- Tell the students why you're doing the lesson or reading the material.
- Keep it real. Middle schoolers thrive for authenticity, so if you are required to teach a lesson that is simply test preparation, tell them. But you can go a step further and explain the real-life lesson in the test preparation and try to make it as fun as possible, explaining that hard things in life can be fun if you make them fun.
- You might say: "There will be times at work that you may be tasked with an assignment or responsibility that makes no sense or seems futile. But persisting in something you do not want to do and you see no value in cultivates self-discipline. Go ahead and spend five minutes researching what kinds of things you might need self-discipline for."
- Allow students to brainstorm and share all the ways it applies to real life.
- When teaching concepts like the Pythagorean theorem, ask students to do some digging and find out who uses it. Then when they have their list, ask them why any of that is important. With each response, keep asking them why and who it benefits.

 **What does purpose-driven learning look like in a high school classroom?** Connect, connect, connect. How will physics help us in real life? How will reading old classics help us in the future? How does studying history help us with future decisions? We must answer these questions with authentic answers. We may think, "Well, I suffered through AB Calculus, so you will too." But we need to let our students understand that learning from the past can mold our future. When we read novels from ancient times and places, we grow our ability to empathize with others. And when we learn the difficult equations, we see what could be when we persevere and challenge ourselves.

- Assignments that relate to real-life situations can also help students find purpose. For example, introduce blogging as a way to teach writing.
- Replace the traditional research project with a video essay or podcast.
- Allow students to teach each other a new concept. Students know what keeps them engaged during class. Allowing your class to design their lesson plans ignites new ideas and allows you to better understand what your students are interested in.
- Ask students to use the concept being taught and apply it to something they are interested in. Have students prepare a presentation to show their classmates how this concept could be used in real life. For example, students could teach classmates how to balance a checkbook, research stocks, create a resume, etc.

 Stop and Reflect: When a student asks, "How will this help me in real life?" how do you respond? How might I reshape the way I respond to shift a student's attitude from "Why" to "Why not?"

Strategies for Attitude Shifters

Reflection versus Mindset

Remember the movie *Click* with Adam Sandler? Whenever something went wrong, he would take his universal remote control and rewind the situation. This special remote gave him the chance to learn from what he did and try it a different way. Now, it didn't always work the way he hoped. But you get the idea.

Reflection is a critical component of creative and critical thinking. Thinking about how we respond to and in certain situations allows us to consider our next steps more deeply and meaningfully. Reflection is used in everyday life, from academic to personal, to professional instances. If we want to assess whether we need to shift our attitudes to be more open-minded, empathetic, and cooperative, we must take the time to consider our past reactions and determine what improvements need to be made.

When we create something, there must be time to think about how the creation worked, how it met our expectations, or how it needs revision. Plus, by allowing time for reflection, we foster compassion, purpose, or belonging in our schools and classrooms. Think about this: "Actively open-minded thinking is the synapse of critical thinking because it allows for the achievement of objectives, reflection on and/or consideration of alternatives before making decisions" (Merma-Molina et al., 2022). When we are deciding what to do, how to do it, and what to change next time, we are engaging in the reflective process. Merma-Molina goes on to explain that while other essential skills are taught, reflection rarely is. Therefore, let's start teaching how to reflect and shift some attitudes.

 **Practical Tips** for all grade levels.

Teachers:

- At the end of every school day, set aside fifteen to twenty minutes simply to reflect on how the lessons went, how you interacted with students, what went well (academically and relationally with students) and why, what did not go well and why, what you could adjust in the lesson or activity next time you try it, what gaps you recognized in student learning that you need to address the next day, what parts of the lesson were boring that you want to liven up, what elements students were super engaged in, etc.
- Have a teaching reflection journal where you journal through these questions.
- We cannot expect students to be reflective if we are not engaging in the process ourselves.
- At the end of the school year or the beginning of the next year, go back and read your reflection. Consider how you might change your curriculum, your attitude, your culture, and your environment to better suit the learning environment and engage your students in deeper thinking. Keep a list—see what works. Remember reflection is a continual process.

Students:

- Have students spend about fifteen to twenty minutes each week reflecting on their learning process in a journal. Have them answer questions like:
  - What went well today and why? What was difficult and why? What parts of the lesson or activity were challenging and why? How did you approach the challenge and why? What would you do differently and why? How did you work with others today, how did it go, and what could you do differently next time? Were you open to new or unusual ideas from your peers or teacher, how and why?
- Ensure students have time after deep learning to reflect on the process. Maybe give them an everybody-writes activity where the prompt on the board is: Write down what you enjoyed about the lesson/activity, what was challenging about the activity/lesson, what seemed irrelevant in the activity/lesson, and what you would do differently if you were the one teaching the activity/lesson.
- Have students reflect on their assessments. What might they do differently next time?
- When a student has a behavioral issue, ask them to reflect on why. Why did they react that way? What could they do better next time? How might a shift in attitude help them if they reencounter the same problem? Using a Restorative Practice may help students reflect on their actions.

INCIDENT REPORT

Name:_____   Date:_____

What happened?

_____
_____
_____
_____
_____

How did you react to the incident? What did you do?

_____
_____
_____
_____
_____

How did it make you feel or how were you affected?

_____
_____
_____
_____
_____

Who did you tell about what happened?

_____
_____
_____
_____
_____

What could be done to make the situation right?

_____
_____
_____
_____
_____

Try it! Consider your last lesson. What went well? If students were actively engaged, why? Were any students not engaged? If not, why? What would you do differently if you were to reteach the lesson tomorrow?

Reimagining Classroom Relationships to Support Attitiude Shifter

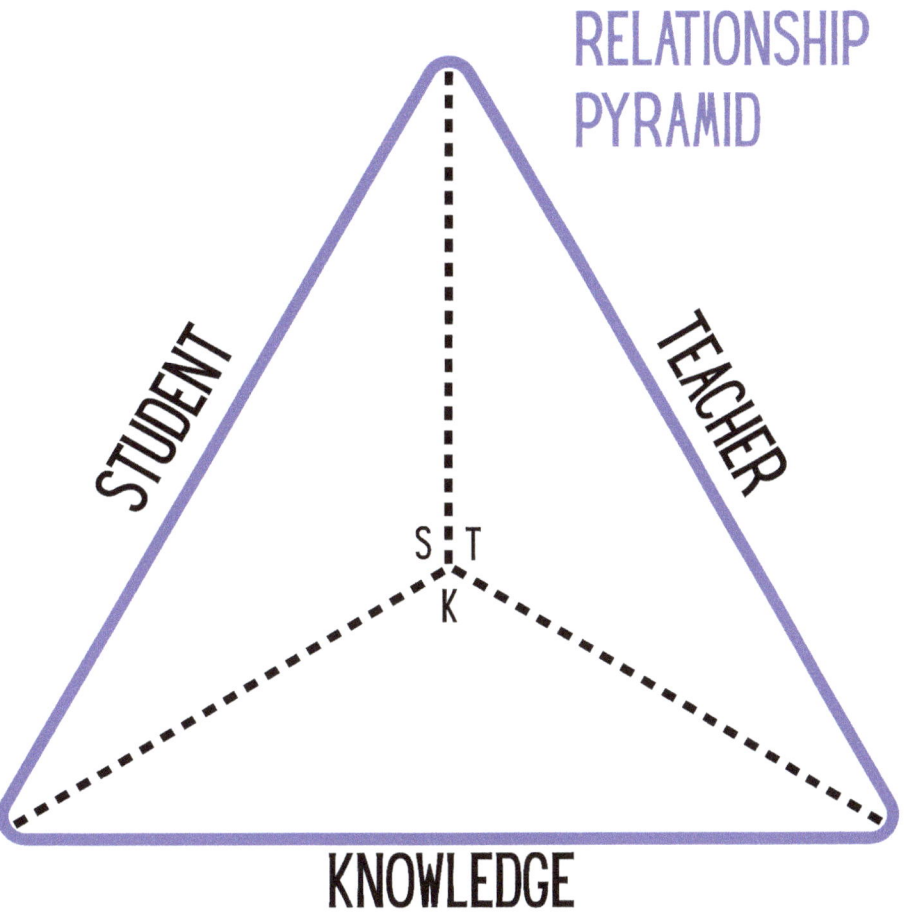

Attitude Shifter

In the final section of "Attitude Shifter," we revisit the educative relationships—all the relationships that exist between the three basic elements needed for classroom learning: the student, the teacher, and the knowledge to be learned. By turning the educative relationship prism and shifting the power dynamic between the elements and relationships, you will find the spaces and places for attitude shifting.

> What would happen to an activity, conversation, lesson, assessment, or unit if you shifted control? Instead of starting with the element or relationship you typically do, shift the prism.

1. Ambiguity. 2. Purpose-driven learning. 3. Reflection over mindset.

TEACHER leads the relationship	T-T	1. Share classroom and content uncertainties and unknowns. 2. Post "our purpose" statements in shared spaces. 3. Review a common lesson informally.
	T-S	1. Model "I wonder" thinking. 2. Highlight the soft skills used to complete learning tasks. 3. Offer tangibles around steps taken as a reflective practitioner.
	T-K	1. Classify content in nontraditional ways to prompt ambiguity. 2. Explore content for more purposeful applications. 3. Post passion topics, units, and activities in an easy-to-see place.
STUDENT leads the relationship	S-S	1. Invite ideas, answers, solutions and questions from others. 2. Challenge each other to identify the "why" behind the content. 3. Discuss the personal process for completing a task.
	S-T	1. Rate comfort level with content. 2. Articulate beliefs around how the content will be used in life. 3. Keep a process journal that is then matched to assessment.
	S-K	1. Identify common misunderstandings around content. 2. Look for practical applications for content beyond those given. 3. Track soft skills used to complete a task requiring hard skills.
KNOWLEDGE leads the relationship	K-K	1. Challenge the concept of needed content, skill progression. 2. Compare/contrast individual content purpose to society's. 3. Consider "what is" versus "what could be."
	K-T	1. Use knowledge hierarchy to shift expectations appropriately. 2. Fracture knowledge into its smallest parts/skills for application. 3. Analyze student performance data to direct change.
	K-S	1. Identify the contents' known open-ended questions. 2. Use answer-first learning to drive purpose. 3. Summarize assessment feedback and staple to next task.

Try it! Considering the unit you are revising, brainstorm all the different attitudes that might need shifting. Why will students react that way to your lesson? Do you have any personal attitudes that you need to reflect on?

Stop and Reflect: Looking back at the strategies in this section, how might you use one or two of them to infuse your lesson with curiosity, creative and critical thinking, and positive attitudes?

Try it! Use this chart as your application piece so that when you are ready to write a lesson plan from your ideas, it is already formatted and easy to find.

Lesson Idea/Creativity Skill

Heighten Anticipation (ignite curiosity and a sense of wonder): *How will you get students excited or curious about the lesson or content?*

Deepening Expectations (deep diving into the lesson; students are consistently actively engaged): *How will you make it hands-on? How will they explore different perspectives? How will it be relevant and meaningful to them?*

Hands-on Interactive Ideas: *What can you bring in, have them create, construct or interact with?*

Connect it to real-life experiences: *List all of the ways this applies to their life, experiences, or dreams. How will you make this connection for them?*

Extend the Learning (how students will apply new-found knowledge and curiosity into the world outside the classroom) *What activities can students do outside the classroom to continue the learning?*

Stop and Reflect:

What new strategies or concepts from this section resonated with you the most? How do you plan to implement them in your classroom?

Reflect on a challenge you might face when applying the ideas from this section. How can you overcome it?

Consider your current teaching practices. How can you integrate the principles discussed in this section to enhance creativity and critical thinking among your students?

How can we can build strong, creative, collabortive teams with contagious energy?

TEAM TRANSFORMER

Team Transformer

"Collaboration drives creativity because innovation always emerges from a series of sparks—never a single flash of insight." ~ R. Keith Sawyer (2008)

Essential Question: How can we build strong, creative, collaborative teams with contagious energy?

The Team Transformer strives to share knowledge in a manner that:

- Embraces empathy.
- Celebrates differences.
- Builds on other's strengths.

Strategies we will examine are:

- Establishing unity.
- Defining effective team characteristics.
- Building empathy.

Definitions

- Groups are typically a collection of students brought together to share information, discuss topics, or perform separate tasks that contribute to a common theme or subject.
- Scaffolding is an educational strategy that provides successive levels of support to help students reach higher comprehension and skill acquisition levels.
- Synergy results from cohesive interactions between students to produce work greater than the sum of its parts (Oxford Languages, n.d.).
- A team is a cohesive unit of students who rely on each other's diverse skills and contributions to accomplish a shared objective.
- Team composition is a strategic and thoughtful arrangement of students into teams, carefully considering factors like their academic abilities, learning preferences, social capital, personal interests, and temperaments to ensure the teams are balanced, diverse, and capable of performing effectively.

Activity

If you were to give your classroom a team name, what would it be, and how does it reflect your desired team atmosphere?

Introduction

Education is evolving, and it's time to shift our focus from individual performance to collaboration. The world needs workers who can thrive in team settings where common goals are achieved through collective effort. To cultivate this spirit, teachers must become facilitators, empowering students to recognize their unique abilities and contribute meaningfully to the community.

In a dynamic classroom, each student's character and talents inspire the rest, creating an environment that fosters curiosity and creativity. Students elevate their thinking and navigate challenges with innovative solutions by embracing the idea that strengths and weaknesses can balance and enrich the team.

Team-based learning transforms the educational experience from "work" to an exciting journey of discovery. When students feel valued for their contributions and connected to a team, they unleash their full potential. With the teacher leading by example, students learn the power of collaboration and become leaders who serve, encourage, facilitate, and inspire their teammates.

> **Team-based learning transforms the educational experience from 'work' to an exciting journey of discovery.**

But what sets a team apart from a group? A group shares information and carries out tasks around a common theme, but a team is a cohesive unit that relies on each other's diverse skills to accomplish a shared objective. In a team, the outcome depends on effective synchronization and collective efforts, much like a sports team working toward victory.

Differentiating Groups and Teams

Groups	Teams
• Collection of individuals joined to share information. • Discuss topics or perform separate tasks that contribute to a common theme or subject. • May have designated a leader. • Members work relatively independently (A. Higby & E. Zeff, 2002).	• A highly cohesive unit. • Members interdependent roles with interdependent contributions. • Members bring unique skills and perspectives. • The team's success relies on harnessing different capabilities effectively. • Unity happens when the collective output of a team is greater than individual contributions. • May have a common goal (A. Higby & E. Zeff, 2002).

Team-based learning goes beyond collaboration. It nurtures essential social and emotional skills, such as communication, problem-solving, and negotiation. By respectfully listening to each other's stories, students empower one another and validate their worth as human beings. These skills will serve them well in all aspects of life.

Moreover, team-based learning encourages critical thinking and diverse viewpoints, amplifying the educational value of each exercise. Students also learn accountability and responsibility when they are relied upon for their team's success. Ultimately, team-based learning equips students with the skills they need to excel in the future. It unlocks the potential of collaborative learning and shapes a generation of agile, innovative thinkers.

Team Transformer includes:

- Embracing the ability to be a close listener.
- Exhibiting patience while deferring judgment.
- Capitalizing on one's strengths while revising one's weakness.

Learning objectives for a team transformer:

This section will explore:

- What it means to be a Team Transformer.
- Strategies to create lessons that encourage collaborative learning.
- Ways to build diverse learning communities.

A teacher as a Team Transformer:

- Creates a curriculum that challenges students to embrace their weaknesses and share their strengths.
- Becomes a mentor, showing students how to work with people from diverse backgrounds.
- Challenges students to take various roles, at times being a leader and at times the follower.

A student as a Team Transformer:

- Embraces and celebrates the differences in their peers.
- Challenges themselves to be open-minded and empathetic toward their teammates.
- Demonstrates the ability to lead and also the ability to listen.

Stop and Reflect: What are the first three obstacles that come to mind when you consider adding more teamwork to your curriculum? How might you overcome those challenges?

Grouping Students

Before we jump into strategies, let's talk about the question we are asked the most: "What is the best way to group students?"

We know that in today's diversified educational landscape, one of the essential components of effective teaching is fostering collaboration and teamwork among students. Doing so can cultivate an environment of curiosity and creativity among learners (Oakley, 2004; Pociask, Gross, & Shih, 2017). How students are grouped can significantly impact their academic achievement, interpersonal skills, and overall classroom dynamics (Achieve NJ, 2015). From traditional practices to innovative methods, teaming strategies have evolved to meet students' unique needs and educational goals. Whether it is grouping students based on ability, interest, or even completely randomly, these strategies form the building blocks for a cooperative and engaging learning environment.

Understanding the foundation of cooperative learning and the research behind it can inform approaches to building teams in a way that fosters integral traits necessary for continued growth.

> **How students are grouped can significantly impact their academic achievement, interpersonal skills, and overall classroom dynamics (Achieve NJ, 2015).**

Ability Teaming	Tailored to meet students' performance levels. Homogeneous grouping provides targeted instruction, while heterogeneous grouping offers peer teaching opportunities.
Higher-lower Pairing	Encourages peer support by pairing students with differing abilities, allowing for mentorship and collaborative learning.
Random Teams	Fosters inclusivity; Ensures students work with different peers, enhancing social skills and promoting a united classroom environment.
Interest-Based Teams	Align teams with students' passions, interest-based groups inspire engagement and motivation for project-based learning.
Personality-Based Teams	Create a balanced team dynamic. Groups students according to personality types, ensuring a mix of leaders, thinkers, and doers.
Role-Based Teams	Assign specific roles, catering to students' strengths and developmental needs.
Pre-Nominated Teams	Allowing students to choose their teammates can build trust and ease collaboration, but must have a strong team culture must be built first.
Teacher-Selected Teams	Based on insights into student relationships and dynamics, educators can form intentional and productive groups.
Rotational Teams	Ensure everyone collaborates with everyone else over time, building a cohesive classroom community.

Try it! Looking at the list, consider when each type of grouping would work in your current class. While these types of teams can be beneficial, it's imperative to remember that for teams to function successfully, they need to be scaffolded so students can learn how to work in these various forms.

Ability Teaming	
Higher-lower Pairing	
Random Teams	
Interest-Based Teams	
Personality-Based Teams	
Role-Based Teams	
Pre-Nominated Teams	
Teacher-Selected Teams	
Rotational Teams	

Unlocking Student Potential: The Power of Scaffolding and Team Composition

Scaffolding, a game-changing approach, provides the support needed for students to soar while striking the perfect balance between challenge and assistance. This concept is probably familiar to you. Scaffolding seamlessly transitions to the realm of teams, where the benefits of scaffolding are equally transformative. Imagine carefully crafting teams, considering academic strengths, learning preferences, social skills, personal interests, and more. The result? A dynamic and inclusive learning environment where each student thrives.

Scaffolding: Providing the Support for Success

Scaffolding is an instructional strategy that involves breaking complex tasks down into smaller, more manageable steps. The teacher provides support and guidance as students complete each step, gradually removing the scaffolds as the student gains mastery of the task. This method helps students build upon their existing knowledge and skills, allowing them to take on challenges that may have seemed daunting otherwise. By providing just the right amount of assistance, scaffolding enables students to stretch their abilities and reach their full potential.

But what makes this strategy truly powerful is its flexibility. Scaffolding can be tailored to meet individual student needs, allowing for personalized instruction and support. Gradually fading away the scaffolds as students become more proficient empowers students to take charge of their own learning.

Team Composition: Creating the Perfect Balance

Just as scaffolding supports individual students, careful team composition can provide a strong foundation for collaborative learning. Teachers can ensure each team has a balanced mix of talents and abilities by thoughtfully selecting team members based on factors like academic strengths and social skills. This can lead to greater academic success as students complement each other's strengths and provide support where needed. It also promotes social and emotional growth as students learn to work together, communicate effectively, and appreciate different perspectives. In addition, strategic team composition allows for creation of diverse teams that reflect real-world dynamics. This prepares students for future collaborative endeavors and fosters a sense of inclusivity and understanding among classmates.

The Impact on Student Potential

When scaffolding and team composition are combined, the results can be remarkable. Scaffolding supports individual students in tackling challenging tasks while strategic team composition creates an optimal learning environment for group collaboration.

Together, these strategies empower students to take risks, explore their full potential, and achieve greater success. By providing the necessary support and creating a balanced team, educators can unlock the full potential of each student and pave the way for academic and personal growth. Here are some helpful tips for scaffolding groups to help elevate collaboration in the classroom.

- Start by grouping familiar classmates—this may ease the stress of working in a new environment with unfamiliar peers (Van de Pol et al., 2015).
- Place the more experienced or skilled students with struggling learners. This can provide advanced students the opportunity to assist their classmates and to act as facilitators who guide and motivate their team (Lin et al., 2011).
- Begin with simpler tasks and a high degree of guidance and structure as a way to introduce students to the idea of collaborative learning.

Reduce the level of guided teacher support, encouraging students to learn better communication, collaboration, and problem-solving skills.

What does scaffolding look like in an elementary school classroom? Scaffolding is a natural part of all good teaching, especially in the elementary classroom! Young students learn at different rates and have a wide range of social and academic needs. Here are some ways you can scaffold to meet the needs of your students:

- Use graphic organizers to visualize connections in concepts and solidify learning.
- Help students break larger tasks down into smaller chunks. This might include introducing new concepts or topics with reading aloud so students can build background knowledge before diving into the meat of the content.
- Allow for productive struggle to a point. We've all had that moment in the classroom when we realize our lesson is falling flat and students are not with us. In these moments, you can stop the lesson and try to see it differently. This can include moving to a different part of the room for a change of scenery, completing more guided practice, and having students model their processes!

What does scaffolding look like in a middle school classroom? Middle schoolers are dying for independence but often need guidance in difficult projects. There are various ways to allow them to struggle productively through work while giving a healthy amount of guidance and structure.

- I do, we do, you do.
  - When teaching a concept, take a few minutes to model the exact task students will be doing independently. Next, have them work on it with a peer or group while you walk around and give constructive feedback and/or encouragement. Finally, have them practice independently while you walk around and give constructive feedback and/or encouragement.
- You do, we do, I do.
  - When teaching a concept where you want students to lead their own learning, you might lead with centers around the skill. You do: For example, if you are teaching a math class on double-digit multiplication, you will have three different centers where students rotate practicing, struggling, or teaching one another the concept. This is always built on prior knowledge. We do: Put a problem on the board and have the class collectively walk through it with the information, skills, struggles, or questions they have. I do: Students have realized they need more information to complete the assigned task or lesson—because they have already struggled through it, they know they need to listen attentively through your mini-lesson to get some basic knowledge.

A quick note on the above strategies: As with anything in the classroom, it is essential to know your objective and make a purposeful decision on which of the strategies would be the most effective way to teach the skill.

There will be times when I do, We do, You do will be the prominent choice, and there will be lessons in which You do, We do, I do will be the most effective.

- Discuss objectives with students and have them share the outcome in their own words.
- Break big projects down into smaller steps with checkpoints for students to assess their own progress, strengths, and areas for improvemen

What does scaffolding look like in a high school classroom? High school students seem most comfortable working with people they know. We must challenge them to work with people who may differ from them in thought. It may take, when scaffolding, to build the trust and open-mindedness needed for the team to effectively work together. However, if we keep high schoolers in the same friend group, they will miss experiencing different perspectives.

- English students could be a part of a writing, poetry, and literature group. This allows them to hear different perspectives and experience different levels of support.
- Physical education and special education students can be teamed together, offering support and guidance as they learn different sports.

 Stop and Reflect: How can I use scaffolding to help my students group in collaborative work?

211

STRATEGIES FOR TEAM TRANSFORMER

Establishing Unity

The team mentality is a critical life skill often left untaught in classrooms. Most students do not innately know how to be part of a team or why a team is so essential. One of the core components of transforming a class into a team is providing opportunities for building unity among classmates. Unity removes the focus from the self and places it on the team, allowing strengths to be shared and weaknesses to be covered. When students feel they belong to a team in the classroom, they are more likely to be vulnerable, take risks, and benefit from shared experiences. Unity happens when the collective output of a team is greater than individual contributions.

What does unity look like in a classroom?

- Team members come together, leverage their strengths, and compensate for each other's weaknesses.
- Creativity is fostered. Problem-solving is more efficient and leads to more comprehensive solutions (Zeff & Higby, 2002).
- Peer-to-peer learning, goal setting, and problem-solving enhance academic performance.
- Students are prepared for future professional environments.
- Opportunities are provided to develop and apply critical life skills while deeply engaging with academic content.
- Active learning is promoted and the development of vital interpersonal skills such as communication, leadership, and conflict resolution is encouraged.
- A sense of shared responsibility and accomplishment is fostered, emphasizing the advantages of working together and optimizing conditions for effective functioning.

How is Unity Built?

With unity, teams are intentionally composed.

- Students' strengths, weaknesses, and learning preferences are considered to create balanced and diverse teams.
- There is clarity of objectives, roles, and expectations, ensuring everyone understands their contributions to collective goals.
- Open communication, respect, and mutual support are encouraged, creating an environment of collaboration.
- Regular feedback and reflection are integrated to continuously improve performance and personal growth.
- Students see that they have more in common than they know.

Building unity takes time. Teams must engage in team-building activities before diving into major projects. A sense of community needs to be established. As educators, we often run out of time and cut this step due to content constraints. However, building trust and rapport is essential to transforming a team.

 Practical Tips: Here are some general activities for all content areas that promote purposeful team building.

- Have students go on a "classmate scavenger hunt." Lots of different templates are available online, but as students look for "someone who is the oldest in their family," or "someone who loves pizza," they find areas of intersection with their classmates, which creates a natural foundation on which to build.
- Implement a morning meeting routine where students take turns sharing a story about their weekend or about something happening in their lives that week. Students of all ages also love show-and-tell.
- Have a puzzle made from a class picture. This is easily adjustable for all grade levels (puzzles with fewer pieces for younger grades and with more pieces for older students!) This can live in a center or as a free choice activity. Students will love to work together to complete a challenging puzzle!

What does building unity look like in a middle school/high school classroom?

- Play the "stand up if" game—start with several low-level risks and move to higher risks slowly.
  - Stand up if you've ever puked on a roller coaster (low level).
  - Stand up if you've ever been scared to speak in front of others (middle level).
  - Stand up if you've ever been harmed by someone you trusted (high level).
  - Debrief: Students can share out loud or journal first or vice versa. Were you surprised by how many others stood up with you? How does knowing you're not alone make you feel?

English/Humanities

- Have students write and share a scene from their life.
- Play a game of Pictionary with items that relate to your content.
- Have students write a poem or song about themselves.
- Have students create a video or podcast interview introducing themselves.
- Have students create and share a vision board.

Sciences

- Chemistry: Create a chemical makeup of yourself (one part personality traits, two parts family background, three parts hopes and dreams).
- Biology: Draw a picture of an empty cell and its components. Ask students what components they would include if they were the cell. Ideas include athleticism, books, kindness, etc.
- Environmental science: If you were an element of the environment, what would you be and why? For example, I would be an oak tree because—.
- Physics: What makes you move? What gives you energy? What are your projected dreams, landing, or direction? (Newton's law of motion says for every action, there is a reaction. What is one major thing that happened in your life and how did you react or how did it form or change you into who you are?)

Math

- Geometry: If you were a shape, which one would you be and why? For example, I would be an octagon because I have eight different activities I am interested in, including—.
- Give all students a triangle. Students have to build a square using their triangle. Debrief: What was challenging about it? Was it possible to build a square with all triangles? What other shapes were needed to make this work? How does this relate to us as a team? What happens if we all have the same skills and strengths? How does it benefit the team that we all have different skills, talents, and strengths?
- Create an equation of your life (birth + [list experiences here] = who I am, what I like, who I want to be). It could have bubble equation letters where they need to write it all.

Special Education

- During resource periods, have students draw a picture of themselves using words that make them unique.
- Draw a map or timeline of all the significant events that have happened in your life so far and how they influenced who you are today.
- Make a playlist of your life. What songs best represent you and your personality, challenges, and strengths?

Remember it's important to debrief after each activity. The deeper the debrief, the more social-emotional learning happens, and the more students will get out of it. For example, have teammates share their responses and then debrief by asking:

- What are some things we have in common, and how can we work together using our commonalities?
- How do these commonalities make us stronger together?
- What are some differences among us?
- How do we benefit from having different experiences and qualities?

Stop and Reflect: On a scale of 1 to 10, how do I rate the importance of building unity in my classroom?

① ② ③ ④ ⑤ ⑥ ⑦ ⑧ ⑨ ⑩

We have all experienced situations when students refuse to work together. How might you use some of the above strategies to encourage students to collaborate?

Defining Effective Team Characteristics

What makes a team effective? There is no clear formula here; teaching our students how to work with a diverse group of peers in different situations will build their confidence and their ability to think critically. By creating different team scenarios, students will expand their knowledge and learn when to be flexible and when to hold strong.

Simply asking students "What makes a great team?" can inspire them to think about their favorite team (sports, music, school, etc.) and what positive characteristics surround them. In the age of COVID-19, many students shy away from teamwork. The skill of collaboration needs to be reawakened and practiced. We are now in a fresh environment to lay the foundation for the incredible possibilities of effective teamwork.

Thoughtful Transition From Groups to Teams Based on research from Galbraith & Webb, 2013.			
	Groups	**Transition**	**Teams**
Composition	Casual or based on individuals' proximity.	Analyze students' strengths, weaknesses, learning preferences, and personalities.	Analyze students' strengths, weaknesses, learning preferences, and personalities.
Objectives	General goals related to the subject, team, and project.	Define clear, specific, and measurable objectives that require a collective effort to achieve.	Common goals that promote interdependence, shared responsibility, and further collaboration.
Roles	General roles related to the subject.	Articulate and assign roles based on a student's abilities and potential growth areas.	Clear, formal roles that contribute to the overall team function.
Communication	Occasional group discussions, mainly individual input.	Foster an environment of open communication. Encourage students to express ideas, ask questions, and give feedback.	Constructive communication, both for academic and interpersonal matters, is provided in a variety of ways.
Conflict Resolution	Handled mainly by the educator.	Teach and model conflict resolution skills. Allow students to manage disagreements under guided supervision.	Managed within the team with minimal external intervention.
Assessment	Individual evaluation based on contributions.	Introduce team-based assessments in addition to individual evaluations.	Evaluated as a team, emphasizing both process and product.

Our students are constantly growing and transforming. Their personalities, strengths, and weaknesses evolve throughout the years. It is crucial to push them by providing chances to develop their leadership skills. Surprisingly, some of the most reserved students shine as exceptional leaders. However, we face challenges when the same students are repeatedly nominated for leadership roles.

An essential lesson for any leader is to learn the art of listening and allowing others to take charge. When students switch roles, they gain firsthand experience and improve their ability to be effective team members. As educators, we are responsible for cultivating leadership skills in all of our students, not just those who appear to be natural leaders. By providing opportunities for students to step into leadership roles and switch roles within a team, we can help them build confidence and strengthen their communication and problem-solving abilities. Furthermore, allowing students to rotate through different leadership positions helps prevent burnout and fosters a sense of inclusivity within the group. It allows every student to shine and contribute their unique skills and perspectives.

In addition to developing leadership skills, it is important for educators to emphasize collaboration and teamwork. Successful leaders delegate tasks, communicate effectively, and work toward a common goal with their team. Promoting a collaborative and supportive environment can prepare our students to become effective leaders in any setting.

What does an effective team look like in an elementary school classroom? Working together in a group is an essential skill that can be incorporated into all aspects of an elementary school day.

- Helping foster effective teamwork in elementary school can be as simple as seating arrangements. Placing students in groups and having them work together toward a common goal or incentive is a great start.

- Model and practice the language students should use when working with their teams. How should they collaborate and share ideas? How should they address conflict? Create scenarios and let students role-play and practice using respectful and productive language.

- Mix up groupings of students in games or lessons so students become accustomed to working with different personalities and different classmates. At the end of a group activity or project, ask students to reflect on how their team worked well together and if there are any areas of improvement.

 **What does an effective team look like in a middle school classroom?** Operating as a team is a challenge for middle schoolers as they face a variety of social insecurities, anxieties, and upheavals. It is critical that we teach and model how to work effectively as a team.

- Team skills are essential for professional and personal growth.
  - Group students and give each group a little piece of paper with a scenario. "You are a journalist who has been asked to collaborate with four other journalists. One of the others has been making disrespectful remarks to another one of your colleagues. What are all the ways you could handle this appropriately? What are some inappropriate ways to handle this?"
  - After they create a list of solutions, allow time for each group to share their scenario and their solutions. This is a time for you to share other solutions or ideas that may be a better way to handle it than what they came up with.
  - Make the connection to real life; they are being prepared to collaborate in various situations after school.
- Every day should present an opportunity for team building.
  - Try using the first five minutes of every class for two weeks to do a short team-building activity. Try to avoid games like Kahoot that have students on screens. We want them to practice important social skills like looking one another in the eye, speaking to others, and engaging in conflicting and fun situations.
- Team skills should be taught, verbally encouraged, practiced, and praised each day.
  - What are essential team skills? Looking someone in the eyes, listening to their ideas, encouraging them when they feel defeated, respectfully challenging them when they are unkind, asking clarifying questions, etc. Teach these skills and have students practice them during a typical assignment like Think, Pair, Share. It might sound like this: "Okay, I want you to turn and share with your partner other ways we could use measurements. Look each other in the eyes when speaking and listening and ask clarifying questions or challenge the thinking."
- When students want to work or operate alone, agree only if you have given them other opportunities to work with a team that day.

 **What does an effective team look like in a high school classroom?** As we discussed earlier, product-based learning allows students to work as a team in order to solve a problem. Oftentimes, the same student will be chosen to take the lead because the other team members know Student A will take control and basically do the entire

project while the rest sit back and check out their phones. Student A likes to be in control, so there is no problem taking control. But Student A needs to learn to follow, listen, and delegate. By rotating roles, students can experience being the leader, the note-taker, the researcher, etc. Students learn not only about different roles but also about themselves.

At the high school level, teachers should stay in the background during teamwork time. Our goal is to watch and listen. Who is getting along? Who is working? What you can learn by walking around and just listening to what our students talk about is amazing. Of course, there will be times when they are off task, but discovering who brings them back on topic is priceless. Think back to when we discussed productive struggle; be careful not to jump in at the first sign of trouble. At this stage, we want students to learn how to solve problems. There will come a time when you have to intervene, and it may be tough to watch them struggle, but the reward is worth it.

As always, allow students to reflect on their role within the team.

- What role did I feel most comfortable in?
- What role do I need to work on?
- What strengths can I bring to a team?
- What made this team work well?
- How could our team improve?

 Stop and Reflect: Think back to when you were on a productive and effective team. How would you describe that team? How can you use that experience to teach your students how to be impactful team players?

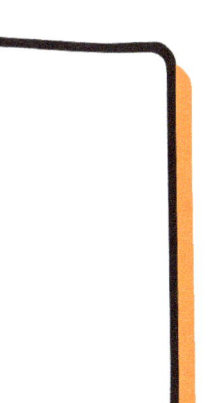

Building Empathy in Team Settings

Empathy, when paired with curiosity and creativity, has the extraordinary ability to transform classrooms into dynamic environments that foster the holistic development of students. While academic pursuits are important, nurturing empathy is equally crucial for personal and societal growth and is a trait that seems to be quickly disappearing.

By integrating curiosity and creativity into collaborative activities, we can cultivate a new generation of empathetic and understanding learners. Collaboration goes beyond mere teamwork; it requires understanding, patience, and the ability to see things from others' perspectives. This is where empathy plays a key role.

When students approach group tasks with an empathetic mindset, they don't just focus on being heard themselves but actively listen and value the input of their peers. This shift from "me" to "we" ensures every member feels valued, creating a transformative collaborative environment.

As we prepare students for a diverse and interconnected world, it's essential to equip them with knowledge and emotional intelligence. By fostering an environment that encourages curiosity and values creativity as a means of emotional expression, we set the stage for a future where collaboration is founded on mutual respect and empathy.

It's also helping students see that differences are not a threat but a necessity to help us cover each other's weaknesses with our collective strengths. While one student may be a visionary, every visionary needs a detail-oriented thinker so tasks are completed in a unique but thorough manner. Always-positive people need someone to see the whole, gaps, or weaknesses. Thus, as a unified team, we accentuate our differences to benefit the team and we remember we are always better together. Below, we will go through some basic team-building activities and more content-relat-ed strategies to build unity in your classroom or with your staff.

 Practical Tips:

- Teach point-of-view. By understanding everyone has their unique perspective, individuals can learn to appreciate diverse opinions and work toward finding common ground. This also helps with conflict resolution, as individuals are more likely to listen to and understand each other's viewpoints.

- Teach active listening skills. Practicing the art of listening is essential for all ages. Asking follow-up questions and actively participating in a conversation is a skill that can be taught. Allow students to interview their peers, listen to podcasts and TED talks, and then summarize what they heard, what questions they have, and what they will do with the information they learned.

- Teach empathy using literature. Have you ever read *The True Story of the Three Little Pigs* by A. Wolf (1996)? It's a great way to teach that everyone has a different perspective regarding the same situation. Encouraging students to reflect on their reactions versus the reactions of other characters can expand their understanding of emotions and actions.

- Encourage group discussions and debates. We mentioned Socratic seminars earlier in "Experience Navigator." Allowing students to discuss and debate different sides of the same issue opens minds, and dialogue can begin.

 **What does building empathy look like in an elementary school classroom?** An empathy map is an effective way to help students visualize their feelings. The center box can represent the student or the entire class. Students can share these ideas with their peers to explain how they feel about a given topic, situation, event, etc.

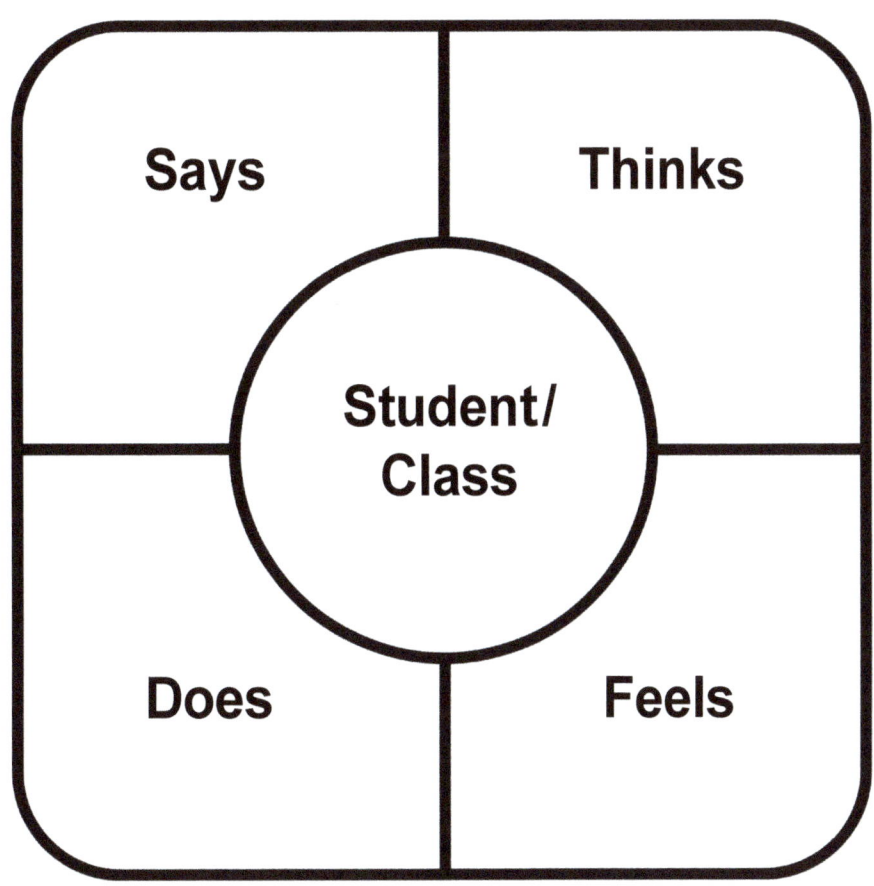

If students are reluctant to share, one option is to draw the map on your writing board and give students four Post-it notes. They can place the Post-it notes in the pertinent box. Then, as a class, you can discuss the different emotions and ways of thinking about the subject. The empathy map can be used extremely effectively with K–2 students during reading aloud to help them think about the perspective of a character.

What does building empathy look like in a middle school classroom? Because middle schoolers are innately self-focused as they navigate physical, emotional, and social changes, it is critical that we provide them ample opportunities to see the perspectives of others and to picture themselves in someone else's shoes. Before empathy and respect can be taught, trust must be built in the classroom between students and teachers and between students and peers. Getting students to understand that their classmates share the very insecurities, fears, and hurt they experience is essential.

- Have students watch video clips of people sharing their stories/perspectives on specific experiences. Allow students to share if they can relate to that experience and share theirs.

- Give strips of paper with specific scenarios and ask students in groups to discuss how that person might feel based on that situation. Allow them to share with the class.

- Have students write down all the mean things someone has said to or about them (if profanity was used, simply have them write the word "profanity" rather than the words). Have students write down how it made them feel and what thoughts went through their heads. Then have them write about a time they treated someone else like that and how it must have made them feel.

- When a student is redirected or confronted about how they've treated another student, they must have some alone time to write a reflection on how their behavior might have made the other person feel. Sometimes, you may have to ask more questions, such as, "How have you felt or how would you feel if someone did that to you or someone you love?"

What does building empathy look like in a high school classroom? High schoolers tend to think they know everything. The two words "I know" seem to be permanent in classrooms. Students may know where they stand on issues, but not the other side of the issue. One strategy is to use Four Corners. This allows students to use movement while they are visually demonstrating how they feel about a subject. When using Four Corners, your classroom becomes the stage, with each corner representing the following: strongly agree, agree, disagree, strongly disagree. Depending on the content, create five to ten open-ended questions. These questions should allow for discussion. Give students the questions beforehand so they can process their thoughts. Then read each question aloud and have students go to the corner they feel best describes their viewpoint. Ask students to share their thoughts and discuss why they feel the way they do. This will allow classmates to see where they may differ plus hear various viewpoints.

When the activity is completed, don't forget to reflect. What did we learn about our classmates? What topic most interested you? The learning could be extended by allowing students to choose one of the topics to further research. This is an excellent way to introduce students to the themes of a new novel or the ethics surrounding a new science unit.

Stop and Reflect: What does empathy look like to you? Create an emoji for empathy. How could you use that emoji to remind your students to be more empathetic?

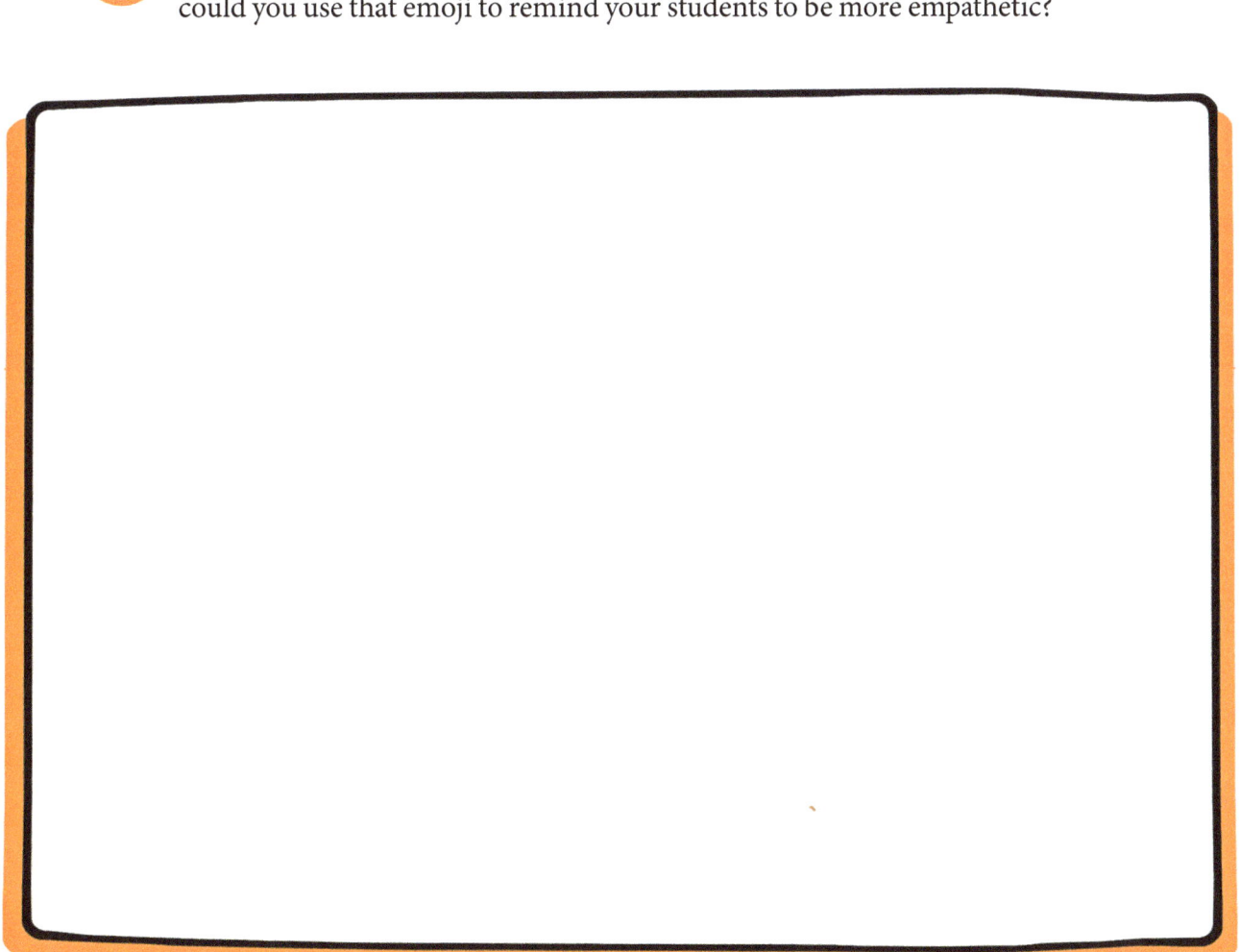

Teacher Teams

Students are not the only ones who can thrive in teams. Collaboration between teachers creates a collective knowledge pool in which teachers leverage each other's strengths and compensate for individual weaknesses. Like any effective strategy, its success is contingent on various factors, which include administrative support, cultural influences, and the well-being of the educators themselves.

 **A Collaborative Environment**

For a school to thrive, collaboration must be at the forefront. But how can administrators support and prioritize collaboration effectively? Here are some tangible actions they can take to make it happen.

1. Facilitate regular professional development sessions. By providing opportunities for teachers to learn and grow together, administrators can foster a culture of collaboration (Johnson & Johnson, 1999).

2. Provide resources for collaboration. Whether it's access to technology or materials, giving teachers the tools they need to work together is crucial (Lin et al., 2011).

3. Schedule dedicated time for collaboration. Within the busy school day, administrators can carve out specific hours for teachers to meet, ensuring collaboration remains a priority (Post et al., 2020).

4. Communicate the benefits of collaboration. Decision makers must understand how collaboration can enhance student outcomes and lead to innovative teaching strategies. By highlighting these advantages, administrators can make a compelling case for its importance (Van de Pol et al., 2015).

Why is collaboration so vital?

1. Improved student outcomes. When teachers work together, they can develop effective strategies that benefit all students, leading to better overall performance (Post et al., 2020).

2. Healthier work environment. Collaboration fosters a sense of shared purpose and responsibility among teachers, combating feelings of isolation and creating a more supportive atmosphere (Johnson & Johnson, 1999).

3. Shared problem-solving. By working together, teachers can tackle challenges collectively, reducing stress and creating a strong support system that sustains their passion and commitment.

4. A shared workload. Collaboration can alleviate the burden of tasks such as lesson planning and resource creation, allowing teachers to share the workload and make their jobs more manageable.

Collaboration is not just nice to have in schools—it's essential for success. By implementing these actions and understanding the benefits they bring, administrators can create an environment where collaboration thrives and everyone, from students to teachers, reaps the rewards.

For educational institutions to flourish, nurturing a culture of collaboration is paramount. Whether drawing inspiration from successful and interactive models or understanding its myriad benefits, the evidence is clear: collaborative teaching can be transformative (Schleifer et al., 2017). Looking at interdisciplinary course models or setting up guest lectures from teachers within an institution in areas of interest or expertise can be the first steps in establishing a collaborative environment.

Collaborative teaching is an investment in the present and future of education, ensuring teachers are supported, enriched, and ready to offer their best to their students. In the grand tapestry of education, collaboration is the intricate weave that strengthens the fabric, allowing it to withstand challenges and adapt to changing times. Embracing this collaborative spirit is not just beneficial—it is imperative for the future of education.

> **For a school to thrive, collaboration must be at the forefront.**

Reimagining Classroom Relationships to Support Team Transformer

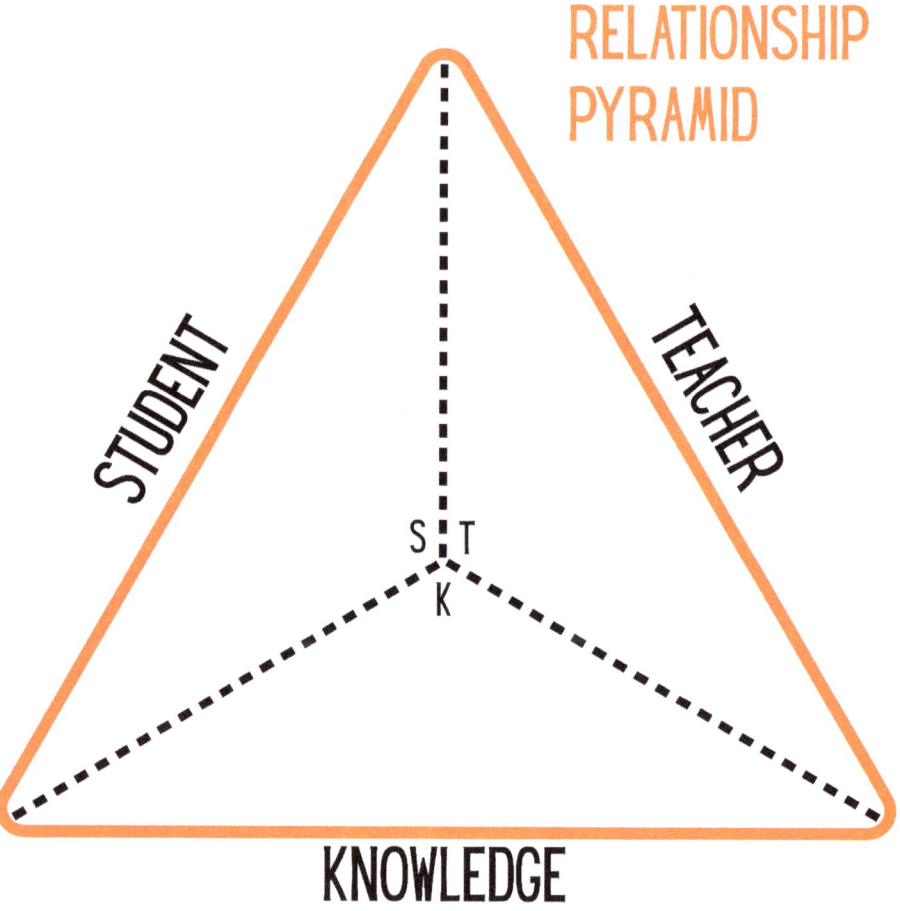

In the final section of "Team Transformer," we revisit the educative relationships—all the relationships that exist between the three basic elements needed for classroom learning: the student, the teacher, and the knowledge to be learned.

By turning the educative relationship prism and shifting the power dynamic between the elements and relationships, you will find the spaces and places for team transformation.

> What would happen to an activity, conversation, lesson, assessment, or unit if you shifted control? Instead of starting with the element or relationship you typically do, shift the prism.

1. Building unity. 2. Effective team characteristics. 3. Building empathy.

Ways to Support Team Transformer in the Relationship Pyramid

TEACHER leads the relationship	**T-T**	1. Encourage informal peer-to-per observation. 2. Rotate roles within formal (PLC) and informal collaborations. 3. Schedule community-building activities out of school.
	T-S	1. Implement gamification strategies to create common goals. 2. Create SLCs that thrive on rotating team formations. 3. Use resources for the purpose of building empathy.
	T-K	1. Form topic teams or preview partners for specific content. 2. Jigsaw professional journals/creators to follow and share. 3. Seek out professional knowledge that promotes empathy.
STUDENT leads the relationship	**S-S**	1. Use frequent rotating informal groupings to create community. 2. Manage teams internally to shift as work progresses. 3. Support each other's stated strengths and weaknesses.
	S-T	1. Create a shared class goal to include teacher(s). 2. State the types of roles wanted/needed in a group setting. 3. Share the daily mindset via an established check-in routine.
	S-K	1. Develop teams based on shared interests or talents. 2. Create and define group roles based on project needs. 3. Share a topic of interest to create classroom connections.
KNOWLEDGE leads the relationship	**K-K**	1. Examine interdisciplinary content for connections. 2. Compare/contrast personal and structured team definitions. 3. Articulate commonalities across realms of learning.
	K-T	1. Understand the benefits of all team roles. 2. Incorporate researched strategies for team formation. 3. Approach empathy as a stand-alone unit of instruction.
	K-S	1. Compare highly successful teams' structure and philosophy. 2. Dissect naturally occurring teams (family/friends) for patterns. 3. Define soft skills for the purpose of student literacy.

Try it! Take a look at the unit you are revising. How might you transform the dynamics in your classroom and lesson planning by implementing teams?

Lesson Idea/Creativity Skill
Heighten Anticipation (ignite curiosity and a sense of wonder): *How will you get students excited or curious about the lesson or content?*
Deepening Expectations (deep diving into the lesson; students are consistently actively engaged): *How will you make it hands-on? How will they explore different perspectives? How will it be relevant and meaningful to them?*
Hands-on Interactive Ideas: *What can you bring in, have them create, construct or interact with?*
Connect it to real-life experiences: *List all of the ways this applies to their life, experiences, or dreams. How will you make this connection for them?*
Extend the Learning (how students will apply new-found knowledge and curiosity into the world outside the classroom) *What activities can students do outside the classroom to continue the learning?*

Stop and Reflect:

What new strategies or concepts from this section resonated with you the most? How do you plan to implement them in your classroom?

Reflect on a challenge you might face when applying the ideas from this section. How can you overcome it?

Consider your current teaching practices. How can you integrate the principles discussed in this section to enhance creativity and critical thinking among your students?

How can we encourage curiosity and creativity so that students can manage, monitor, and modify their own learning?

EVALUATION DESIGNER

Evaluation Designer

"It is wrong to suppose that if you can't measure it, you can't manage it —a costly myth." ~W. Edwards Deming (2018)

Essential Question: How can we encourage curiosity and creativity so students can manage, monitor, and modify their own learning?

An Evaluation Designer creates methods that assess:

- Motivation and curiosity.
- Different modes of creative thinking.
- Student voice.

Strategies we will examine are:

- Methods to manage, monitor, regulate, and modify student learning.
- Using effective formative and peer feedback.
- Student-owned grading practices.

Definitions

- An assessment is a holistic, ongoing process that focuses on understanding an individual's learning progress, skills, strengths, and areas for growth.
- An evaluation is designed to measure and judge performance against a set standard or benchmark.
- Feedback is a nuanced process of honesty and constructive criticism that, when executed effectively, can guide students toward deeper comprehension and enhanced performance.
- Hard skills are specific, measurable abilities acquired through formal education, training, or experiential learning.
- Soft skills are interpersonal skills and qualities such as curiosity and creativity that pertain to human interactions and emotional intelligence.
- Traditional assessments are primarily characterized by standardized tests, essays, and quizzes.

 **Activity**

What if there was a robot capable of evaluating all of your assignments? What skills would that robot have? Draw your idea of a grading machine.

Introduction

In the world of cinema, directors like Christopher Nolan, Greta Gerwig, and Steven Spielberg skillfully craft captivating stories that enthrall audiences. In the realm of education, Evaluation Designers play a similar role, orchestrating a variety of assessments to measure student learning. Instead of traditional methods focused on memorization, these designers recognize the importance of diverse evaluations that engage students as active participants in their own learning journey. Each student brings a unique perspective and set of talents that can be directed into a cohesive narrative.

> **ASSESSMENTS SERVE AS PERSONALIZED MAPS, LEADING LEARNERS ON A JOURNEY OF SELF-DISCOVERY AND GROWTH.**

Just like a movie director brings out the best in their cast, an Evaluation Designer enables students to showcase their strengths and areas of growth. They go beyond testing knowledge and tap into motivation, curiosity, and creative thinking. By understanding each student's individual strengths, designers can create balanced assessment systems that value student choice and voice. For example, students may struggle with written tests but excel in practical or oral assessments. By providing a variety of evaluation platforms, like different scenes in a movie, students are allowed to shine in their own way.

Like skilled directors, Evaluation Designers create scenarios that challenge students to think creatively and approach problems from different angles. Just as a filmmakers experiment with camera angles and lighting, Evaluation Designers encourage students to explore beyond the boundaries of traditional learning.

How can this pedagogy be applied without abandoning traditional methods? Just as each movie genre has its unique style and tone, Evaluation Designers must tailor their approach to resonate with their students. It's crucial for students to feel integral to the "film" of education, where their roles are not just acknowledged but also celebrated.

Assessments go beyond mere evaluations. They serve as personalized maps, leading learners on a transformative journey of self-discovery, strategy refinement, and curiosity nurturance. The feedback gained from assessments is a precious resource enabling students to navigate their strengths and weaknesses, embrace challenges, and chart their own path toward success.

Teachers become Evaluation Designers by successfully guiding students through varying ways of demonstrating mastery while becoming creative and critical thinkers with their peers.

Evaluation design includes:
- Clearly defining how different skills will be achieved.
- Being open to various evaluation methods.
- Responsibility and ownership over products presented.

Should read Learning Objectives for an Evaluation Designer:

This section will explore:

- What it means to be an Evaluation Designer.
- Differences between assessment and evaluation.
- Strategies to create lessons that assess creative and critical thinking.
- Ways educators and students can collaborate in designing evaluations.

A teacher as an Evaluation Designer:

- Creates assessments that allow feedback.
- Inspires students to self-monitor, self-regulate, and self-modify.
- Challenges students to take various roles—at times being a leader and at times a follower.

A student as an Evaluation Designer:

- Discovers different ways to effectively monitor personal growth.
- Pushes themselves and their peers to revise work by offering solid feedback.
- Demonstrates the ability to honestly evaluate the effectiveness of learning.

 Stop and Reflect: When you think of assessments, what are the first three words that come to mind? Are they positive or negative words? Can you change any of the negatives to positives?

What's the Difference? Hard Skills versus Soft Skills

In the realm of education, the distinction between hard and soft skills is paramount. Hard and soft skills have risen to prominence in education due to their combined ability to holistically prepare individuals for the complexities of the modern world.

Hard Skills

- Hard skills are quantifiable and lend themselves to standardized assessment. Tests, certifications, and practical evaluations measure proficiency, accuracy, and practical application. This tangible nature allows for clearer evaluation, making matching specific skills with job requirements easier.
- Hard skills lay the foundation for academic and professional success.
- Hard skills are specific, measurable abilities acquired through formal education, training, or experiential learning. These skills encompass technical proficiency, domain-specific expertise, and specialized knowledge such as mathematics, coding, or linguistic fluency.
- Hard skills lay the groundwork for tasks that demand precision and technical finesse.

Soft Skills

- Soft skills, often referred to as interpersonal skills or people skills, embody qualities that pertain to human interactions and emotional intelligence.
- Soft skills encompass attributes such as empathy, communication, adaptability, and creativity.
- Soft skills are nuanced, reflecting an individual's ability to connect with others and navigate complex social landscapes.

As educators, we yearn for our students to achieve personal and academic growth, and that requires balancing hard and soft skills. While these skills may seem different, their true power lies in how they work together. A successful individual is not just technically competent but also can communicate, innovate, and collaborate.

In today's rapidly changing world, it's crucial to develop both types of skills to thrive. By recognizing the unique qualities of each skill set and finding ways to integrate them, individuals can aim for excellence and adaptability. The interaction between hard and soft skills mirrors the intricate dance of human capabilities on the journey to success.

Assessing Soft Skills

Whenever we do a workshop on the CREATE Method, the question of assessing soft skills seems to be a sticking point. How do we collect tangible data on skills that are difficult to quantify? The key is to shift our approach from assessing to observing. Instead of trying to quantify soft skills, we can observe and evaluate them through behaviors and interactions.

Behaviors that demonstrate strong soft skills include active listening, effective communication, conflict resolution, adaptability, and problem-solving. These behaviors can be observed during group projects or even in day-to-day interactions in the classroom. By paying attention to how students handle different situations and communicate with others, we can gain insights into their level of soft skill proficiency.

Classrooms that encourage questioning, treat mistakes as learning opportunities, and provide platforms for students to showcase their creative endeavors are the ones where curiosity and creativity thrive. By adopting innovative assessment techniques and fostering an environment that champions said traits, educators can ensure students are equipped with the tools they need to thrive in the ever-evolving world. Through the first section of this workbook, we dove into several soft skills, including curiosity and creativity. How exactly do we go about evaluating these two important skills?

> **CLASSROOMS THAT ENCOURAGE QUESTIONING, THAT DO NOT PENALIZE MISTAKES BUT TREAT THEM AS LEARNING OPPORTUNITIES, AND THAT PROVIDE PLATFORMS FOR STUDENTS TO SHOWCASE THEIR CREATIVE ENDEAVORS ARE THE ONES WHERE CURIOSITY AND CREATIVITY THRIVE.**

Assessing Curiosity

When we started this journey together, we discussed how curiosity is the driving force behind lifelong learning. It prompts students to dig deeper into subjects, ask thought-provoking questions, and make connections between different fields. Assessing curiosity requires more than just a simple quiz. Evaluation Designers use reflective journals, allowing students to document their learning journey or open-ended projects.

As a refresher, curiosity is:

- An indispensable soft skill.
- Acts as the driving force that propels learners to venture out, question, and seek a deeper understanding of the world that surrounds them.
- Naturally inclined to seek out novel solutions and adopt innovative approaches to challenges.

When assessing curiosity, educators should observe a student's:

- Proclivity to pose questions.
- Tenacity in pursuing answers.
- Adeptness at drawing connections between seemingly unrelated pieces of information (Casali & Meneghetti, 2023).

The depth, breadth, and quality of questions students raise can serve as reliable indicators of their inherent curiosity.

To effectively measure curiosity, educators can:

- Utilize techniques such as inquiry-based learning assessments. These assessments evaluate students based on the depth and quality of their questions (Richardson & Krstic, 2021).
- Observe students' participation and engagement levels during class discussions.
- Perceive a student's enthusiasm to delve into new subjects.
- Discern a student's relentless pursuit of answers (Casali & Meneghetti, 2023).

 Practical Tip: Offer students the chance to spearhead class discussions or present on subjects they are passionate about. Remember show-and-tell in elementary school? Allowing students to teach their peers about things that interest them will ignite their curiosity.

Assessing Creativity

Creativity involves generating new ideas and solving problems in innovative ways. To assess creativity, an Evaluation Designer may assign tasks with multiple valid solutions, encouraging students to showcase their original thinking.

As a refresher, creativity is the ability to make something:

- Novel (new).
- Appropriate.
- Useful.

When assessing creativity, educators should observe a student's:

- Deep understanding of the content's many dimensions.
- Ability to use divergent thinking, fluency, flexibility, elaboration, and originality.

To effectively assess creativity, educators can:

Prioritize students' ability to think outside the box, come up with original solutions, and adapt to different situations.

- Assign open-ended tasks or projects.
- Create assignments that allow students to showcase their creative thinking and innovative problem-solving skills.
- Incorporate peer reviews and self-assessments into the curriculum.

Practical Tip: Instead of replicating a given piece of art, challenge students to create a piece that conveys a specific emotion or theme, allowing their imagination to shine.

Stop and Reflect: Assess yourself! What grade would you give yourself when it comes to curiosity and creativity? Why? How are you measuring yourself?

TO EVALUATE OR TO ASSESS?

While the terms are often used interchangeably, assessment and evaluation serve distinct purposes in the educational and professional realms. Assessment is a holistic, ongoing process that focuses on understanding an individual's learning progress, skills, strengths, and areas for growth. It emphasizes feedback, guidance, and opportunities for improvement, positioning the learner in a cycle of continuous learning and development.

Conversely, evaluation is a more summative approach designed to measure and judge performance against a set standard or benchmark. While evaluation often culminates in a grade or a rating, assessment nurtures growth through constructive feedback. Thus, assessment is not just about the end point but the journey, supporting learners in realizing their potential over time.

To Evaluate or to Assess

Assessment and evaluation, while often used interchangeably, serve distinct purposes in the educational and professional realm. **Assessment is a more holistic, ongoing process** that focuses on understanding an individual's learning progress, skills, strengths, and areas for growth. It emphasizes feedback, guidance, and opportunities for improvement, positioning the learner in a cycle of continuous learning and development. **Conversely, evaluation is a more summative approach** designed to measure and judge performance against a set standard or benchmark. While evaluation often culminates in a grade or a rating, assessment nurtures growth through constructive feedback. Thus, assessment is not just about the endpoint but the journey, supporting learners in realizing their potential over time.

To Evaluate	The Difference?	To Assess
Focused on final outcomes or results	Scope of focus	Focused on the ongoing learning process
Often yields a grade or score	Outcome	Yields feedback to support further learning
Summative in nature	Purpose	Formative, aimed at understanding and improvement
Quantitative and judgment oriented	Nature	Development-oriented, highlighting strengths/areas of growth
Often conducted at the end of an instructional period	Timing	Conducted throughout the learning journey
Determines if objectives were met	Goal	Identifies learner's needs and areas for growth

STRATEGIES

Self-Assessment

Methods to Manage, Monitor, and Modify Student Learning

Students tend to look to us, the teachers, for the "right answer," resulting in mimicking rather than learning. Often, when shown a model of excellent work, students will just regurgitate what they see instead of thinking about how they can add their own creative and critical thinking to the assignment. Self-assessment is an essential strategy, and instructing our students on how to evaluate their work will lighten our load and expand their ability to think critically.

Unlike traditional methods that focus on what a student knows, holistic assessments delve into how a student thinks, approaches challenges, and adapts to new situations. *Assessment Strategies for Self-Directed Learning* (2005) by Arthur L. Costa and Bena Kallick provides a deep dive into the intricacies of holistic assessment techniques, emphasizing soft skills such as curiosity and creativity. Central to this approach is the idea of learners analyzing their performance to adjust accordingly. This self-assessment is not an isolated act; it thrives on a sequence of self-assessment skills that facilitate the development of a keen, introspective learner.

These self-assessment skills—self-monitoring, self-regulation, self-management, and self-modification—work synergistically, fostering a cyclical process vital to effective self-directed assessment. Focusing less on quantifiable skills and more on the student as a whole can elevate learning.

Self-Monitoring

One of the keys to continuous academic and personal improvement is self-monitoring. This introspective process involves evaluating and assessing performance, behaviors, and emotions, giving valuable insights into progress toward certain goals. By paying attention to students' actions and consequences, you can make informed decisions and determine what needs adjustment. In an educational setting, self-monitoring means students can regularly check their understanding of a topic, identify areas of difficulty, and seek assistance when necessary. In everyday life, it means being aware of emotional reactions and understanding the triggers for certain behaviors.

The real power of self-monitoring lies in its ability to provide immediate feedback, allowing for quick adjustments and refinements to a student's approach. Self-monitoring can empower students to regulate, manage, and modify their behavior.

What does self-monitoring look like in an elementary school classroom? I did a lesson once with a second grade reading group and was modeling my thinking out loud. One of my students stopped me. "Wait! I didn't know I was supposed to think while reading!" What an "Aha!" moment this was for me. I knew I needed to do a LOT more modeling of my thinking so students could peek into my brain as I process content, my emotions, how I am (or am not) actively engaged, and more.

- A simple but extremely effective way to encourage self-monitoring is checklists—their applications are endless! Small printed checklists can remind students of what they are supposed to do when they arrive at school, how to "give me five" and show the teacher you're paying attention, etc.

- Ask students to reflect on the purpose of what they're doing during the day. Asking them the why behind their activity or lesson will keep them focused and allow them to reflect on their learning.

- Think aloud during challenging math lessons.

What does self-monitoring look like in the middle school classroom? Because of the social development of middle school students, much of the self-reflection will be aimed at helping them recognize appropriate and inappropriate behavior patterns and interactions. For example, they may have inappropriate interactions, like talking about themselves excessively while conversing to demonstrate they can relate. We want to teach them that making friends appropriately means conversations are two-sided, and rather than spinning the conversation to highlight themselves, they should ask questions of the friend they are speaking with. Another example might be rather than always wanting to work alone or pick up their phones to distract themselves from the fear of feeling rejected or left out, we teach them the signs of self-sabotage in social situations and how to be friendly, inviting, social, and interact well with others. Not all students will struggle with these social aspects, but teaching self-reflection and offering time for it at the end of a class is critical. At this stage, they need the expected behaviors modeled.

- Model self-monitoring and have conversations with students about your progress. For example, "Yesterday, on my drive home, I was thinking about our frustrating class period. I realized I was a little short-tempered and impatient with you guys. I should have been more understanding that it was a hard assignment, and maybe my instructions weren't as clear as they could have been. So I'm sorry for not being more patient and I will work on that in today's class."

- List a series of social interactions on strips of paper and pass them out to groups. Have students role-play how to handle those situations appropriately. Leave time for a discussion on why it was incorrect or appropriate.
- Have a rubric for both academic attitude and social interactions and allow students to self-assess how they did at the end of each class period with a note on what they could have done better and will work on next time.

 **What does self-monitoring look like in the high school classroom?** Much self-monitoring comes from self-reflection. Allow high school students to reflect on what was difficult. What did they need to do to find the answer? When teaching a difficult subject such as poetry, a new calculus equation, or a new scientific method, it can be helpful for students to write a difficulty paper.

Basically, this paper is designed for the student to write on what they found difficult and what they did to overcome the difficulty. As they walk through the challenging concept, they ask themselves:

- Where am I confused?
- What is making me confused?
- What questions do I have regarding this content?
- How did I overcome this challenge?
- If I didn't overcome the challenge, what might I do differently?

These papers allow students to use their voice and to be open and honest. They give you insight into your students' thinking process. Usually, the only grade attached to these is a completion grade; it is another chance for students to take a risk and be vulnerable without consequence. This also provides excellent formative feedback on where students are experiencing productive struggle.

 Stop and Reflect: How might you use self-monitoring in your classroom?

Self-Regulation

Self-regulation is the key to unlocking a person's full potential. It encompasses the ability to control one's thoughts, emotions, and behaviors so as to achieve long-term goals. Imagine if students could resist short-term temptations and distractions and instead focus on achieving their dreams.

In the world of education, self-regulation is paramount. It allows students to effectively manage their cognitive processes, such as attention and memory, for optimal learning experiences. But self-regulation goes beyond academics. It plays a crucial role in all aspects of life.

When you excel in self-regulation, you gain better emotional control, become more resilient in the face of challenges, and adapt to changing situations with ease. It's a skill that sets you up for success in all areas of life.

The journey to becoming an Evaluation Designer involves developing self-regulation skills. It combines intrinsic factors like personality and external factors like environment and upbringing. By understanding and honing your self-regulation abilities, you can help students pave their path to success.

What does self-regulation look like in the elementary school classroom? We've all seen children who are emotionally dysregulated. They need a break! There are many great (and fun!) ways elementary school students can self-regulate their emotions. Here are some ideas you can try in your classroom!

- Brain breaks! Many YouTube videos give students an easy and fun way to give their bodies a chance to move and their brains a break. These can be used as transitions between lessons or to break up a long piece of content.

- Breathing exercises are an easy way to help students calm down and connect their minds and bodies. Some of my favorite breathing exercises for K–5 children are to use their fingers to "smell a flower" (breathe in) and then "blow out a candle" (breathe out). K–2 students in particular love this one, but I've seen it work just as well with upper-grade elementary students!

- Create a "calm corner" students can visit for a specified time. You can include a timer and coloring sheets, journal pages, or small fidget toys students can use when they need a little break from the routine.

What does self-regulation look like in the middle school classroom? Middle schoolers are emotionally all over the place, learning how to manage unfamiliar and confusing feelings, thoughts, and hormones. Part of teaching self-regulation is giving them the language to identify feelings and emotions, giving them safe opportunities to mess up, and holding them accountable to identify their needs choices, and make amends for their mistakes.

- Give students the language to identify what they are experiencing and feeling. A feelings wheel could be printed and placed on the wall or in a take-a-break spot in your classroom. You could even give each student a journal and have them glue or tape a copy of the feelings wheel in there.

- A Zones of Regulation curriculum teaches that big problems require big responses and small problems require small responses. You can teach students to identify big problems versus small problems. Then ask them if their response matched the size of the problem. The curriculum includes activities that allow students to learn ways to cope or regulate depending on what zone they're in. This could be something they journal about after a redirection. It can seem very elementary, but they are critical skills for middle school that can be adapted to fit the age level appropriately.

- Teach students about physical signs in our body that we are coming emotionally undone. For example, "The jaw is clenched or tightening, our face gets hot, our mind swarms with responses, and we ball up our fists." Then give students a list or let them brainstorm a list of healthy ways to address those responses before it ends in an emotional explosion. For example, getting a drink from the fountain, pulling out a journal and get it out, sitting at the take-a-break section and playing with a fidget toy, going to the gym to jog a couple of laps, or going to the gym and throwing a couple of punches at a pad.

- Have students pair up and practice responding appropriately to situations that they often become emotionally dysregulated in. For example, "When the teacher tells me to stop talking and I was not talking, instead of shouting, 'I wasn't talking,' I could 1) say okay, 2) ask to talk about it later, or 3) tell the teacher I was just explaining the directions."

What does self-regulation look like in the high school classroom? High school students should be able to self-regulate without your assistance, but there may be times when a friendly reminder on how it is helpful to think before we act can be beneficial.

- You know the student who loves to call out the answer, even if that answer is incorrect. Give them three note cards to help them recognize how often they are calling out the answer. Take a note card each time the student calls out—this will bring attention to the call-out but in a silent and noninvasive manner.

- You know the student whose hand is constantly raised and who rarely allows other students to answer the question or may become agitated because you are not calling on them. Have that student lead the discussion instead of participating. Give them a set of questions you want answered and allow that student to take the lead.

- You know the student who never turns an assignment in on time. Give them a calendar and allow the student to create their timeline (within a timeline that works for you). For example, have a one-week window for the student to turn in the assignment. If the student misses the deadline they created, have them write a reflection on why the deadline was missed and attach a plan on how they will remedy the situation. Some students are better when they have a weekend to work on the assignment, while others would rather turn it in and be done. If we allow this flexibility, students learn to take responsibility for their own decisions.

 Stop and Reflect: How might self-regulation look in your classroom?

Self-Managing

Self-management skills allow students to take control of their lives. Self-managing means being your leader, making decisions that align with your goals, and taking responsibility for the outcomes. In today's fast-paced world, navigating countless options and choosing a path that resonates with your aspirations is important.

This involves setting clear goals, planning how to achieve them, and executing those plans with diligence and determination. Self-management also encompasses time management and organizational skills, as efficiently structuring your time and resources is essential. Mastering self-management is key to becoming an Evaluation Designer for you and your students.

 **What does self-managing look like in the elementary school classroom?** In elementary school, self-management is about teaching students routines and structures that will keep them organized and productive. Here are a few simple strategies to try in your class!

- Help students stay organized through simple structures like color-coded folders (red for math, green for science, yellow for social studies, etc.).
- Make using a classroom planner part of the daily classroom routine so students get into the habit of using it and keeping track of their assignments, homework, due dates, and more.

- Help students develop an awareness of time management and how they're working toward completing tasks. This can sound like, "We're ten minutes into our fifteen-minute work block. Please look at what you've accomplished so far and decide what you'd like to wrap up in the next five minutes." Older students can also benefit from more explicit directions like "We're about ten minutes into our work time, and you should be about halfway through your work. Take a moment to evaluate where you're at and where you'd like to be when we finish up in about five minutes."

What does self-managing look like in the middle school classroom? Middle schoolers get pulled in many directions as they are deciding who they want to be. They desire independence but need guidance to be independent responsibly. As a result, a few strategies provide opportunities for self-managing.

- Teach and provide activities and opportunities to identify what is most important. For example, you can give students a couple of scenarios and have them collaborate to determine which priorities are most important and why. "You have basketball practice after school, you have a three-page paper due in two days, and a math assignment is due in the third period tomorrow. You also promised your neighbor you would mow his lawn. How do you make all of this work? Do you attempt it all? Which are the most important and why? How would you handle this? How would you make time to recharge after so much at once?" Debrief about prioritizing, the risks of taking on too much, and the challenge of pushing through when you feel overwhelmed.
- Teach them how to have academic conversations with their teachers.
    - Remind them of their desire to be more independent and that independence starts with owning their learning.
    - "When you are unclear about an assignment, talk to the teacher about it rather than just not completing it and telling us later you didn't understand."
        - Ms. _____, when you explained the assignment, I wasn't quite sure what to actually do."
    - "When you are struggling with an assignment, email me and tell me what you're struggling with and what you've tried. Part of owning your learning is reaching out when you're unsure rather than waiting until the next day to tell me you did not know what to do."
    - "When you miss a class, you need to ask me what you missed and how to make it up."
- Teach them how to stay organized.
    - Write in a planner.
    - Make a routine habit of checking the planner.
    - Organize assignments still in their possession.

 **What does self-managing look like in the high school classroom?** Executive functioning skills are an essential component of the high school classroom. High schoolers juggle multiple classes, extracurricular activities, jobs, friends, and family responsibilities. At this stage, students will have varying levels of organization. Some will use a paper student planner while others may use a digital one. Some students are overly organized while others use no organization at all. Their backpacks are overflowing with miscellaneous papers and lack a system. It's important to help students see that whatever method they use for self-management is fine—as long as they self-manage.

- For larger projects, allow students to design individual checkpoints by breaking down the steps and setting their deadlines.

- If a student is handing in late assignments, ask the student to create a plan and share it with you. What will be done? By when? What steps will you take to complete these tasks? What obstacles do you anticipate? How will you address those obstacles?

- Have periodic check-ins with students. Allow time to meet with each student during a larger project. Asking students to show how they complete a task can be powerful. It helps the student clarify their ideas and allows you an opportunity to mentor the student.

 Stop and Reflect: How might you incorporate more self-managing?

Self-Modifying

Self-modifying is the key to continuous growth and improvement. It's all about harnessing the insights gained from self-monitoring and using them to make necessary adjustments in your strategies, behaviors, and actions.

In the realm of learning, a self-modifying student knows when to pivot from a study strategy that isn't delivering the desired results. They have the adaptability to switch gears and try a different approach. In everyday life, self-modifying means identifying unproductive habits and actively working to break free from them.

This invaluable skill starts with being flexible and open-minded. It's about recognizing that there's always room for improvement and taking proactive steps to achieve it. Assessments play a crucial role in adopting a growth mindset. They become exciting challenges that offer development opportunities. Setbacks become mere stepping stones to even greater achievements.

What does self-modifying look like in the elementary school classroom? Self-modifying in elementary school is about coaching social situations and helping students consider when their actions or behaviors aren't getting them the desired outcome. Teachers can help students brainstorm alternative ways to respond to issues and role-play to practice using a new skill or strategy.

- Student A cuts in front of Student B in line. Student B gets mad and shoves Student A, leading to them getting in trouble. We can help Student B think about other options for responding when someone cuts (take a deep breath, step to the side, ask the student to go to the back of the line, raise your hand and ask the teacher for help).

- Students LOVE to role-play! Create common classroom scenarios and put them in a bowl. Have students sit in a circle and create a fishbowl activity (we're on the outside looking in!). Pairs, small groups, or students can take turns in the middle of the circle and act out the scenarios. Ask the students sitting in the circle to observe how they respond to the issues and have them brainstorm other alternatives.

What does self-modifying look like in the middle school classroom? Middle school is the first time students really have to study or develop habits for maintaining a grade and working hard for an assessment. As a result, there will be a lot of trial and error in what works for which students. In fact, there tends to be an assumption that when you have a test, you simply read over the material, write out note cards, and practice saying them. But as we know, there are different ways to memorize, study, and learn. We have the opportunity to teach students to try several different strategies and to adjust when the one they try does not work for them or a particular assignment.

- Give students a list of scenarios and have them share ideas for how they would prepare. Have them devise reasons those ideas may not work and what they would try or adapt if that were the case. For example, "Tomorrow, I will give you a quiz on what we read on the seven reasons information has to be read with discretion. How could you prepare for that?"
- Have a list of common studying strategies and have students talk through which one they've tried if it worked and, if not, what they tried next.
  - Using notecards.
  - Rewriting the material.
  - Taking notes.
  - Rereading notes.
  - Creating a song or poem to remember the content.
  - Drawing pictures to help remember important concepts.
  - Reviewing material with a friend.
  - Listening to calm music while writing out concepts to remember.

What does self-modifying look like in the high school classroom? Many high schoolers use strategies that don't work for them because they were taught only one way to accomplish a task. In high school, we must give students the flexibility and autonomy to design their way of learning. Taking notes is a perfect example of this. Some students may:

- Write in their textbook or use Post-it notes.
- Use a digital notebook on their computers.
- Create visual notes by drawing pictures.

We want students to learn what works best for them—not for us. When students use their creative and critical thinking skills to discover what works and what doesn't, they make their learning and thinking their own. What's important is that students learn the benefits of taking notes—how they go about that is up to them.

Stop and Reflect: How might you use self-monitoring in your classroom?

Overall, teaching students to self-assess ensures students are equipped with these skills and are ready to navigate the complexities of the modern world. As the world becomes more interconnected and complex, our assessment methods must evolve to capture the multifaceted nature of modern learners. By adopting self-assessment standards, we ensure education remains relevant, comprehensive, and truly transformative, preparing students for the challenges and opportunities of the future.

Providing Feedback

As teachers, we are responsible for ensuring our students learn effectively. Formative feedback is a powerful tool that helps us understand our students' learning needs, track their progress, and give them the guidance they need to succeed. Let's define formative feedback. Simply put, feedback helps students improve their work while they are still learning (Poulos & Mahony, 2008). Whereas summative feedback (such as exam results) aims to evaluate a student's overall understanding of a subject and count toward their final grade, formative feedback is intended to guide and help students improve their performance (Hattie & Timperley, 2007). It often includes suggestions for next steps, highlighting areas to focus on, and explaining what they have done well.

Why is formative feedback so important? Think about the last time you gave an assignment back. You spend all that time at home or after school grading papers, and when you finally hand them back—boom—students look at the grade and throw it in the recycling bin. They don't even look at your feedback. They are only concerned with the final grade.

That's why formative feedback is so important. It helps students feel more invested in their learning. Students feel supported and more willing to take risks in their learning. They will learn from any mistakes they make and can focus on their strengths and weaknesses. Students often look at their final grades and ignore all the feedback. Once the assessment is graded, is there another opportunity for them to use the feedback? Oftentimes, the answer is no.

Another benefit of formative feedback is that it allows teachers to track students' progress. By providing regular feedback, you can identify where students are struggling and adjust your teaching accordingly (Taras, 2003). This ensures all students progress at their own pace and do not fall behind. Students can use the feedback immediately as they continue to progress toward the summative assessment.

 Practical Tips: Here are practical tips for using formative feedback effectively.

1. Make feedback a regular part of your routine.
2. Ensure feedback is specific and actionable.
3. Encourage students to reflect on their feedback.
4. Use software such as Google Docs where you can provide instant feedback by leaving comments and questions.
5. Conduct one-on-one conferences with the students where they walk through their upcoming assessments with you.
6. Ask students a question. Have them write the answer on a Post-it note (no names) and place it on the door as they walk out. You can see the overall class understanding of a concept.

Effective Feedback	Ineffective Feedback
Delves into nuances	Ambiguous
Strikes balance between what the student does well and what needs improvement	Leaves students without clear directions on how to fix what needs fixing
It is timely	Lacks personalization
It is actionable	Too late - only given once students receive a summative grade and are not allowed to put the feedback into practice.

 Practical Tips

1. Have students hand in only the first section of the assignment. Giving feedback on a smaller portion is less time-consuming.

2. Have students list the top two areas in which they want feedback. This will allow you time to focus on those two areas and not look at all the details.

3. Use standard feedback codes. I have teachers tell me they use certain symbols to represent common mistakes, such as * to indicate unclear, ? to indicate this section needs more evidence, + to indicate this section works well, etc.

4. Use student exemplars, With the student's permission, walk the class through a paper as you verbally give feedback.

There are numerous examples in books and online on incorporating formative feedback. It's important to remember that Evaluation Designers engage in multiple opportunities and methods to provide feedback. This may take time to administer, but by the time you arrive at the summative assessment, you should be able to read it, mark the rubric, and move on, unless the students will be doing that assignment again and they can use the feedback—you know what will happen—recycling bin!

Stop and Reflect: What common mistakes do students make in your content area? What image would you associate with that mistake? Try making your own shorthand for grading.

Common Mistake	Image

Peer Feedback

The dynamic of peer feedback introduces an additional layer of complexity. When students step into the shoes of an evaluator, they not only offer diverse perspectives, often highlighting aspects overlooked by educators, but also hone their critical thinking. Analyzing a peer's work demands a level of analytical rigor, fostering a deeper understanding of the subject. Moreover, the act of articulating feedback refines their communication skills.

However, the success of peer feedback hinges on the environment. Educators must cultivate a space where students feel secure, both in giving and receiving feedback, and learning what feedback to give. Constructive critique should be encouraged while negative or disparaging remarks should be curtailed. Students must be taught how to give feedback.

- Glows and grows. Have students list three areas where the assignment works well and two areas where the assignment needs improvement.
- Sandwich feedback. Have students start with a compliment, add a piece of constructive feedback, and then end with another compliment.
- Model peer feedback by giving clear peer feedback worksheets and activities.

What does peer feedback look like in an elementary school classroom? Getting elementary school-aged children to share feedback with their peers requires a strong classroom culture and a foundation of mutual respect and trust between students. Here are some ways to get your K–5 students engaged in peer feedback.

- Encourage students to initially focus their peer feedback on reflections and on things they noticed in their classmate's work.
- Create a protocol for students to follow when providing peer feedback. This might be as simple as "Tell your classmate one thing you noticed about their work, and ask them one question."
- Create an anchor chart with different sentence stems students can use to get their ideas started.

 **What does peer feedback look like in a middle school classroom?** Middle schoolers are incredibly fragile regarding feedback, especially from peers. As a result, peer feedback can happen only after a strong community has been established. Peer feedback can be incredibly beneficial when there is common respect, empathy, and positive interaction as a community.

- Create ground rules as a class.
    - Good feedback always starts with empathy: How would I feel if I received the feedback I am about to give?
    - Feedback is never personal but always helps me become the best version of myself.
    - Feedback highlights what I do well and what I need to improve on.
    - Feedback is skill-focused.

- Model giving feedback both verbally and on a rubric.
    - What language to use and not use.
    - Sandwich approach: One positive, one area of improvement, another positive.

 **What does peer feedback look like in a high school classroom?** Oftentimes, when looking at a model assignment, students are asked to give a critique and grade the assignment using the rubric. It's incredible how they can edit someone else's work but cannot yet edit their own. Giving peers feedback in a constructive and meaningful way is essential to building deeper thinking.

- Have students read their assignment out loud to a small group, then ask:
    - What stands out the most to you?
    - What questions are left unanswered?
    - How could I improve on this assignment?
- Combining the Team Transformer and Evaluation Designer roles, have students gather into their teams and rotate the assignment, adding on the previous teammate's feedback.
- Have students use the rubric to guide their peer feedback. Not only will the student become more familiar with the rubric, but it will serve as an organization tool for their feedback.
- Allow feedback to be recorded instead of written—giving students a choice in how they deliver the feedback will allow for a more honest evaluation.

Self-Editing/Peer Feedback Activity

Lesson plan example—this activity will work with any writing assignment.

An important step in writing is being able to self-edit. In fact, one of the standards we are addressing today is: "Students will be able to develop and strengthen writing as needed by planning, revising, editing, rewriting, or trying a new approach, focusing on addressing what is most significant for a specific purpose and audience." As a writer, you want to make sure your paper is clear, concise, organized, focused, and ultimately proves what you want to prove with strong solid support.

Polishing Activity

1. Highlight in YELLOW your thesis and topic sentences. Do all of your topic sentences relate to your thesis?

2. Highlight in BLUE all lines that are YOUR words. Are you analyzing rather than summarizing? Is your essay balanced? You do not have to include your introduction and conclusion.

3. Highlight in GREEN all the support from the text. Do you have enough textual support? Did you cite each quote?

4. Highlight in ORANGE all the support from OUTSIDE RESOURCES. Have you cited at least three different sources and addressed the counterclaim?

5. Take your pen and CIRCLE all of your transitions (words and phrases), both between paragraphs and inside your paragraphs.

6. Reread your introduction and conclusion. Are they cohesive? Do you have an attention-getter?

Editing Activity

1. Underline any places within the essay where there are tense shifts. Remember this needs to be written in literary present tense.

2. Start any words that could be stronger—use powerful nouns, verbs, and adjectives!

3. Place a square around any incorrect citations.

4. Draw a squiggly line under any awkward sentences, wordy sentences, fragments or run-ons. Remember reading out loud can help.

5. Square any repetitive sentence beginnings. Don't let your paper be choppy!

Reflection Activity

After you have finished completing this activity, you will write a reflection on what you noticed in your paper. On a separate sheet of paper, answer the following:

1. Write your best sentence. Why do you think this was your best sentence?

2. List two strengths in your writing and give examples.

3. List three areas of improvement and give specific examples.

4. Write a "to-do" list for your editing process. What are the major areas you need to focus to improve your paper?

Stop and Reflect: Looking at your unit, consider the following questions:

	Critically Thinking and Understanding Assessment Methodologies	
	As you design your next evaluation tool consider the following questions	
WHO?	are we assessing?	Consider the students' demographic, age group, and learning abilities of the students. Understand the unique needs and backgrounds of each student. How does the assessment cater to individual differences?
	are we directing this toward?	Is the assessment tailored for a specific group? Is the evaluation accessible for all groups?
	decided this assessment was valid and worthwhile?	Who stands to benefit from this assessment? Does this benefit the educator, the student, or a third party?
	will be "marking" this assessment?	Is this assessment being graded by yourself, by an assistant, a third party, the student, or in a group setting?
	will be looking at these data?	Consider who will receive the results of the assessment. How does this information help them?
WHAT?	are we assessing?	Identify the specific skills, knowledge, or competencies being evaluated.
	are we focusing on?	What are the primary objectives of the assessment?
	are we not assessing?	Recognize any gaps or areas not covered in the assessment. How might these gaps impact overall understanding?
	sort of feedback will this assessment provide?	Does this assessment intend to grow a student's realm of understanding and skills, or rather is it meant to measure a student's development?
	will be the key takeaway from this assessment?	What are you looking to measure?
	are we working toward this?	What are the long-term goals or outcomes are expected from this assessment?

WHEN?	are we assessing?	Consider the demographic, age group, and learning abilities of the students. Understand the unique needs and backgrounds of each student. How does the assessment cater to individual differences?
	will the students be able to use this feedback from this assessment in future learning?	Does this assessment build toward something greater? Are students being guided to grow in any way, shape, or form? Will your feedback be timely and meaningful?
	will the students receive this feedback?	Understand the anxieties that come while awaiting feedback. Keeping students informed on the grading process can work to alleviate worry, and give students a date to look toward.
	will students be assessed in different ways than this assessment?	Is every assessment the same? In what ways do assessments vary?
	are we building from this?	When will you be expanding upon the skills developed now?
WHERE?	is this feedback being recorded?	Do students have a reliable place to view feedback? Can students comment on feedback?
	does this assessment fit in the student's understanding of assessment and feedback?	Think about the assessment from the perspective of your students. Does the assessment fit what is being assessed? Is there a way to make the assessment better fit your students' needs?
	are we assessing this?	Consider the environment: is it in class, online, at home, or in a lab? How does the location impact the assessment's effectiveness? Can you change the environment to make it less stressful?

WHY?	are we assessing?	Understand the purpose: is it for grading, feedback, placement, or self-assessment? This is a key question - does this need to be an assessment or can I turn it into an activity?
	this assessment type, format, priority?	Understand the purpose: is the type of assessment beneficial for the educator and the students, and is it necessary?
	now?	Could students benefit from more time before an assessment? Consider why the assessment should occur at this moment. Is this assessment relevant?
	does this need to be accessed?	What is the underlying reason for this focus? Is it curriculum-driven, based on student needs, or other factors?
	are we assessing this?	Reflect on the reasons some areas are left out. Is it due to time constraints, irrelevance, or other factors?
	are we working towards this?	What's the bigger picture or ultimate goal behind this assessment? Remember, we want creative and critical thinking to shine.

🔍 **Stop and Reflect:** What are all the ways you can use the above questions when you design your next evaluation tool?

Reimagining Classroom Relationships to Support an Evaluation Designerr

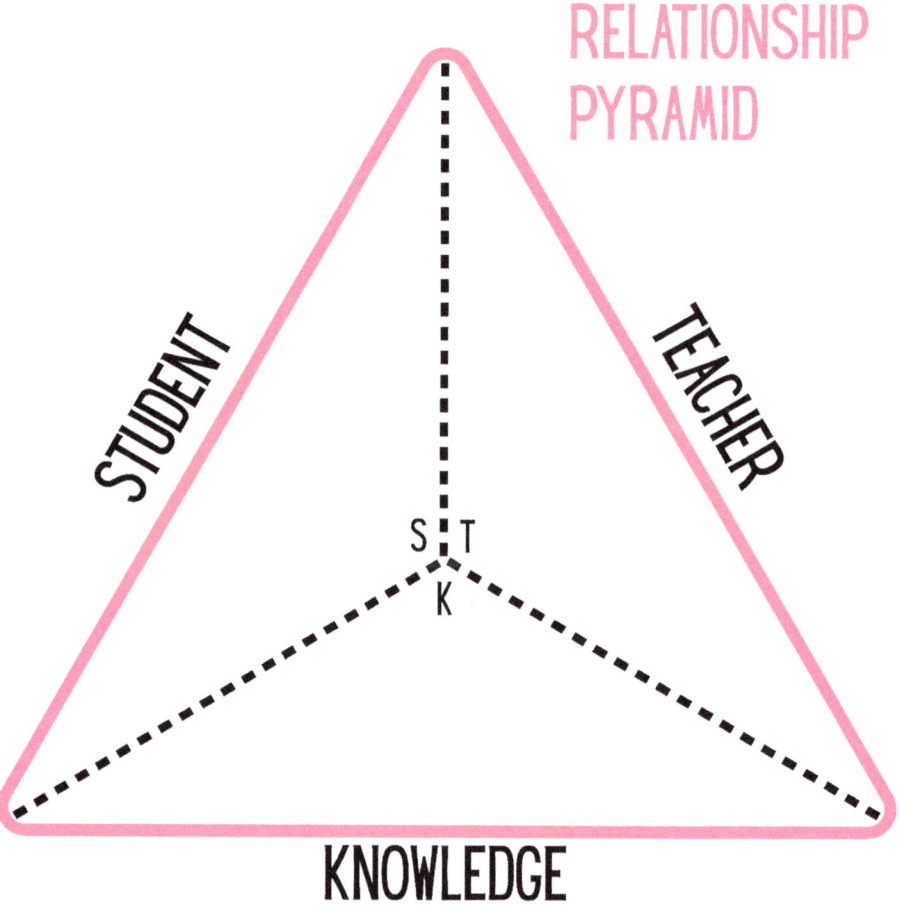

In the final section of "Evaluation Designer," we revisit the educative relationships—all the relationships that exist between the three basic elements needed for classroom learning: the student, the teacher, and the knowledge to be learned. By turning the educative relationship prism and shifting the power dynamic between the elements and relationships, you will find the spaces and places for evaluation design.

> What would happen to an activity, conversation, lesson, assessment, or unit if you shifted control? Instead of starting with the element or relationship you typically do, shift the prism.

1. Methods to manage, monitor, and modify student learning. 2. Using effective formative and peer feedback. 3. Student ownership grading practices.

TEACHER leads the relationship	T-T	1. Revise assessments using shared data across class, grade, etc. 2. Engage in peer observation for the purpose of feed "forward." 3. Create vertical/horizontal standards for student-owned grading.
	T-S	1. Integrate self-assessment strategies into daily practice. 2. Discuss the purpose of feedback and how to use it. 3. Scaffold assessment discussions to support ownership.
	T-K	1. Approach the classroom with the "teach students not content" motto. 2. Create failed assessment resources as institutional records. 3. Retain student exemplars to use in future lessons.
STUDENT leads the relationship	S-S	1. Discuss "self" process to help brainstorm strategies. 2. Set up a peer mentors system of feedback. 3. Develop editor/author partnerships for feedback opportunities.
	S-T	1. Self-assess on a range of items from skill to engagement. 2. Provide formative feedback to the teacher on content/instruction. 3. Select content areas for feedback and assessment.
	S-K	1. Use self-strategies to direct the learning path. 2. Self-select content areas for feedback and assessment. 3. Match exemplars to each level of mastery.
KNOWLEDGE leads the relationship	K-K	1. Track strategies as students move from personal to content knowledge. 2. Match student data to types of feedback/scaffold. 3. Compare personal critique to formalized assessment.
	K-T	1. Research tips to become reflective practitioner. 2. Use evaluation feedback and peer dialogue as inspiration. 3. Consider what students need and want in a teacher.
	K-S	1. Use assessment data to set personal learning goals. 2. Rate and revise feedback based on its perceived usefulness. 3. Research the purpose, usability, and versatility of the assessment.

Try it! Take a look at the unit you are revising. How might you transform the dynamics in your classroom and lesson planning by implementing teams?

Lesson Idea/Creativity Skill

Heighten Anticipation (ignite curiosity and a sense of wonder): *How will you get students excited or curious about the lesson or content?*

Deepening Expectations (deep diving into the lesson; students are consistently actively engaged): *How will you make it hands-on? How will they explore different perspectives? How will it be relevant and meaningful to them?*

Hands-on Interactive Ideas: *What can you bring in, have them create, construct or interact with?*

Connect it to real-life experiences: *List all of the ways this applies to their life, experiences, or dreams. How will you make this connection for them?*

Extend the Learning (how students will apply new-found knowledge and curiosity into the world outside the classroom) *What activities can students do outside the classroom to continue the learning?*

Stop and Reflect:

What new strategies or concepts from this section resonated with you the most? How do you plan to implement them in your classroom?

Reflect on a challenge you might face when applying the ideas from this section. How can you overcome it?

Consider your current teaching practices. How can you integrate the principles discussed in this section to enhance creativity and critical thinking among your students?

The CREATE Method and Social and Emotional Learning

Social and emotional learning (SEL) is instrumental in cultivating a holistic educational environment emphasizing cognitive development and interpersonal and intrapersonal growth. As in the CREATE Method, SEL principles nurture traits like curiosity and creativity. By fostering emotional intelligence and self-awareness, SEL empowers students to better understand and regulate their emotions, providing them with a safe space to ask questions and explore unfamiliar territories.

As students learn components of the CREATE Method such as risk-taking, open-mindedness, and empathy, there will be an increase in self-confidence and a reduced fear of failure. In contrast, students become more open to taking creative risks, brainstorming novel solutions, and approaching problems with an innovative mindset (Von Thienen et al., 2017). Additionally, SEL's emphasis on empathy and understanding aids in promoting collaborative endeavors, where different perspectives meld, further fueling curiosity and stimulating creativity, all of which complement a student's ability to grow socially and emotionally.

	C	R	E	A	T	E
SEL promotes empathy, understanding, and effective communication. For teachers, this means collaborative lesson planning and sharing best practices and resources whilst supporting one another. A classroom environment where educators model collaboration directly benefits students by demonstrating teamwork.		X		X	X	
SEL empowers students with communication skills, empathy, and conflict resolution. These skills lay the foundation for effective student collaboration in group projects or classroom discussions. Students learn to respect diverse perspectives and work collectively towards common goals.			X	X	X	
The interplay between different fields or units of knowledge is pivotal. With SEL, students and teachers alike can find interdisciplinary connections, fostering a richer understanding and promoting a collaborative approach to broad learning.	X					X
A teacher's relationship with knowledge is not static. Through SEL, educators become lifelong learners who continually seeks to expand their understanding and pedagogical techniques. This adaptability ensures they present information in a way that resonates with students, fostering an inclusive classroom.	X	X				X
SEL techniques instill curiosity, resilience, and a growth mindset in students. This relationship with knowledge drives them to collaborate, seek help when needed, and value the learning process as much as the outcome. Persisting through difficulties helps develop a positive and constructive relationship with the content.	X	X	X			
With SEL, teachers better understand students' emotional and social needs. This leads to stronger relationships, making students feel valued and understood. Such a connection naturally encourages active participation, feedback, and collaboration.	X	X	X	X	X	X

Before we finish our journey together, let's revisit the kettlebell activity we did at the beginning. Remember that deeper thinking in the classroom starts with us, the educators. Therefore, we must ensure we infuse the CREATE Method into our lives, not just our classrooms.

Take a minute to reflect on what you have learned and how you can work to ensure balance in your professional and personal life.

Content Curator

Note down the most pressing content-related challenges you're facing both personally and professionally. How can you curate your current knowledge to address these pressures?

Risk Facilitator

Write about the risks that cause you concern. How can embracing these risks transform your approach to your personal and professional life?

Experience Navigator

Identify experiences that currently feel overwhelming. What strategies can navigate you toward a more meaningful and manageable personal/professional experience?

Attitude Shifter

Reflect on the attitudes or perspectives that add to your stress. How can a shift in attitude help you view these challenges differently?

Team Transformer

Consider the team dynamics that may be contributing to your workload. How can you leverage your team's (personal and professional) strengths to lighten the collective load?

Evaluation Designer

Think about the pressures of assessment and evaluation. How can you design evaluations that are less burdensome yet effective and engaging for both yourself and your students?

WHAT NEXT? FINAL THOUGHTS ON CREATING A THINKING CLASSROOM

Phew! That was quite a process. It may seem overwhelming as you work through your first lesson, but the more you use The CREATE Method, the more ingrained it will become.

HERE ARE A FEW TIPS TO HOLD ON TO:

Not every CREATE letter applies to every lesson.
Pick and choose what is best for you and your students.

Take time to reflect on what worked and what didn't. That way the next time you teach this lesson, you will know how you want to refine it.

Keep your own attitude in check. Teaching is hard. Our reaction will impact our student's reactions so try to model the kind of attitude we want our students to demonstrate.

Don't be afraid to be vulnerable with your students. Share times of failure, joy, and frustration. By building this connection, students will feel more open to sharing their thoughts and feelings.

Try new strategies. Try to take risks by incorporating new ideas and asking for input from peers and students. There are incredibly talented teachers sharing ideas on different internet sites. Try one, adapt it to your classroom, and experiment!

 6. This is a process. This is not a quick solution to all your classroom challenges.

 7. Not every lesson is going to be engaging, not every student will embrace the concept, and not every parent will agree. Give yourself grace. Be patient.

 8. Give yourself permission to not grade everything. Remember feedback comes in all different sizes.

 9. Collaborate! Work with other teachers to brainstorm ideas. Teaching should not be a lonely profession.

 10. Give yourself permission to not grade everything. Remember feedback comes in all different sizes.

 11. Embrace joy - have fun while you are teaching. Use your passions, your curiosities, and your unique teaching style to ensure your classroom is inviting, creative, and inspiring.

At the very beginning of our journey together, we asked you to remember a time when learning was meaningful to you... **INFUSE YOUR CURRICULUM WITH CREATIVE AND CRITICAL THINKING AND MAKE YOUR CLASS A LEARNING EXPERIENCE TO REMEMBER!**

AUTHOR INFORMATION

Katie Trowbridge, M.A.T. and M.ED.

Katie Trowbridge has over two decades of experience as a teacher and mentor. Katie bolsters creative and critical thinking, social-emotional learning, creative problem-solving, communication and collaboration, and team building. She focuses on helping educators and students find their best creative selves by designing practical, relevant, and student-focused curricula.

Growing up in Chicago, Katie's passion for education allowed her to start educational non-profit organizations, assist school districts in writing SEL curricula, design programs for adults and students to encourage collaboration and communication and mentor new teachers to find their voice. As a result, Katie received several Teacher of Excellence and Outstanding Educator awards.

Creating professional development for her peers has been a highlight in her career. She designed and delivered courses such as: What is Growth Mindset? How to Use Effective Feedback, What's the Big Deal about Inquiry-Based Learning? How to Incorporate Creative Thinking and Community through Blogging; Rethinking the Research Paper: Using Video Essays to Encourage Creativity and Critical Thinking.

She is now President and CEO of a non-profit organization, Curiosity 2 Create, whose mission is to infuse creative and critical thinking into classrooms by offering tailored professional development and coaching centered around the CREATE method. She travels nationwide, speaking at conferences, presenting workshops, and coaching educators.

Katie is passionate about building a community of educators who support each other in creating creative classrooms. Therefore, Katie and Dr. Cyndi Burnett co-founded the Creative Thinking Network, which aims to empower educators worldwide through community, collaboration, and knowledge to amplify creative thinking in any classroom.

She is pursuing her Ed.D in Innovative Teaching and Learning at Northeastern University in Boston.

Acknowledgements

It is impossible to thank everyone who helped make this workbook possible. Thanks to my mom, June Barnard, and daughter, Katelyn Moon, the founders of Curiosity 2 CREATE. They trusted me enough to take this fantastic non-profit and run with it. My dad, Dr. Thomas Schmidt, gave me a love for learning and Shakespeare. My step-father, Ron Barnard, pushed and encouraged me to get a degree in teaching and do what I love best. My stepmother, Dr. Barbara Gibson-Schmidt, is an excellent sounding board for all my education questions.

To my Board of Directors and incredible staff — thank you for always being my cheerleaders and keeping me grounded. A leader is nothing if he/she/they don't have a strong team offering guidance and wisdom. I am fortunate to have a team full of creative and critical thinkers.

Thank you to all of my co-workers at Naperville North High School who helped shape me into the teacher I am today. You all inspired me and challenged me to keep working until I created the classroom I dreamed of. Thank you to Helena Hitzeman, who is the best department chair and co-teacher a person could ask for — she allowed me to take risks with my curriculum and encouraged me to never give up.

To the students who have impacted my life, thank you for making me the teacher I am today. Room 246 at Naperville North High School will always have a place in my heart because of each and every student who walked through that door. You each taught me the importance of compassion and creativity.

To Jason Silva, when I first hired you as an intern, I had no idea you would be such a superstar. Without your research dedication and creative ideas, the CREATE method would still be in my head. Thank you for all you did to help make this workbook happen.

Lastly, to my husband, Todd Trowbridge, I don't think I would have an ounce of sanity left without your love, patience, humor, and ability to get me to step away from the computer.

SPECIAL ASSISTANCE FROM JASON SILVA CHELSEA STENVIG

Jason Silva

Jason Silva is a Creative Content Creator and Researcher at Curiosity 2 Create, where he focuses on furthering creativity and curiosity-based education in the classroom. His profound enthusiasm for fostering mental well-being can be seen in his pursuit of a degree from Boston University, majoring in psychology and minoring in education.

This educational background has equipped him with a nuanced perspective on the interplay between mental health and learning environments, which he eagerly explores in his professional endeavors for Curiosity 2 Create.

Away from work, Jason is an avid reader and rock climber. Fueled by coffee, Jason can often be found reading in between climbing sessions, favoring non-fiction literature on education, psychology, and history.

Jason's relentlessly positive outlook is the cornerstone of his approach to life and work. No challenge is too daunting, no mountain too high—whether in his rock climbing adventures or in his pursuit to make a tangible impact in the mental health community. With a spirit imbued with optimism and a mind sharpened by rigorous academic and professional experiences, Jason Silva is a burgeoning force in the intersection of creative content development, research, and mental health advocacy. His journey symbolizes a blend of intellectual rigor, creative zest, and an unwavering dedication to aiding others in navigating the intricacies of mental health.

Acknowledgements

Every step of this journey was truly only made possible with the guidance of Curiosity 2 CREATE. Without each person on the team, I don't think this could have happened. Thank you all.

My friends and family, lending their unwavering support, were the backbone of this endeavor. Without all of your small acts of kindness, I would not be me. Thank you to each and every one of you.

I would last like to thank my parents– Joseph e Fatima Silva. Agradeço profundamente por tudo o que fizeram por mim e por sempre inspiraram-me a ser um estudante dedicado. Vocês me encorajaram a ser um melhor Açoriano e um melhor Americano, e uma melhor pessoa. Obrigado.

Chelsea Stenvig, M.A.

Chelsea has a heart for serving others. She is passionate about mentoring urban youth and helping children grow in the areas of faith, learning, health, and character.

Originally from the Chicago area, she earned her bachelor's in secondary education and English from Concordia University Wisconsin and a master's in leadership and Innovation from Wisconsin Lutheran College.

Chelsea formerly taught English at New Berlin Eisenhower High School in New Berlin, Wisconsin as a long-term substitute but then quickly realized her heart was in the inner city. She taught 5th grade all subjects at the Institute of Technology and Academics in Milwaukee, Wisconsin for one year and then became the 6th-8th grade ELA teacher and also spent time teaching writing and social studies. Chelsea later became the Dean of Students at ITA, where she coached teachers in classroom management, lesson engagement and led a variety of professional developments for staff regarding student engagement and classroom management.

Chelsea was selected by the Center for Urban Teaching to participate in their leadership training program in which she learned to coach teachers and then became a co-principal during two summer school programs. She was selected to participate in the first cohort of a master's program through the Center for Urban Teaching and Wisconsin Lutheran College, in which she obtained a masters in Leadership and Innovation, which focuses on turning around failing urban schools or starting up high-performing urban schools.

Acknowledgements

Thank you:

Kim Taylor, for teaching me everything I know about education. You modeled loving students, humility, and boldness, backed up your staff, and taught us the power of vision. There is no one I respect more in the field of education than you.

Kevin Festerling, for walking into my classroom that day and encouraging me when I felt defeated and planned to leave education altogether.

Everyone at the Center for Urban Teaching, you are why our kids in Milwaukee have a chance at a quality and promising future!

Heather Piontek and Rupal Kumbhani, you were my lifeline - teacher's aides really are the backbone of the classroom.

Mallory Umar, for being the best instructional coach and for working tirelessly to get me from boring lessons to a project-based mindset.

Katie Trowbridge, thank you for taking a chance and allowing me to be part of this team. Your passion for shaking up education inspires me.

The Lord who put me in the right places at the right times with the right people to make it all possible.

To the professor my freshman year who said college wasn't for me and I should go back home to a community college. You have been the inspiring story I share with my students that only we get to decide how far we'll go.

To my students in Milwaukee, you have walked hard roads no child should ever have to experience. You truly taught me more than I could have ever taught you, and I love every last one of you. May you continue to pour out your passion into others!

REFERENCES

Adobe. (2019). Get Hired Study. Adobe. www.adobe.com/content/dam/cc/uk/en/schools/Adobe_Get_Hired_EMEA.pdf

Amabile, T. M., Conti, R., Coon, H., Lazenby, J., & Herron, M. (1996). Assessing the work environment for creativity. Academy of Management Journal, 39(5), 1154–1184. www.doi.org/10.2307/256995

Andersen, P. H., Kragh, H., & Lettl, C. (2013). Spanning organizational boundaries to manage creative processes: The case of the LEGO Group. Industrial Marketing Management, 42(1), 125–134. www.doi.org/10.1016/j.indmarman.2012.11.011

Angelou, M. (2023). Caged Bird Legacy, LLC.

Argabright, K. J., McGuire, J., & King, J. (2012). Extension through a new lens: Creativity and innovation now and for the future. Journal of Extension, 50(2). www.doi.org/10.34068/joe.50.02.39

Aristotle, Bartlett, R. C., & Collins, S. D. (2011). Aristotle's Nicomachean Ethics. University of Chicago Press.

Austen, J. (1813). Pride and Prejudice. Penguin.

Balkin, A. (1990). What is creativity? What is it not? Music Educators Journal, 76(9), 29–32. www.doi.org/10.2307/3401074

Bandura, A. (1977). Self-efficacy: Toward a unifying theory of behavioral change. Psychological Review, 84(2), 191–215

Basadur, M., Taggar, S., & Pringle, P. (1999). Improving the measurement of divergent thinking attitudes in organizations. Journal of Creative Behavior, 33(2), 75–111. www.eric.ed.gov/?id=EJ591207

Beghetto, R. (2020). On creative thinking in education: Eight questions, eight answers. www.static1.squarespace.com/static/52d6f16be4b0770a479dfb9c/t/5eeb9189e4514244c48d6431/1592496523508/Creative%2Bthinking%2Bin%2BEd%2B%28Beghetto%2C%2B2020%29+copy.pdf

Bennet, D., & Bennet, A. (2008). The depth of knowledge: surface, shallow or deep? VINE, 38(4), 405–420. https://doi.org/10.1108/03055720810917679

Bolander Laksov, K., & McGrath, C. (2020). Failure as a catalyst for learning: Towards deliberate reflection in academic development work. International Journal for Academic Development, 25(1), 1–4. www.doi.org/10.1080/1360144x.2020.1717783

Bullmaster-Day, M. (2014). Productive Struggle for Deeper Learning. Studylib. www.studylib.net/doc/18815883/productive-struggle-for-deeper-learning

Burnett, C. & Worwood, M (Host). (2023, March 28). The thinking teacher is a creative teacher (S6. E100) [Audio podcast episode]. Fueling Creativity in Education podcast. www.fuelingcreativity.podbean.com/e/thinking-teacher/

Cárdenas, D., & Garza, S. (2007). Restructuring student and teacher roles: Dealing with struggle. Journal of Scholarship of Teaching and Learning, 7(1), 34–44. www.files.eric.ed.gov/fulltext/EJ854933.pdf

Casali, N., & Meneghetti, C. (2023). Soft skills and study-related factors: Direct and indirect associations with academic achievement and general distress in university students. Education Sciences, 13(6), 612–612. www.doi.org/10.3390/educsci13060612

Comer, J. (1995). Relationships and learning: Clarification on a Popular Quote. Education Service Center, Houston, Texas. Retrieved from www.theeffortfuleducator.com/2018/05/09/relationships-and-learning-clarification-on-a-popular-quote

Cook, P. (1998). The Creativity Advantage. www.citeseerx.ist.psu.edu/document?repid=rep1&type=pdf&doi=560fddfad03bfc4161de67d9ccf6721ec15811da

Costa, A., & Kallick, B. (2004). Assessment strategies for self-directed learning. Corwin Press.

Cremin, T., Glauert, E., Craft, A., Compton, A., & Stylianidou, F. (2015). Creative little scientists: Exploring pedagogical synergies between inquiry-based and creative approaches in early years science. Education 3-13, 43(4), 404–419. www.doi.org/10.1080/03004279.2015.1020655

Dawson, S. (2023). Embracing uncertainty and complexity to promote teaching and learning innovation. Pacific Journal of Technology Enhanced Learning, 5(1), 15–16. www.doi.org/10.24135/pjtel.v5i1.171

Deming, W. E. (2018). The New Economics for Industry, Government, Education. MIT Press.

Doron, E. (2017). Fostering creativity in school aged children through perspective taking and visual media based short term intervention program. Thinking Skills and Creativity, 23, 150–160. www.doi.org/10.1016/j.tsc.2016.12.003

Eisen, D. (2012). Developing a critical lens: Using photography to teach sociology and create critical thinkers. Teaching Sociology, 40(4), 349—359 Published by: American Sociological Association. www.jstor.org/stable/41725518

Emmanuel, G., & Delaney, H. (2014). Professors' influence on students' beliefs, values, and attitudes in the classroom. Journal of College and Character, 15(4). www.doi.org/10.1515/jcc-2014-0029

Fabris, M. A., Roorda, D., & Longobardi, C. (2022). Editorial. Student-teacher relationship quality research: Past, present and future. Frontiers in Education, 7. www.doi.org/10.3389/feduc.2022.1049115

Figliotti, J., & Burnett, C. (2015). 20 lessons to weave creative thinking into your curriculum.

Figliotti, J., & Burnett, C. (2021). Weaving Creativity into Every Strand of Your Curriculum.

Foundation for Critical Thinking. (2023, December 11). K-12 Instruction: Critically. Critical Thinking. www.criticalthinking.org/pages/critical-thinking-professional-development-for-k-12/432

Galbraith, D. D., & Webb, F. L. (2013). Teams that work: Preparing student teams for the workplace. American Journal of Business Education (AJBE), 6(2), 223. www.doi.org/10.19030/ajbe.v6i2.7687

Guildford, J. P. (1967). Creativity: Yesterday, today and tomorrow. Journal of Creative Behavior, 1(1), 3–14. www.doi.org/10.1002/j.2162-6057.1967.tb00002.x

Harvard Business Review. (2022, August 3). Why your students are disengaged and what you can do to draw them back. Harvard Business Publishing Education. www.hbsp.harvard.edu/inspiring-minds/why-your-students-are-disengaged

Hattie, J., & Timperley, H. (2007). The power of feedback. Review of Educational Research, 77(1), 81–112. www.doi.org/10.3102/003465430298487

Helfand, M., Kaufman, J. C., & Beghetto, R. A. (2016). The four-c model of creativity: Culture and context. The Palgrave Handbook of Creativity and Culture Research, 15–36. www.doi.org/10.1057/978-1-137-46344-9_2

Heljakka, K. (2023). Building playful resilience in higher education: Learning by doing and doing by playing. Frontiers in Education, 8. www.doi.org/10.3389/feduc.2023.1071552

Hennessey, B. A., & Amabile, T. M. (2010). Creativity. Annual Review of Psychology, 61(1), 569–598. www.doi.org/10.1146/annurev.psych.093008.100416

IBM Global Business Services. (2010). Executive Report. www.compromisorse.com/upload/estudios/000/54/GBE03350USEN.pdf

Jederlund, U., & Von Rosen, T. (2022). Teacher–student relationships and students' self-efficacy beliefs. rationale, validation and further potential of two instruments. Education Inquiry, 14(4), 1–25. www.doi.org/10.1080/20004508.2022.2073053

Johnson, D. W., & Johnson, R. T. (1999). Making cooperative learning work. Theory into Practice, 38(2), 67–73. https://doi.org/10.1080/00405849909543834

Jussim, L., & Harber, K. D. (2005). Teacher expectations and self-fulfilling prophecies: Knowns and unknowns, resolved and unresolved controversies. Personality and Social Psychology Review, 9(2), 131–155. www.doi.org/10.1207/s15327957pspr0902_3

Katz-Buonincontro, J. (2012). Creativity at the crossroads: Pragmatic versus humanist claims in education reform speeches. Creativity Research Journal, 24(4), 257–265. www.doi.org/10.1080/10400419.2012.726574

Kim, K. H. (2011). The creativity crisis: The decrease in creative thinking scores on the torrance tests of creative thinking. Creativity Research Journal, 23(4), 285–295. www.doi.org/10.1080/10400419.2011.627805

Lin, T.-C., Hsu, Y.-S., Lin, S.-S., Changlai, M.-L., Yang, K.-Y., & Lai, T.-L. (2011). A review of empirical evidence on scaffolding for science education. International Journal of Science and Mathematics Education, 10(2), 437–455. www.doi.org/10.1007/s10763-011-9322-z

LinkedIn. (2019). 2019 Workplace Learning Report. www.learning.linkedin.com/content/dam/me/business/en-us/amp/learning-solutions/images/workplace-learning-report-2019/pdf/workplace-learning-report-2019.pdf

LinkedIn. (2020). 2020 Workplace Learning Report. www.learning.linkedin.com/content/dam/me/learning/resources/pdfs/LinkedIn-Learning-2020-Workplace-Learning-Report.pdf

Manning, A. (2016, May 10). Divergent vs. Convergent Thinking: How to Strike a Balance. Professional Development at Harvard DCE. www.professional.dce.harvard.edu/blog/divergent-vs-convergent-thinking-how-to-strike-a-balance/

McDonald, N., & Messinger, D. (2011, January). The development of empathy: How, when, and why. ResearchGate. www.researchgate.net/publication/267426505_The_Development_of_Empathy_How_When_and_Why

McGregor, S. L. T. (2020). Emerging from the deep: Complexity, emergent pedagogy and deep learning. Northeast Journal of Complex Systems, 2(1). https://doi.org/10.22191/nejcs/vol2/iss1/2

Melville, H. (1851). Moby-Dick. W. W. Norton.

Merma-Molina, G; Gavilán-Martin, D., Urrea-Solano, M. (2022). Actively open-minded thinking, personality and critical thinking in Spanish adolescents: A correlation and predictive study. International Journal of Instruction, 15(2), 579–600.

Murdock, M., & Keller-Mathers, S. (2008). Teaching and learning creatively with the torrance incubation model. The International Journal of Creativity and Problem Solving. www.semanticscholar.org/paper/Teaching-and-Learning-Creatively-with-the-Torrance-Murdock-Keller-Mathers/d16d15d9963e0392ee28c3955db4da5f560c2a83

New Jersey Office of Evaluation. (2015). Collaborative teams toolkit tools to support collaborative team structures and evidence-based conversations in schools. www.state.nj.us/education/AchieveNJ/teams/Toolkit.pdf

Oakley, B., Brent, R., M. Felder, R., & H. Elhajj, I. (2004). Turning student groups into effective teams. ResearchGate. www.researchgate.net/publication/242350622_Turning_student_groups_into_effective_teams

Oxford Languages. (2023). Synergy. In Oxford Language Dictionary. Retrieved from www.oxfordlanguages.com

Oxford, R. (1992). Who are our students? A synthesis of foreign and second language research on individual differences with implications for instructional practice. TESL Canada Journal, 9(2), 30. www.doi.org/10.18806/tesl.v9i2.602

Pianta, R. C. (2001). Student-teacher relationship scale: Professional manual. Psychological Assessment Resources.

Piers, E. V., Daniels, J. M., & Quackenbush, J. F. (1960). The identification of creativity in adolescents. Journal of Educational Psychology, 51(6), 346–351. www.doi.org/10.1037/h0042669

Pociask, S., Gross, D., & Shih, M.-Y. (2017). Does team formation impact student performance, effort and attitudes in a college course employing collaborative learning? Journal of the Scholarship of Teaching and Learning, 17(3), 19–33. www.doi.org/10.14434/josotl.v17i3.21158

Post, M. L., Barrett, A., Williams, M., & Scharff, L. (2020). Impact of team formation method on student performance, attitudes, and behaviors. Journal of the Scholarship of Teaching and Learning, 20(1). www.doi.org/10.14434/josotl.v20i1.24128

Poulos, A., & Mahony, M. J. (2008). Effectiveness of feedback: The students' perspective. Assessment & Evaluation in Higher Education, 33(2), 143–154. www.doi.org/10.1080/02602930601127869

Richardson, S., & Krstic, S. (2021). Evidencing creativity and curiosity in IB schools. www.doi.org/10.37517/978-1-74286-638-3_7

Robinson, K. (2013, May 13). How to escape education's death valley. YouTube. www.youtube.com/watch?v=wX78iKhInsc&vl=en

Runco, M. A. (1993). Divergent thinking, creativity, and giftedness. Gifted Child Quarterly, 37(1), 16–22. www.doi.org/10.1177/001698629303700103

Runco, M. A., & Acar, S. (2019). Divergent thinking: New methods, recent research, and extended theory. Psychology of Aesthetics, Creativity, and the Arts, 13(2), 153–158. www.doi.org/10.1037/aca0000231

Runco, M. A., & Jaeger, G. J. (2012). The standard definition of creativity. Creativity Research Journal, 24(1), 92–96. www.doi.org/10.1080/10400419.2012.650092

Sawyer, K. (2008). Group Genius. Basic Books.

Schleifer, D., Rinehart, C., & Yanisch, T. (2017). Teacher collaboration in perspective: A guide to research. In ERIC. Public Agenda. www.eric.ed.gov/?id=ED591332

Stein, M. I. (1953). Creativity and Culture. Journal of Psychology, 36(2), 311–322. www.doi.org/10.1080/00223980.1953.9712897

Suárez, N., Regueiro, B., Estévez, I., del Mar Ferradás, M., Guisande, M. A., & Rodríguez, S. (2019). Individual precursors of student homework behavioral engagement: The role of intrinsic motivation, perceived homework utility and homework attitude. Frontiers in Psychology, 10. www.doi.org/10.3389/fpsyg.2019.00941

Taras, M. (2003). To feedback or not to feedback in student self-assessment. Assessment & Evaluation in Higher Education, 28(5), 549–565. www.doi.org/10.1080/02602930301678

Thomas Stearns Eliot. (1931). Preface to "Transit of Venus" (Poems by Harry Crosby).

Treffinger, D. J. (1986). Research on Creativity. Gifted Child Quarterly, 30(1), 15–19. www.doi.org/10.1177/001698628603000103

Truss, D. (2019, November 5). Teacher as compass. www.pairadimes.davidtruss.com/teacher-as-compass/

Van de Pol, J., Volman, M., Oort, F., & Beishuizen, J. (2015). The effects of scaffolding in the classroom: Support contingency and student independent working time in relation to student achievement, task effort and appreciation of support. Instructional Science, 43(5), 615–641. www.doi.org/10.1007/s11251-015-9351-z

Von Thienen, J. P. A., Clancey, W. J., Corazza, G. E., & Meinel, C. (2017). Theoretical foundations of design thinking. Understanding Innovation, 13–40. www.doi.org/10.1007/978-3-319-60967-6_2

Vonnegut, K. (1969). Slaughterhouse-Five. Laurel.

Wiggins, G., & McTighe, J. (2005). Understanding by design (2nd ed.). Association for Supervision and Curriculum Development.

Wolf, A., Scieszka, J., & Smith, L. (1996). The true story of the 3 little pigs. Puffin Books, New York N.Y., U.S.A.

World Economic Forum. (2016). Factors for enabling the creative economy. www3.weforum.org/docs/WEF_2016_WhitePaper_Enabling_the_Creative_Economy.pdf

World Economic Forum. (2023). Future of Jobs Report 2023. www3.weforum.org/docs/WEF_Future_of_Jobs_2023.pdf

Wulf, G., & Lewthwaite, R. (2016). Optimizing performance through intrinsic motivation and attention for learning: The OPTIMAL theory of motor learning. Psychonomic Bulletin & Review, 23(5), 1382–1414. www.doi.org/10.3758/s13423-015-0999-9

Young, J. (1985). What is creativity? Journal of Creative Behavior, 19(2), 77–87. www.doi.org/10.1002/j.2162-6057.1985.tb00640.x

Zeff, L. E. & Higby, M. A. (2002). Groups versus Teams. Rapid Intellect. www.rapidintellect.com/AEQweb/6jan2118j2.htm

Zusak, M. (2005). The book thief. Alfred A Knopf.

www.ingramcontent.com/pod-product-compliance
Lightning Source LLC
Chambersburg PA
CBHW040003040426
42337CB00033B/5211